Designing Families

TITLES OF RELATED INTEREST FROM PINE FORGE PRESS

Sociology of Families *by David Newman*

Sociology of Families: Readings *by Cheryl Alders*

Gender and Families *by Scott Coltrane*

The Gender of Sexuality *by Pepper Schwartz and Virginia Rutter*

Exploring Social Issues Using SPSS for Windows 95/98 Versions 7.5, 8.0, or Higher *by Joseph Healey, John Boli, Earl Babbie, and Fred Halley*

Social Prisms: Reflections on Everyday Myths and Paradoxes *by Jodi O'Brien*

This Book Is Not Required: An Emotional Survival Manual for Students, Revised Edition *by Inge Bell and Bernard McGrane*

Media/Society: Industries, Images, and Audiences, 2nd Edition *by David Croteau and William Hoynes*

Crime and Everyday Life: Insight and Implication for Society, 2nd Edition *by Marcus Felson*

Building Community: Social Science in Action *edited by Philip Nyden, Anne Figert, Mark Shibley, and Darryl Burrows*

Race, Ethnicity, Gender, and Class: The Sociology of Group Conflict and Change, 2nd Edition *by Joseph F. Healey*

Riddles of Human Society *by Donald Kraybill and Conrad Kanagy*

The McDonaldization of Society, Revised Edition *by George Ritzer*

An Invitation to Environmental Sociology *by Michael M. Bell*

Schools and Societies *by Steven Brint*

Designing Families: The Search for Self and Community in the Information Age

John Scanzoni

PINE FORGE PRESS
Thousand Oaks • London • New Delhi

For information:

Pine Forge Press
A Sage Publications Company
2455 Teller Road
Thousand Oaks, California 91320
sales@pfp.sagepub.com

SAGE Publications Ltd.
6 Bonhill Street
London EC2A 4PU
United Kingdom

SAGE Publications India Pvt. Ltd.
M-32 Market
Greater Kailash I
New Delhi 110 048 India

Production Editor: Wendy Westgate
Production Assistant: Patricia Zeman
Designer/Typesetter: Danielle Dillahunt
Cover Designer: Ravi Balasuriya
Indexer: Molly Hall

Printed in the United States of America

00 01 02 03 04 10 9 8 7 6 5 4 3 2 1

Library of Congress Cataloging-in-Publication Data

Scanzoni, John H., 1935-
    Designing families: The search for self and community in the information age / by John Scanzoni.
      p. cm.
    Includes bibliographical references (p.) and index.
    ISBN 0-7619-8683-9 (cloth: acid-free paper)
    ISBN 0-7619-8566-2 (pbk: acid-free paper)
    1. Family. 2. Marriage. 3. Sex roles. 4. Community. I. Title.
    HQ734 .S3756 2000
    306.85—dc21   99-6324

For Jo,

who challenged and inspired me
to write this book in the first place

ABOUT THE AUTHOR

John Scanzoni is Professor of Sociology at the University of Florida. He has a long-standing interest in the connections between gender issues and family change. His concern has been how couples—within the context of external factors such as the educational and marketplace systems—might be able to move more effectively toward gender equity. He continues that interest by widening the range of external factors to include the type of collaborative community known as the New Everyday Life (NEL). That label was coined by a group of Scandinavian scholars who also term their proposal for families of the future a Nordic Feminist Vision. They believe that this vision holds promise for balancing the interests of women, men, and children alike. Scanzoni elaborates their proposal by suggesting ways in which those competing interests might indeed be balanced. He also describes how an NEL approach might address the interests of lone parents, older citizens, and those who are economically disadvantaged.

ABOUT THE PUBLISHER

Pine Forge Press is a new educational publisher, dedicated to publishing innovative books and software throughout the social sciences. On this and any other of our publications, we welcome your comments, ideas, and suggestions. Please call or write to:

Pine Forge Press
A Sage Publications Company
2455 Teller Road
Thousand Oaks, CA 91320
805-499-4224
E-mail: sales@pfp.sagepub.com

Visit our World Wide Web site, your direct link to a multitude of on-line resources: www.pineforge.com

An old world is collapsing and a new world arising; we have better eyes for the collapse than for the rise, for the old one is the world we know.
John Updike, 1992

The endurance and universality of the concept of family testify to its strength and vitality. Family patterns vary and compositions alter, but the need to belong to something larger than oneself is innate and compelling. This need is demonstrated over and over again by groups that refer to themselves as "family." . . . Children play "family," and elders reinvent it when it does not exist.
Margaret Mahoney, 1986

We must abandon any illusion that we can or should revive some largely mythical traditional family. We need to invent new family traditions and find ways of reviving older community ones.
Stephanie Coontz, 1992

The good-provider role may be on its way out, but its legitimate successor has not yet appeared on the scene.
Jessie Bernard, 1981

The real problem is not . . . the loss of old contexts but rather the failure of our present democratic and industrial scene to create new contexts of association and moral cohesion.
Robert A. Nisbet, 1953

The contours of the new institutions that will emerge to take the place [of the old] are still hidden in the dawn of a new century.
Katherine McFate, 1995

Genuinely satisfying alternatives to conventional housing and communities will emerge only as we are able to visualize scenarios of the future based on the reconceptualization of work, family life, and gender roles.
Leslie Kanes Weisman, 1992

Transcendence is the need of man to feel his own house as a room in some greater, all-embracing structure in which he is at home, [and] to feel that the other inhabitants of it with whom he lives and works are all acknowledging and confirming his individual existence.
Martin Buber, 1958

He that will not apply new remedies must expect new evils, for time is the greatest innovator.
Francis Bacon, early 17th century

Dream No Small Dreams: They Lack Magic to Stir Men's Blood.
Daniel Burnham, 1871, upon being asked to
redesign Chicago after the Great Fire

Contents

◆◆◆————————————————————————

PREFACE

◆◆◆────────────────────────────────────

This book is about figuring out how people can make better families— better for themselves, and better for the society around them. The book explores "terrain that usually remains untrod due to social scientists' self-imposed exile—the regions between what is and what might be." [1]

To one degree or another, ordinary citizens in North America and in Europe, in hopes of pursuing a better life, have been reinventing families for some 200 years. [2] But in the past 30 years, the tempo of that reinvention has picked up dramatically. Some social critics view what has been happening recently with considerable alarm. In particular, they are concerned about children. Nevertheless, most of today's citizens, like our forebears, are simply trying to do the best we can. We don't lack for suggestions about what to do. We get all kinds of advice from a vast array of politicians, social policy analysts, clergy, and social scientists. This book adds to the long list of proposals concerning how to make better families.

However, this book is different from most existing proposals in a number of ways. For one thing, it places the reinvention, or design, of families squarely within the context of the new kind of society into which many parts of the world seem to be moving. Some observers have noted that the First Wave of human history was the agricultural era. [3] The industrial

age constituted the Second Wave. In the First Wave, the family style practiced by most people in most parts of the world is known as the *extended
family.* The essence of that style was mutual help. Typically, a man and a
woman would live in a hut or tiny cabin (often little more than a hovel)
with their own children. Their household was frequently sited near to other
households containing blood relatives of one sort or another. This cluster
of relatives often had to work together in order to coax a bare subsistence
from the soil. Everybody helped out in caring for infants and small children.
And as soon as they were old enough, children began to participate in the
extended family's struggle for economic survival.

In the late 1700s, Scottish engineer James Watt perfected a new, and
much improved, design for the steam engine. His engine became the catalyst
for the industrial age—the Second Wave—that began around 1800. By the
start of the 19th century, persons in England and North America had been
experimenting with a new style of family life for a couple of hundred years.
Its essence was independence from the authority and control of blood
relatives. For some time, husband-wife households—called *nuclear families*—
had been moving out of the countryside and away from their relatives to
the cities of England or to North America. They were pursuing both
personal freedom and economic opportunity. The 19th and early 20th
centuries are known as the period of the industrial age. During that time,
among most citizens, the nuclear family style gradually became the preferred way to live. The extended family style was discarded in large part
because it did not fit with the industrial age. The nuclear family style was
preferred in large part because it did fit.

However, in the last half of the 20th century, another invention appeared that was just as revolutionary as the steam engine. The computer
helped shut down the industrial age, just as Watt's engine had undermined
the agricultural era. Hence, we now live in a postindustrial society. This
period is also called the Third Wave, or the information age, and it will
chart the course of the 21st century. At the same time that Europe and
North America were beginning to slip into the postindustrial mode, the
nuclear family style began to fall on hard times. There were several reasons
for this, and I consider them in later chapters. But the basic question I ask
in this book is quite simple: Does the nuclear family style fit with the
information age? The shift from the agricultural era to the industrial age

was monumental. The emergence of the postindustrial, information age is equally unprecedented and significant. The former shift signaled the ascendance of a new style of family. Might the latter shift suggest another new style? If not, why not? And if so, what style or styles might appear?

This book is about ancient family values, and yet at the same time a new family style. It explores the notion of the reinvention of mutual help patterns across households described as "fictive kin" rather than among blood kin. The households themselves are free to pursue the rich diversity that has come to characterize the postindustrial age. *Cohousing* is a label used to describe some currently existing neighborhoods made up of households that are sited close together and are socially connected. Cohousing households are both independent and interdependent at the same time.

The idea of cohousing was conceived, born, and matured in Scandinavia. Scandinavia is also the source of a proposed innovation on the cohousing model called the New Everyday Life (NEL). Advocates of NEL envision it as a series of cohousing communities that pay particular attention to the interests of women, men, and children alike. They describe the New Everyday Life as "a Nordic Feminist Vision." It is one example of what Anthony Giddens calls "utopian realism." [4] This book explores whether or not that vision of family and community might somehow fit with the information age.

It goes without saying that I am hugely obliged to numerous persons for their inputs to and influences on this book. They include valued colleagues at the University of Florida (notably Bill Marsiglio) and elsewhere. The following reviewers for Pine Forge Press were very helpful:

Jane Bock, *University of Wisconsin, Green Bay*

Elaine David, *Campbellsville University*

Elizabeth Hartung Freimuth, *California State University, Fresno*

Linda Green, *Normandale Community College*

Larry McCallum, *Augustana College*

David Pollock, *Berry College*

Barbara Ryan, *Widener University*

Jean Pearson Scott, *Texas Technical University*

Beth Anne Shelton, *University of Texas, Arlington*

Georgia Stevens, *University of Nebraska, Lincoln*

Pamela Turner, *Kansas State University*
Elaine Wethington, *Cornell University*
Carol S. Wharton, *University of Richmond*

I would also like to thank the staff at Pine Forge Press (especially publisher Steve Rutter), long-suffering friends, and my children. All have been both quite candid and very helpful in providing criticisms, insights, and encouragement.

I must add special thanks to my students who in recent years in a variety of classes had to contend with earlier drafts of this book. Their often blunt comments regarding its shortcomings were a continuing stimulus for me to make it stronger. In that regard, permit me to quote and paraphrase slightly the conclusions of Professor Wayne C. Booth, a member of the Carnegie Commission that issued the widely endorsed 1998 Boyer report on the need to restructure undergraduate teaching:

> My books would have been quite different—and to me less valuable—if I had produced them in solitude or after talking only with professional colleagues. It was not just that thinking about how to teach students to read responsibly led me to ideas that I would otherwise have overlooked. Responding to students' rival readings actually changed my [thinking on how to write my own book]. For this and other reasons, teaching and publishing have always felt absolutely inseparable.[5]

Most of all, I am indebted to Professor Mary Joyce (Jo) Hasell—friend, colleague, spouse—for convincing me about the significance of cohousing in particular and of spatial features in general. Like many social scientists in recent years, I once took people's housing and neighborhoods for granted. They were simply there—they were little more than "givens." I paid virtually no attention to the dynamics between families and physical spaces. Although by no means intentionally, I overlooked the ways in which spatial features surround and influence families, and how in turn families might affect those very same features—a rather bizarre stance, if one thinks about it, especially when it comes to families. It is obvious, after all, that most families reside in housing and neighborhoods of one kind or another. Hence, from her perspective as an interior architect, Jo argued that reinventing families for the information age must include a spatial as well as a social component. Although at first I staunchly resisted the idea, the longer I wrestled with it, the clearer it became that I could not avoid making their interface a central element of this book. Whatever else it entails, designing families includes the experience of "producing space." [6]

1

NEW FAMILIES—NEW IDEAS

◆◆◆ ——————————————————————————

During the summer of 1996, while riding the train from Stockholm to Copenhagen, I couldn't help overhearing a conversation between two passengers seated behind me. He was a Swedish man in his 20s, she a German woman in her 70s. Communicating in English, they were remarking enthusiastically about the many children traveling with us. She was saying how delightful it was to have her own grandchildren call her Grandma, and he was sharing fond memories of his grandparents. She then volunteered that when people marry, "children must come first. When I married, I gave up my profession for many years, and that way we stayed married and raised good children." They then both lamented how "people today get married and then divorced many times over." He commented, however, that he could fully sympathize with today's young couples. Although regrettable, he said, there are often "good reasons for breaking up." She responded sadly how her daughter-in-law had recently divorced her son, taking their daughter with her, so she could have her "profession."

As their conversation drifted to the spectacular Nordic summer sky and to the surrounding pristine dairy farms, it occurred to me how curious it was that two people from different generations and genders, different cultures, and different languages, and communicating in a tongue foreign to them both, could agree on something pervasive to virtually every Western society. Americans are not alone in feeling anxious and uneasy about what is taking place among today's families and at the same time feeling helpless to do very much about it. We sense that society is changing rapidly around us, and so are families. Many citizens, like the German woman, yearn for the more comfortable past. Yet she and millions of other women like her paid a dear price for that "comfort." In spite of our nostalgia, most persons in the West do not want to go back. Instead, we are groping for something that works in the present as well as the future.

And that is what this book is about. It is about figuring out how people can make better families—better for themselves and better for the society around them. This book explores the "terrain that usually remains untrod due to social scientists' self-imposed exile—the regions between what is and what might be." [1] Most citizens are quite eager to explore what might be. They take quite seriously Thomas Jefferson's words about our "inalienable rights," such as "life, liberty, and the pursuit of happiness." Today's citizens, no less than Jefferson, want to pursue better lives.

To one degree or another, ordinary citizens—in hopes of pursuing better lives—have been reinventing families for a long time.[2] During the past 30 years, the tempo of reinvention has picked up dramatically. Some social critics (as they have for 200 years) view what is happening with considerable alarm. In particular, they are concerned about children. Nevertheless, most of today's citizens, like our forebears, are simply trying to do the best they can. We have no lack of suggestions about what to do. We get all kinds of advice from a vast array of politicians, social policy analysts, clergy, and social scientists. This book adds to the long list of proposals concerning how to make better families.

THE INFORMATION AGE

"So what makes your book different from all the rest?" asked a colleague. It is different because it places the reinvention, or design, of families within the context of the new kind of society into which the entire world seems to be moving. Some call it the postindustrial society, or the information age. Still others refer to it as the knowledge age, or the Third Wave.[3] The

First Wave, they say, was the agricultural era, and the Second Wave was the industrial period. Another way to describe this new era is to say that it is *posttraditional*.[4] Posttraditional does *not* mean that it is antitradition or that there is an absence of tradition. It simply implies that in this period no tradition—that is, no established way of doing things—can compel allegiance merely because it did so in the past. "But we've always done it this way!" is to defend tradition in the traditional way. However, in this new age, every tradition must now justify itself, and perhaps reinvent itself. No tradition is exempt from continual scrutiny, and none can ever be taken for granted. Out of this constant ferment new traditions are created, some old ones are sustained, and some are discarded.[5]

As the story of my 1996 Scandinavian train ride indicates, it is not just the United States that is becoming posttraditional. A number of social scientists agree that the posttraditional movement is going global.[6] Globalization, or the emergence of the "global village," implies far more than the idea of international economic competition, although that is surely part of it. More broadly, globalization means that the everyday lives of ordinary citizens throughout the world are becoming increasingly interconnected— at least via the media and other forms of technology. It also implies that throughout the course of the 21st century, the everyday lives of citizens the world over are likely to bear an ever greater resemblance. And one of the most vital similarities will be the habit of examining traditions and requiring that those traditions justify themselves.

This book, for instance, is about an ancient tradition—old family values—that some say we should reinvent. The old tradition was the blood, or extended, family lodged within its community. It was a tradition that prevailed for thousands of years prior to the Industrial Revolution. However, throughout the 1800s and 1900s, people gradually discarded it. Nonetheless, some argue that perhaps it is now time to reinvent that tradition. It is an old tradition whose time may have come again. However, reinventing that "older" tradition implies rigorous scrutiny of the "newer" tradition of the nuclear family. Scrutiny—that is, careful examination—of the nuclear family style is by no means recent. It has been going on at least since the late 1800s.[7] Recently, however, both the sources and the frequency of that scrutiny have increased significantly.

Over the years, I have written a great deal about the reinvention of the nuclear family tradition or style.[8] It has seemed to me, as it has to many others, that the centerpiece of its reinvention should be gender equity. Many of us have been convinced that gender equity is the basis for satisfying adult relationships as well as the foundation of effective parenting. I believe that today more strongly than ever before. Nevertheless, at the same time, I share the concerns of some observers who wonder whether the nuclear family style is the most appropriate vehicle for achieving and maintaining the objective of gender equity. Consequently, Part I of this book is about requiring that "newer" tradition—the nuclear family style—to justify itself.

The gist of Part I is that the newer tradition, the nuclear family style, has not quite lived up to its promise, particularly for women. It has not allowed women the same degree of independence and freedom as it has men. And so for the past 30 years, women (and men) have been struggling to invent a family tradition that will supply the independence denied to women by both the extended and the nuclear styles.

But what is to be done about the shortcomings and fragility of the nuclear family tradition? In Part II, I offer a response. Why not consider reinventing the older tradition of the extended family embedded within its community? But that option poses monumental obstacles. Could we actually bring those older family values up-to-date? And how would a contemporary version of that ancient tradition fit within the posttraditional, information age? That ancient tradition is such a forgotten and obscure way of doing things that even talking about it makes it feel almost radical. Bear in mind, however, that *radical* simply means "taking things by the roots." [9]

SIX PRINCIPLES FOR A NEW FAMILY POLICY

British sociologist Anthony Giddens believes it is time for the Western democracies to design new public policies in general, and family policy in particular, based on what he calls the "radical center." [10] The typical conservative (right) and liberal (left) approaches to public policy have exhausted themselves and worn thin.[11] Both sides seem to lack fresh ideas for untangling the unique dilemmas and puzzles of postindustrial society.[12] As a result, Giddens wants to replace both sides, yet retain their best ideas.

These ideas, as he sees it, consist of at least six principles, and he wants to base the construction of fresh social policy on those principles. Using them implies going to the root of things. I shall adapt the following principles to fashion a family policy for the information age:

1. A balance of freedom with responsibility
2. Special attention to women's interests
3. Personal and political empowerment for women, men, and children alike
4. Participation in dialogic, or democratic, decision making
5. Positive welfare aimed at both advantaged and disadvantaged households
6. The direct confrontation of violence

Considering these principles as the basis for family policy forces us to go to the root of things; it is, in that sense, a radical family policy. Some of its roots are "liberal," whereas some are "conservative." An example of the policy's liberal roots lies in its making women's interests a centerpiece. Another liberal root is found in the emphasis on the empowerment of the economically disadvantaged. At the same time, the policy draws on several ideas that are highly significant to conservatives. Chief among these is the matter of personal responsibility for individuals beyond oneself and one's household—a sense of obligation for what sociologist Daniel Bell calls the "public household." [13] Furthermore, the proposed family policy places the well-being of children in a whole new light—a matter of tremendous importance to conservatives and liberals alike, and indeed to all citizens.

It has been observed that any policy statement is a vision of the future.[14] Visions of the future are based on the obvious fact that "not everything that will exist has existed or does exist." [15]

A policy statement is a conception of how we want things to be. We believe that if certain things are made to happen, people will be better off than they are right now. In the early 1960s, for instance, President Kennedy gave the nation and the world a vision of the future by stating, "We shall put a man on the moon by the end of the decade." Once that broad vision became official U.S. policy, hundreds of specific technical programs were put in place in order to achieve the goal. Similarly, the family policy proposed in this book is a vision of the future. It is a picture of what we can derive from the best of what we were.

Repairing Damaged Solidarities

The first principle of an innovative family policy, or vision of the future, requires the "repair [of] damaged solidarities." [16] The term *solidarity* implies a group that is solid, and that means a group that is able to reconcile effectively the ever-competing demands of freedom with the need for responsibility. On one side of the equation are autonomy, independence, liberty, and rights; on the other side are duty and obligation. A group is damaged when it gives more weight to one side of the equation than the other. For example, up through the 1950s, the nuclear family was damaged because it was out of balance. [17] Women experienced far more limitations than freedoms in this family form, and men enjoyed many more freedoms than limitations. But beginning in the 1960s, ordinary individuals began trying to repair the damage. For more than 30 years, women and men have been struggling to achieve a better balance between freedom and responsibility for both genders.

Self and Community

However, some critics worry that because most of us have concentrated so much on freedom, we have tended to ignore responsibility, especially toward children. [18] The result is that today's families are damaged, they say, although for the opposite reason from the 1950s family. The subtitle of this book points to the contemporary search for both self and community. The *search for self* is another way to describe the quest for independence and autonomy. The *search for community* is another way to describe our yearnings for responsible connections with others. Accordingly, any family policy or design we propose must rise to this first test: To what extent does it bring about *in*dependence and *inter*dependence at the same time? To what degree does the design facilitate both autonomy and responsibility? How does the design accommodate undeniable demands for freedom as well as unquestionable requirements for responsible social arrangements? How would those arrangements balance the ever-competing, and equally compelling, interests of women, men, and children?

Women's Interests

If the first principle of an innovative family policy emphasizes something we have overlooked, namely, responsibility, then the second cautions us that we cannot minimize liberty, or what Giddens calls "emancipation."[19] Few of us are prepared to relinquish the hard-won freedoms not only of the past 30 years, but of the prior centuries as well. Nor should women, in particular, be asked to do so. If anything, we may expect that greater numbers of women in the West and around the world will seek and obtain increasingly higher levels of autonomy. Ever since the 1500s, people in the West have struggled to rid themselves of arbitrary political power as well as material deprivation.[20] The struggle has been fundamentally a politics of social class. The have-nots have tried to better themselves, sometimes (but not necessarily always) at the expense of the haves. Until quite recently, the public policy objective was to increase every *man's* chances for educational and economic opportunity.[21] As men's lives improved, the men's dependent women and children were believed to benefit accordingly.

Giddens argues that it is now time to make the politics of gender as pivotal as the politics of social class. Doing so mandates that women's emancipation from arbitrary male power should become a central political issue. To the extent that the United States has had anything like a family policy, it has centered chiefly on assisting poor people in becoming self-sufficient.[22] A more comprehensive family policy would retain that goal and add to it the objective of women's autonomy.

Empowerment:
Personal and Political

Gender politics is about making life better for women—expediting women's *personal* empowerment. But it is also about political empowerment. Furthermore, personal and political empowerment are not just for women. Empowerment is just as vital for men and children as well. Hence, personal and political empowerment for all citizens is a third principle of an innovative family policy, or vision of the future.

Giddens offers a simple definition of empowerment: "Individuals and groups" are empowered, he says, when they're able "to *make things happen, rather than have things happen to them.*" [23] Up to now, public policy has been conceived typically as something that politicians do, after consulting with experts and being lobbied by special interests. For this and related reasons, today's citizens tend to feel quite alienated from politics and to have very little sense of personal political efficacy. However, in this post-traditional, information age, Giddens believes that citizens must construct ways to participate more fully in the range of political issues that influences their everyday lives. [24] Although "empowerment" is sometimes a cliché, in this case it is not. It captures the idea of women, men, and children alike being able to make things happen.

Accordingly, if citizens have an interest in designing family policies that address both responsibility and autonomy, they cannot wait on politicians to do it for them. Throughout the industrial era, many people held to a sharp disjuncture between the personal realm on the one hand and the public, or political, domain on the other. Because family was located in the personal realm, it was thought to lie outside the political domain. However, as we move into *post*industrial times, that rift needs to be bridged. The same citizens who make healthy families must become active partners with government in designing ways to support their efforts. They themselves must take the responsibility for making things happen, and they must have the authority to do so.

Dialogue

The fourth principle of an innovative family policy is what Giddens call "dialogic democracy." It is a process that underlies, and is essential for, both personal and political empowerment. As Giddens sees it, relationships at every level of society should be "ordered through dialogue rather than through embedded power." [25] Dialogue means that persons get to participate effectively in the decision making that affects their everyday lives. To participate effectively means to be able to help shape the outcomes of their discussions and/or negotiations. The overall scenario is like an upward spiral. In order to take part in dialogue effectively, one must possess a certain degree of empowerment, and the more one takes part in dialogue, the more empowerment one develops. And so it goes.

Dialogue, says Giddens, should be the basis for dyadic love relationships, for parent-child relationships, and for relationships among friends and kin across household boundaries.[26] Furthermore, he argues that individuals' practice of dialogue in their personal relationships contributes to their effective use of dialogue in the political arena. For at least two centuries, women have been struggling to get men to deal with them on the basis of dialogue rather than embedded male power. In recent decades there has been, at least in the West, a discernible movement toward gender dialogue.[27] Nevertheless, embedded male power remains a significant force in male-female relationships in the West and throughout the world. Hence, information-age family policy must address the issue of designing ways to facilitate gender dialogue.

Positive Welfare

The four principles of a new family policy discussed thus far feed into what Giddens calls "rethinking the welfare state." Designing a new approach to welfare is the fifth principle of a family policy for the information age. The welfare state was conceived in Europe in the late 19th century, and after World War II it matured there to a much greater degree than in the United States. However, on both sides of the Atlantic, the welfare state is now under siege: The "grounding assumptions on which traditional welfare programs were built have melted away." [28] Those assumptions were "tied to an implicit model of traditional gender roles, presuming male participation in the paid labour force, with a 'second tier' of programmes directed towards families without a male breadwinner." [29]

The welfare state was an uneasy compromise between thoroughgoing socialism on one side and the continuation of an unbridled, and often irresponsible, capitalism on the other.[30] Among other things, it assumed a "top-down dispensation of benefits." Citizens were merely clients; they had virtually no political or economic empowerment. Very often, they became the responsibility of caseworkers. Moreover, the welfare state tended to be reactive. It aimed to "pick up the pieces" after citizens experienced unforeseen mishaps, such as unemployment, accidents, illnesses, or disabilities.

Giddens calls such mishaps examples of "external risk"—events over which workers had virtually no control. During the industrial period, the persons most vulnerable to external risks were men who labored at physically demanding, working-class occupations.

However, in the emerging information age, external risk has spread everywhere throughout the class structure. New technologies lean toward obsolescence as soon as they become popular. To take but one example, a well-educated man or woman involved in high-tech support, development, manufacture, or sales may suddenly and unexpectedly find him- or herself out of a well-paying job. And when he or she finds another, there is no guarantee whatsoever how long either the job or the company will be around.[31] A quip from a computer trade magazine says it well: "Q: How many programmers does it take to get information out of your company's database? A: None. Six Windows query and reporting packages promise to help you get it yourself without any programmers."[32]

Manufactured Risk

According to Giddens, not only is the information age characterized by the growing pervasiveness of external risk, it is marked by the acceleration of what he calls "manufactured" uncertainty, or risk. These are risks that women and men encounter as a result of choices they make in their pursuit of freedom and autonomy.[33] Such choices may lie in the occupational realm—for example, individuals may opt to leave or to take certain jobs and/or educational opportunities. Or the choices may lie in the personal realm—an individual may choose to leave a spouse or partner and may take along (or not take along) his or her children. Or the choices may lie in the forming of new relationships, even for individuals who may already be in relationships.[34] Or the choices may lie in a person's becoming a parent, even though he or she may or may not currently have a partner.[35] Options for manufactured risk appear everywhere throughout posttraditional society. Furthermore, an adult's manufactured risk may be stressful for his or her children, even though the children have taken little or no active part in the adult's decision.

To deal with the spread of external risk, and to cope with the growth in manufactured risk, Giddens argues for what he calls "positive" welfare policies. Those would be new policies and programs aimed at persons of both genders in the middle class, working class, and lower class alike. Instead of merely picking up the pieces, those innovative policies "would have to be redirected and reorganized in such a way as to promote responsible decision-making." [36] Besides enabling persons to bear the consequences of external risk, positive policies would help persons from all social classes to assume their manufactured risks in a responsible, or accountable, manner.

Positive welfare (principle 5) rests squarely on the first four principles. First of all, positive welfare requires a balance between freedom and responsibility. Second, it addresses women's interests but pays equal attention to the interests of men and children. Third, positive welfare stems from empowerment that is both personal and political. Fourth, it requires decision making that springs from dialogue, not unilateral authority. In short, positive welfare is something that could *not* easily be put in place. It would be a daunting task to design specific programs that might appeal to advantaged and disadvantaged families alike.

Confronting Violence

Trying to weave a coherent family policy from the five preceding principles is difficult enough. Nevertheless, Giddens insists that radical politics must further address the issue of violence, stretching "all the way from male violence against women through casual street violence to large-scale war." [37] Violence, he believes, is increasingly untenable at the international level.[38] In its place, dialogue is becoming a matter of compelling national self-interest. Thus, the sixth principle of a posttraditional, information-age family policy is to challenge and denounce violence in a much more open and direct manner than we have so far.

"The topic," Giddens admits, "is a big one." Everyone is against violence, yet we authorize soldiers and police to use violence against those who would harm us. The inclination to accept the inevitability of official violence tends to seep into the personal realm. Indeed, parents are authorized to use a certain degree of physical force on their own children.[39] And in the past, patriarchal tradition legitimated men's use of violence toward women.[40] Today, no one would defend that tradition, yet gender violence continues. Male violence, or aggression, may be sexual as well as physical, and all too often it is both. Moreover, women may sometimes inflict violence on children.

What is lacking is a new set of cultural traditions regarding violence in the realm of personal, or primary, relationships. At the core of those new traditions is principle 4—dialogue. A great deal of men's violence against women "can be understood as a generalized refusal of dialogue." And when "dialogue stops, violence begins." [41] That being the case, the objective must be to maintain dialogue. As long as people are talking (even heatedly), they are less likely to become violent. But dialogue does not exist in a vacuum. It is found in a context of freedom balanced with responsibility, of political efficacy, of women's interests, and of positive welfare.

Hence, the task is to design a family policy—a vision for the future—that declares unequivocally that personal interaction should be violence-free. That policy would also identify the structural, or situational, arrangements that might help to reinforce the new tradition. And in order to bolster nonviolence, those situational arrangements would necessarily reinforce freedom and responsibility, personal and political efficacy, dialogic decision making, women's interests, and positive welfare.

CONCLUSION

We are rapidly leaving the industrial period and entering the murky contours of the postindustrial era. This period has also been called the Third Wave, and it is also known as the information age or posttraditional society. Family policy that may have served reasonably well during the industrial period no longer seems adequate. What is now required is an innovative family policy fashioned around the six highly interconnected principles described in this introductory chapter:

1. A balance of freedom with responsibility
2. Special attention to women's interests
3. Personal and political empowerment for women, men, and children alike
4. Participation in dialogic, or democratic, decision making
5. Positive welfare aimed at both advantaged and disadvantaged households
6. The direct confrontation of violence

Part I of this book examines the historic and contemporary background for this innovative approach to family policy. Part I shows that the nuclear family style is faltering in large part because it is unable to fulfill these six principles. For example, Chapter 2 asks, How did we get to the point in the mid-20th century where families were damaged because of the elevation of women's obligations over their freedoms? In Chapter 3 the question is, How did we get to the present, where some critics worry that freedom is overwhelming responsibility? And Chapter 4 asks, What does it mean to describe cohousing as a strategy for reforming family? Part II shifts to offering a strategy aimed at fulfilling these six principles.

PART I

DESIGNING FAMILIES PAST AND PRESENT

2

AN UNFINISHED REVOLUTION: THE 1940s NONCONNECTED FAMILY STYLE

◆◆◆ ──────────────────────────────

During the middle decades of the 1700s—just prior to America's war for independence—a growing number of social critics were complaining that the extended family style was "damaged." [1] It was damaged in the sense described by the first principle discussed in Chapter 1: It was out of balance—obligations far outweighed freedoms. Subsequently, the 200-year history of the nuclear family style may be thought of as a revolution. [2] It is a record of citizens trying to repair the damage by bringing family freedoms into greater symmetry with family responsibilities. In the 18th century, few Americans gave much thought to principles 2-6 as described in Chapter 1. Concerns for women's interests, personal and political empowerment, dialogic decision making, positive welfare, and personal violence hardly existed at all. What did engage most persons was interest in greater freedom in their personal and economic lives, and the connections between the two.

A FOOT IN EACH OF TWO FAMILY STYLES

"One foot in the Romanesque, the other in the Gothic style of architecture," said the tour guide as she directed our gaze upward to the ceiling of the medieval chapel in which we stood.[3] The chapel, she told us, was an example of a building that was not quite in the older Romanesque style, but neither was it in the style of something that would later be called Gothic. She added that during that in-between period (around the 11th and 12th centuries), the designers and builders of churches were not fully aware that they were actually creating a whole new style of church architecture.[4] They were simply trying to improve church buildings—to make better ones—buildings that more adequately expressed their spiritual ideals and aspirations.

As the guide continued speaking, I started thinking about historian Lawrence Stone's study of how family, sex, and marriage gradually changed in England throughout the years 1500-1800.[5] Stone says that during those three centuries, growing numbers of persons were becoming part of an expanding business and merchant class known as the *bourgeoisie*—a forerunner of today's upper-middle class. When it came to the style of family they preferred, members of this class (like the medieval church architects) had one foot in the past and one foot in the future. And like those earlier architects, they were not fully aware that they were creating a whole new style of family. They simply wanted to improve their family style and make it better. They were groping for a family style that more adequately expressed their own values, ideals, and aspirations.

THE CONNECTED FAMILY STYLE

The family style from their past was what we today refer to as the *extended family*.[6] Let's say, for example, that Mr. Cooper (a prosperous farmer) and Mrs. Cooper and their children, aged 7 and 9, lived in a house by themselves located in the English countryside near London. Nearby in one house lived Mr. Cooper's parents, and in a separate house, Mrs. Cooper's parents. In yet another nearby house lived the Cooper's 17-year-old daughter, Lydia, who was married to 19-year-old Tom Crenshaw. Furthermore, those four households might be located near additional households that include a whole range of relatives—siblings, cousins, aunts, uncles—married or unmarried, and with or without children. Although it was not the typical way of living, dire circumstances occasionally forced more relatives to share the same house—for example, an unmarried aunt might care for her infirm mother and several of her nieces and nephews whose parents had died in a smallpox epidemic. Stone tells us that the core feature of that extended, or *connected,* family style of life was mutual support. Anthropologist Edward C. Banfield has observed that although children at that time frequently lost their natural parents to warfare, famine, disease, and assorted mishaps, this did not "mean catastrophe for the children." The reason is obvious: There were "plenty of others to take their place." [7]

The flip side of those mutual help patterns was obligation, control, and sometimes domination and exploitation. The unmarried aunt, for instance, might have pleaded to be allowed to move to London, to "marry the man I love." However, her relatives insisted it was her duty to stay and care for the elderly and the orphaned children, and so she did, even though that meant relinquishing her own desires, including marriage. Stone notes that as the decades rolled by, some members of the bourgeoisie began to resent the amount of control their kin had over their individual destinies. They wanted greater freedom to live their own lives.

THE FREEDOM TO LOVE

At the close of the agricultural era, the most fundamental freedom sought by couples was the right to marry the "one I love." Researcher Willard Waller has observed that "the sentiment of love is the heart of the problem of life in the [nuclear] family." [8] But love was also a serious problem for 18th- and 19th-century extended families. Sociologist William Goode has noted that love has always had enormous potential to disrupt the social order.[9] People in love have virtually zero tolerance for the limitations that others may seek to impose on them. Love is among the most potent expressions of autonomy and individualism. It typically drives a person to choose self-fulfillment and personal satisfaction, and not infrequently to disregard the cost of that choice to others and to him- or herself.

Throughout history, love has gotten in the way of older family members' trying to influence the marriage choices of the younger members. Love's explosive force has been documented in the literature and history of the ancient Hebrews, Greeks, and Romans.[10] Shakespeare's *Romeo and Juliet* shows that young lovers can and will violate their extended families' wishes and go to extraordinary lengths to be together—hopefully in life but, if need be, in death. A much later example of love's erratic and fickle ways captured the entire world's attention when, in 1936, Britain's King Edward VIII fell in love with a divorced woman. His extended family opposed the match, and the Church of England ruled that he was not permitted to wed her. Undeterred, he committed political and social suicide by abdicating his throne in order, he said, "to marry the woman I love." Even the movie *Titanic* revolves around the story of a young woman who feels obliged to marry a rich man so that her mother will not live in penury. But when she falls in love with a poor man, she forgets all about her obligations.

Several of Jane Austen's finest novels (e.g., *Persuasion, Pride and Prejudice, Emma, Sense and Sensibility*) were adapted for television and film in the 1990s, and these adaptations reached wide audiences and received enthusiastic responses. Austen describes premarital love in England during the transition from the First to the Second Wave—the early 1800s. During that time, love very definitely included a physical and sexual yearning, but the urge to merge also included a longing to be married, because that was the only legitimate setting in which couples could consummate their physical desires. Prior to marriage, being in love included sexual desires and a longing for the magical wedding that would unleash their fulfillment. There was also the fervent hope that subsequent to marriage, husbands and wives would continue to love each other as devoted companions. Nevertheless, once married, they were bound by rigid gender-driven rules, including the dictum that they could never divorce. Hence, whether or not they continued to love one another in any sense of that term was irrelevant to the maintenance and outcome of their marriage.

THE NONCONNECTED FAMILY STYLE

As hundreds of thousands of couples moved to cities in Europe and North America throughout the industrial period, they had no idea that they were in the vanguard of a new style of family. They simply wanted a style that "worked" for them—a family pattern that would more fully express their own values, aspirations, and ideals. That usually meant getting out from under the collective thumb of their blood kin. The upshot was that they began to create a new style of family in which, say, Tom and Lydia Crenshaw might begin to make certain choices for themselves even though their kin would strenuously object. They might, for instance, move to London, even though their kin insisted they must not. That kind of individual freedom is the essence of what eventually came to be known as the *nuclear* style of family life. Very likely, most couples who made such changes deeply regretted having to leave the land on which they had grown up and the relatives they loved—they indeed had one foot in the past and the other in a highly uncertain future. Nevertheless, growing numbers of late-18th- and early-19th-century couples made the choice to be relatively *nonconnected* to their relatives in order to be free to love each other and their own children in ways they deemed best.

What was happening, says Stone, was "not so much the replacement of one family type by another as the widening of the varieties. There was a growing diversity of family types, a widening pool of cultural alternatives." [11] If we visualize the extended family style as a train waiting in the station on its own track, the nuclear family style can be seen as another train waiting on a different track. We can say that in the late 18th and early 19th centuries, most passengers were boarding the extended family train, but a few began to board the nuclear family train. As the 19th century wore on, fewer and fewer went extended, and more and more went nuclear. Dizard and Gadlin observe that in spite of the fact that families were constructing a range of varied lifestyle alternatives, "few grasped the full implications" of the enormous changes that were taking place. [12] Keep in mind that a family style that had worked quite well for thousands of years was being seriously challenged. Upstanding citizens were taking steps to create something different in its place: "The circle of people to whom one felt obligated and for whom one felt responsible was shrinking, and conceptions of morality and justice were shifting from a basis in community and family to a basis in individuals themselves." [13]

THE INDUSTRIAL REVOLUTION

Although the quest for independence from kin—including the freedom "to marry the one I love"—had been proceeding for some time prior to the early 19th century, at that point it got a huge jolt forward. The Industrial Revolution—the start of the Second Wave—produced an abundance of well-paying jobs in factories and businesses in the burgeoning cities located on both sides of the Atlantic.[14] Hundreds of thousands of couples like the Crenshaws could find urban employment. Because they were no longer dependent on the land controlled by their extended families, they were free to order their own destinies and those of their children. Had they remained economically dependent on their kin, couples would not have been able to marry and parent in the ways they themselves thought best. Because the economic resources offered by urban factories and businesses were a viable alternative, couples were finally able to pull themselves free from kin authority.

Once early-19th-century couples arrived in the cities in England or the United States, the objective was not merely economic survival, as it had been in the countryside. Instead, the preeminent goal became nuclear family success—especially in the United States. The cities became the stage for poor (mostly white) *men* to try their hands at gaining wealth and prestige by making the American Dream their private reality. A few succeeded, but many did not, and all were subject to the careening boom-and-bust cycles of a rapidly developing, and often ruthless, capitalism.[15] In many urban lower-class and working-class households, survival became as problematic as it had been on the farm. Consequently, just as they had in rural settings, a large number of mothers and children labored many hours a day alongside husbands and fathers—only now their "fields" were sweatshops and unsafe factories. Typically, destitute families had to look to private charities and churches for help, or else migrate back to rural areas where they had kin who might be able to give them a hand.

THE AMERICAN DREAM AND KIN SUPPORT

Throughout the 1800s and early 1900s, hundreds of thousands of people migrated to North American cities from rural areas. In addition, they were joined by millions more who migrated from Europe. Cities were made up of ethnic neighborhoods that possessed a strong sense of shared solidarity. Many of the households in those neighborhoods were linked by blood. It was not uncommon for a nuclear family to migrate to a city and then send money to relatives back home, allowing them to migrate to the same or a nearby neighborhood. Once in place, this household proximity facilitated mutual helping-out patterns comparable to and yet quite distinct from those that pervaded agricultural communities. Kinfolk in cities were inclined to assist each other for any number of reasons, not least of which was the grim reality that very soon they themselves might be forced to seek aid from the very households they were now fortunate enough to be able to sustain.[16] When a household looked to its kin for help, everyone understood that the help would be temporary—"Just until we get back on our feet."

Make no mistake about it—each nuclear family was expected ultimately to stand on its own two feet. Kin help was viewed as sometimes necessary, but always temporary. The kinds of permanent, ongoing exchanges demanded for survival during the agricultural era were viewed as no longer tenable or desirable. Nevertheless, because marketplace conditions often careened wildly from tolerable to disastrous, no household could ever risk making itself too isolated, or nonconnected.[17] A nuclear family never knew when the kin they were helping out today would be needed to assist them tomorrow with unexpected emergencies of their own. Even though 19th- and early-20th-century culture was not explicit about mutual help patterns, everyone knew they existed. The sense of relief that help was available when needed was tied to a sense of regret and embarrassment that it was needed at all.

Social scientist Robert Nisbet underscores the potency of urban assistance patterns when he argues that 19th-century capitalism, as brutal and callous as it was, would never have survived had it not been for urban kin (and ethnic) networks caring for savaged workers of both genders and all ages.[18] Furthermore, although neither as extensive nor as intensive, mutual aid patterns could sometimes be found among households not linked by blood—that is, friends and close neighbors stood by each other in times of need. Those unfortunate men who could not support their wives and children—either by the own efforts or with the help of kin or neighbors— were perceived as "failures." Throughout the 19th century, many of these disillusioned would-be providers simply deserted their families and disappeared, never to be heard from again.[19] Furthermore, after the Civil War, divorce rates began their upward climb—a steady trend that has continued until recently.[20] Then as now, some critics reacted to divorce trends by demanding "tighter restrictions on divorce and tougher enforcement of laws holding parents responsible for the actions of their children." [21]

UNIQUE CONSTRAINTS ON AFRICAN AMERICANS

Throughout the 1800s, and continuing into the 1900s, the ideals of freedom, privacy, and independence signified by the nonconnected nuclear family style spread throughout, and were held ever more firmly by, a rapidly expanding urban population. Although some persons were periodically unable to fulfill its ideals because of economic downturns, that style of life became integral to the American Dream.

By all available accounts, emancipated African Americans believed in the Dream and its nonconnected family style as steadfastly as did their Euro-American counterparts.[22] The big difference was that black men were subject to a state of unremitting economic downturn in the form of racial segregation—legal exclusion from educational and occupational opportunities. Hence, they were unable to fulfill the socially demanded role of Good Provider in the same consistent fashion as white men. Although black women responded by entering the paid labor force so that their families might survive, the low wages they typically received made it exceedingly difficult for their households to make it on their own.[23] Hence, even though they preferred household independence, or at most the temporary helping patterns common in white society, both rural and urban blacks frequently created what anthropologist Carol Stack calls "fictive kin." [24]

Fictive Kin

For many decades, scholars have noted the existence of a "helping tradition" among African Americans that some believe can be traced to preslavery West African tribal customs.[25] During the traumas of bondage, it was quite apparent that adult slaves routinely assumed the care of children torn from their natural parents by either sale or death.[26] Though children may have resided in a particular household, they could not be adopted by it in any formal or legal sense. Instead, children were absorbed by fictive kin—that is, a support network that, because of the chaos and brutality of plantation life, could not be limited to a particular household.

Bereft children, as well as children who for the time being were fortunate enough to have their natural parents, belonged to a network of households and were identified by its adults as "all our children." Some households might have two adults, others more or one, and their ages varied. Although formal marriages were forbidden by law, slaves often created "informal" marriages in their place. However, at any time, adults could disappear without warning (with or without their children) because they were sold. By the same token, newly purchased adults (with or without children) could just as suddenly appear on the plantation and, for the sake of survival, gradually be absorbed into a particular set of fictive kin. Ties of blood and "marriage" were, after all, irrelevant when owners decided to sell or buy slaves. The upshot was that the composition of any given household was by no means as crucial to a person's survival and well-being as was the shared obligation of all the adults and children in the loop to give when they could and receive when they must. Slave households had no choice but to subordinate blood ties to an overriding objective: Within any fictive kin network, every household held the obligation to look out for the well-being of every other household, whether or not the households were linked by blood.

Following the end of slavery in 1865, the need for black citizens to create and maintain fictive kin was as pressing as ever. The pervasive economic discrimination facing black men, even when they were employed, made it exceedingly difficult for them to fulfill the household provider role in the same ways as white men. The result was that fictive kin remained a significant presence in black neighborhoods at least until the 1930s. Stack describes their existence in a northern urban area as late as the 1960s, and a study conducted in the early 1990s has demonstrated their presence in a small southern town.[27] Throughout the long period of legal discrimination known as "Jim Crow," and prior to the advent of New Deal and Great Society programs, survival demands impelled black households to maintain ongoing mutual support networks that included both tangible and intangible help.[28] Among other things, "helping" meant paying attention to every child within the fictive kin network. Adults felt obliged to serve as role models and sources of wisdom for children by, among other things, helping them to figure out how to make it in white-dominated society. The expression "It takes a village to raise a child" is illustrated by these historic patterns of networked households carrying out their shared obligations to receive and to give.[29]

Recall that during this same era, it was not uncommon for friends and neighbors in white neighborhoods to help each other out when needed. However, seldom did those friend-based helping patterns ever assume the significance of blood kin networks. Euro-Americans had never experienced the constraints of chattel slavery, legal discrimination, and pervasive prejudice based on skin color. Accordingly, white citizens seldom if ever felt pressure to create and maintain fictive kin networks for survival purposes. Among white citizens, "helping out" was indeed temporary, because they knew that sooner or later, broader economic conditions would improve. Eventually, white men would be able to find jobs, and thus once again be able to support their families. Among African Americans, by contrast, such optimism would have been unfounded. Even in the urban, industrial North, black men were typically the last hired and the first fired.[30] Hence, in contrast to white neighborhoods, in black neighborhoods fictive kin relationships were a pervasive and permanent feature for many decades.

That feature of the African American experience conveys at least two major conclusions: First, it illustrates Nisbet's argument that no one particular family form is inherently better, and thus more necessary, than any other.[31] People are remarkably inventive in doing what they must in order to survive and, if possible, thrive. What matters is that they create social patterns that "work"—that is, that promote both responsibility and freedom as fully as possible. Writing in the late 1960s, sociologist Andrew Billingsley showed that black fictive kin got high marks on both counts.[32] In view of the awesome formal constraints imposed by the larger society on black Americans, fictive kin were not only necessary, they were also sufficient to meet the emotional and tangible needs of black adults and children. That it was a moral imperative to remove those formal constraints goes without saying. What needs saying is that in spite of them, many blacks figured out effective ways to "overcome." [33]

Second, the black experience adds concrete, "cross-cultural" substance to the idea of people inventing family styles. It illuminates the notion that within a given social environment, people can and do create innovative neighborhood arrangements. Adults will behave in that manner if they perceive that connecting households through strategies that they themselves design could perhaps make life "better" for them and any children within their orbit. Moreover, such connections would neither exclude nor require that households be linked by blood. What is required is a common set of ideas regarding the appropriate balance of household freedom and household obligation, alongside a willingness and ability to participate jointly in ways that express those beliefs. Although African Americans designed neighborhood connectedness as a means to enhance their well-being, by all accounts most preferred the nonconnected family style.[34] They were, after all, Americans, and the dominant American culture praised and reinforced the autonomous and self-contained household. Churches, both black and white, were and are among the most prominent purveyors of that emotionally charged cultural theme.[35]

THE EMERGENCE OF FEMINISM

At the same time that the ideal of household freedom from kin control was steadily gaining popular acceptance, a whole set of new freedoms loomed on the horizon. In the early 1800s, a number of well-educated women in Britain and the United States were active with their husbands in a movement, first, to terminate the international slave trade and, second, to abolish slavery in both countries.[36] But as they actively sought the freedom of others, it gradually dawned on these women that they themselves were not as free as their own husbands. The result was that they became the first organized feminists. As the 19th century wore on, it became increasingly plain that the hoped-for freedoms of the nuclear family style were not being equally distributed. Many feminists (female and male) believed that men were doing a whole lot better than women.

The Seneca Falls Declaration

To try to correct the imbalance in gender-based rights and responsibilities, a national conference was held in 1848 at Seneca Falls, New York, from which came an affirmation of women's freedoms based on the 1776 U.S. Declaration of Independence: "The history of mankind," [said the 1848 declaration] was 'a history of repeated injuries and usurpations on the part of man toward woman, having in direct object the establishment of an absolute tyranny over her.' "[37] Many conference participants believed that the first step in abolishing that tyranny would be for women to gain access to the ballot box. Accordingly, the conference narrowly adopted a resolution advocating universal suffrage—the right to vote for everyone, including women.

Nevertheless, beyond their demand for universal suffrage, the early feminists differed significantly among themselves regarding what it meant for women to have greater independence and freedom. The mid-19th-century British philosopher John Stuart Mill was among the first to advocate explicitly for total equality between the genders in both homeplace and workplace.[38] He believed firmly that for women to be equal with men, they must first gain their economic independence—they must become self-sufficient. By no means did all 19th-century feminists agree with Mill, but many shared the belief that the evolving nuclear family style was doing more for men's interests than for women's, and that something should be done to redress the imbalance. In short, the same argument used in earlier decades to pry the nuclear family free from the extended family was now being used to pry women from the grip of subordination to men within the context of the nonconnected family.

DOMESTIC SCIENCE:
A HALFWAY FEMINISM

Some feminists believed, for instance, that gender equality meant elevating woman's status in the home. Among these was Catharine Beecher (sister of Harriet Beecher Stowe). Beecher's mid-19th-century books on home and family "made her name a household word."[39] She believed that women were "devalued because they were not trained for the complex and varied work in household management." [40] For women to achieve social equality with men, who were clearly dominant in the marketplace, Beecher advocated "female supremacy in the home." [41] Accordingly, she set forth an agenda aimed at enabling wives and mothers to become the social equals of men. Men and women each had their separate spheres of influence, and Beecher declared the two spheres identical in significance. Thus, she asserted that excelling in the domestic sphere was the same thing as excelling in the occupational sphere.

The late-19th- and early-20th-century founders of the "home economics" movement implemented and expanded Beecher's agenda. They believed that the growing pool of stay-at-home mothers should no longer be content with the previously limited definitions of their roles. In the male sphere of the workplace, "more and more jobs were being formalized into professions by virtue of the steady injection of technical know-how." [42] Consequently, following Beecher's arguments, the movement's leaders felt that wives and mothers should think of themselves as holding the lofty profession of "homemaker." Moreover, they, like men in the workplace, should "be informed by the findings of science and the benefits of technology." [43] The domestic half of the homemaker role meant being informed by connoisseurs of shopping and cooking, decorating, health and hygiene, sewing, and cleaning. The parenting half meant that wives and mothers required the advice of experts from rapidly developing scientific disciplines, such as psychology and child development.

Homemaker

Girls and women learned that being an effective homemaker meant rejecting the "old wives' tales" of their mothers regarding how to cook, keep house, and take care of their husbands and children. They could excel "without relying on the advice of their mothers." [44] That message significantly reinforced the cultural image of the self-sufficient, self-contained nuclear household. An effective homemaker need look no longer to her mother, sisters, or cousins for advice and help that, although well-intentioned, might just as easily be misguided and invalid. Instead of following the ancient tradition of seeking advice from kin, she should instead sit at the feet of nationally recognized experts on how to do it all herself. Hence, the belief that the wife no longer required kin assistance for her domestic and child-rearing needs was added to the already existing ideal that the husband should not look to his kin to help out with provider obligations.

Mother

Prior to the 19th century, extended families viewed child rearing as the ancient process of seeing that their offspring learned to become responsible contributors to the well-being of kin and community. Based on their own experience, adults assumed that children's spiritual and personal well-being would proceed from the deep satisfactions of giving to, and the solid security of receiving from, something larger and more important than themselves. Nevertheless, in the United States, experts informed 19th- and 20th-century parents that they needed to amend the ordering of their child-rearing priorities. This reordering was especially difficult for immigrants to grasp, because at that time the nuclear family style was far less strongly endorsed in Europe than it was in North America.[45]

American mothers were told that, first and foremost, they must make the child's emotional well-being, or happiness, their top priority. Everything possible must be done to produce a psychologically healthy child. To be sure, the child must learn to be responsible, but, mothers were told, that would flow from his or her being a happy child, not the other way around. Moreover, parents had to understand that the child's preeminent responsibility must ultimately be to her- or himself, not to the nuclear family, and certainly not to other kin. Clearly, children (especially girls) must learn to cooperate with their parents and to do things around the house. And they must pay attention to their parents, relatives, and schoolteachers. But the requirement to conform must be subordinated to the child's primary responsibility to become an autonomous and self-sufficient individual.

Children

The upshot was that women's interests became intertwined with, and absorbed by, children's interests. A mother's effectiveness was measured in terms of her children's successes in life. Her husband was defined as a Good Provider if he produced money for the family.[46] But being a Good Mother meant, first, that the wife produced sons who would be at least as successful as their father.[47] Second, it meant producing daughters who grew up to be Good Mothers. Because parenting is just as essential as economic production for the well-being of society, and because women were said to be biologically and emotionally fitted for the task of parenting, they were declared to be the equals of men.

At the start of the 20th century, the family revolution that had begun a hundred years earlier had progressed to a declaration of equity between wives and husbands. It was, however, a declaration of equity without independence. Wives still remained reliant on their husbands for identity, status, and economic well-being. The revolution fell far short of the ideal of gender equity advocated by Mill and others. Clearly, it had a long way to go.

REINVENTING SEX AND LOVE: A HALFWAY LIBERATION

The movement toward gender equality inched forward slightly during the decade of the "Roaring Twenties." It shifted because women and men were inventing a range of sexual freedoms unknown to, and unimagined by, the characters of Jane Austen's early-19th-century novels. The 1920s marked the invention of "dating." It was the time of the "first sexual revolution." [48] During that turbulent decade, citizens substantially reinvented their views about premarital sexual desires. They also reconstructed the links between their sexual desires and marriage. Their reinvention contained several aspects, perhaps the most significant of which was that the object of one's desire need not necessarily be one's intended spouse.[49] Not only did sexual longing become a component separate and distinct from future spousehood, the legitimate expression of desire itself was transformed dramatically. Terms such as *necking, petting,* and *French kissing* slowly became part of the everyday vocabulary of respectable middle-class citizens. Sensual behaviors that were thought to be the province of married couples prior to sexual intercourse (i.e., foreplay) were now being routinely practiced among never-married youth who had pledged neither love nor marriage.

Love was being reconstructed. Prior to that time, being in love meant getting married, followed by gratification of the couple's formerly sublimated sexual desires. However, from the 1920s to the 1960s, that predict-able and orderly sequence was effectively undermined. Not only did certain forms of previously forbidden sexual expressions become legitimate for single persons, they were not necessarily preceded or followed by declara-tions of love and promises to marry. Whether or not love and/or marriage would ever follow rested on a highly intricate social process that Waller calls the "Dating Game." [50] For both genders, "winning" the Game meant falling in love (with a beautiful woman or a handsome man) and eventually getting married (to a Good Wife and Mother or a Good Provider).

The Game was like a tennis match, consisting of several sets leading up to the final outcome. Women playing the match were in constant danger of losing their sets if they "gave away" too much sexual pleasure. If they relinquished too many sets, their chances of ever "winning" a trip to the altar with their current or any other desirable "opponent" declined steeply. Men, however, could never lose a set, much less the entire match, simply because they had been sexually overgenerous. On the contrary, men who boasted of sexual exploits were envied and secretly admired by their peers at the same time that the objects of their successes were either pitied or scorned and derided. Obviously, the Dating Game had vastly different implications for women than it did for men. Men, after all, had been engaging in foreplay and actual intercourse with prostitutes since time began. What was suddenly different was that men now had a certain degree of controlled sexual access to a pool of women formerly denied them—that is, women who were eligible to become their wives.

Furthermore, men got this new freedom without having to give up their ancient liberty to consort with prostitutes. Additionally, they could exercise this newfound freedom in one of two ways. They could try to get as much sexual satisfaction as possible without ever promising anything (much less love and marriage) in return. Waller views this as "exploitation." He observes that, in contrast, some men sought to be "honorable." Hon-orable men realized they must be cautious in extracting unrequited sexual favors (e.g., intercourse) from women. Extracting "too many" favors placed the woman's reputation at risk, and thus reduced her value on the marriage market. For "respectable" women, the world of sexual freedom was an entirely novel and perilous experience. They had never been part of, nor were they yet allowed into, the hidden realms of illicit and illegal sex. Men kept them out of that world at the same time that they dominated the new sphere of sexual activity into which "nice girls" had finally been initiated.

As she played the Dating Game, a woman had but one overriding preoccupation—she must be able to finesse the man to be honorable. Although required to supply sexual favors, a woman could never allow herself to be exploited, because that would lower her hopes of eventually making a good match. To make a good marriage, a woman had to titillate, but could never fornicate. A good marriage meant getting a man who was likely to be a Good Provider and a warm companion. Hence, the woman's typical "game plan" was to utilize her available resources (popularity, beauty, and sexual favors) to get the man she loved to requite her love and to marry her. Hence, even though the Dating Game was a new invention, it merely tinkered around the edges of the ancient double standard of sexuality.[51] Though refined a bit, the double standard remained alive and well at least until the 1960s.

THE COLLAPSE AND REVIVAL OF MUTUAL AID

In addition to being the cradle of a sexual revolution, the 1920s were years of virtually unprecedented economic expansion in the United States. Jobs were plentiful, and more couples than ever before were able to afford the highly prized and sought-after nuclear family style. Kin helping out kin became considerably less typical, especially among Euro-Americans, simply because it was less imperative. More so than at any other time during the whole industrial era, nuclear households were, because of their increasing economic self-sufficiency, able to care for themselves apart from their relatives. Researchers Jan Dizard and Howard Gadlin conclude that the 1920s seemed to signal the final "collapse of mutual aid" among kin.[52]

Nevertheless, that nonconnected lifestyle came to a screeching halt in the wake of the Great Depression: "The calamity of the [nineteen] thirties required families [once again] to pull together." [53] Catastrophic unemployment rates meant that many families could not keep up their loan payments. Hence, they lost their cars and houses along with their furniture and appliances. Tens of thousands of small business owners were wiped out. After having worked so hard for so long to achieve freedom from dependence on their kin, many households were unexpectedly forced once more to look to them for help, and in numerous cases this meant actually moving in with them. Couples and their children who had grown accustomed to an autonomous nuclear family lifestyle were abruptly thrust into crowded and distasteful daily living with relatives, and "guilt, anxiety, anger, and psychological depression all flourished." [54] A comparable situation occurred in Mexico during that country's 1995 economic crisis, in which the government cut the living standard of most citizens by 20%. For several years prior to that time, many middle-class Mexicans had been enjoying a higher level of prosperity than they had ever before dreamed possible. At the same time, they had also been experiencing a greater degree of independence than ever before from reliance on their kin. Nevertheless, in order to absorb the economic shock imposed by the government, they suddenly "moved in with each other, and the [extended] family really took the place of social security and unemployment insurance." [55]

MUTUAL AID REPLACED BY THE GOVERNMENT

Although in the short run it compelled U.S. households to work together for survival, in the long run the Great Depression was an unrivaled catalyst for the significant undermining of the ancient family value that kin must help each other out.[56] For example, the 1935 Social Security Act meant that senior citizens were no longer perceived as a "burden" to their children. It also implied that children need no longer worry about their parents' becoming a burden.[57] At the same time, Aid to Families with Dependent Children (AFDC) was created; it was intended to support widows with small children until the children were old enough to permit the mothers and offspring to enter the labor force. The Wagner Act and the 1936 National Labor Relations Act officially recognized trade unions, allowing them to organize and bargain collectively with industry.[58] The labor movement's principal objective was to negotiate labor contracts that would guarantee a "living wage"—that is, a level of wages that could support a nuclear family lifestyle built around the role of the male Good Provider. Among other things, that lifestyle meant freedom from situations of dire need that would force families to seek help from kinfolk.

The seeds of principle 5 (positive welfare) as described in Chapter 1 were being planted in the United States at this time. The Great Depression required the United States to follow the lead of the European democracies by establishing a sense of "national community" in which virtually everyone perceived him- or herself to be a "social citizen." [59] President Franklin Roosevelt declared that every American is his or her "brother's keeper." Every citizen was said to be part of the national community, and as such must contribute taxes as he or she is able. Sometimes circumstances made it impossible to contribute, but no matter. The obligation to give when able was balanced with the duty to take when needed. Every citizen deserved to receive help in the form of national government assistance when she or he had need. Because kin assistance was often inadequate and typically distasteful, the federal government replaced relatives as the ultimate source of help for nonconnected households.

By 1945 and the end of World War II, most Americans believed it archaic to think that kinfolk should or could cushion the effects of economic uncertainties on floundering households. They perceived that ancient "family value" as a vestige of a grim past they fervently hoped was finally left behind. That is not to say that nuclear families somehow ceased completely to exchange money, goods, and services with their kin. [60] Rather, when they did so, it was no longer out of desperation and the need for survival. Bolstered by government guarantees, more nuclear families than ever before could achieve and maintain the highly valued cultural goals of autonomy, privacy, and independence.

POSTWAR SUBURBIA:
THE PINNACLE OF THE NONCONNECTED STYLE

Putting their "grim past" behind them was symbolized vividly by the spectacular migration of nuclear families from cities to suburbs that marked the post-World War II years. [61] The burgeoning postwar suburbs afforded a visual demonstration of how to invent a *spatial* structure superbly suited to reinforce a social structure based on household nonconnectedness:

The design of the houses and the layout of the subdivision itself made it clear that each nuclear family was assumed to be independent. . . . Rooms were arranged in ways that made it clear that only parents and their children were to be at home here. . . . Kinfolk might visit, but stays would be short. The whole marketing strategy concentrated on the nuclear family, its upward mobility, and its independence.[62]

The massive construction of the new suburbs, with their well-paved streets and detached one-family houses, accessed by modern highways, vividly symbolized the conspicuous desirability of the nuclear family lifestyle.[63]

The immense expansion of those spatial features became a visible sign of the belief that this was indeed the most desirable way to live. The nuclear family lifestyle became virtually obligatory, because there were no longer any defensible excuses for living otherwise. The nonconnected nuclear family had at last become the moral domain of every *man* and his family. There is perhaps no more colorful way to capture the essence of postwar suburbia than with the word *Levittown,* the name of certain housing developments that also became a broad designation applied to the many thousands of such developments springing up during that period around practically every U.S. city.[64] In early 1949, people stood in line for several days waiting for developer William Levitt to open his Hicksville, New York, real estate office. By the close of the first day's business, $11 million in vacant land and unbuilt houses had been sold.[65]

For 20 years, the Depression and the war had restrained the surging desires of hundreds of thousands of couples to participate fully in the nonconnected nuclear family lifestyle. The style itself had been around for a long time and was clearly understood. Its foundational element was a self-sufficient couple able to attend to their own material and companionate needs, and thereby to have a "successful" marriage. From that base, the couple progressed to being "successful" parents, raising as many healthy and happy children as they could afford. And all this was to be done "free from the scrutiny of parents and unencumbered by the weight of familial obligations." [66]

Social scientist Kenneth Fox explains that suburban couples sought to distance themselves from their parents because they viewed them as a "potential drain on economic and psychological resources." He adds that parents of suburban couples "bore the scars of the Depression." Those parents were "accustomed to depending on relatives and perhaps neighbors for social and economic stability." [67] Consequently, their parents were "sceptical of suburban life" and opposed the idea of their adult offspring taking on mortgage and consumer debt because that meant they would have fewer dollars to help out their kin when needed. Nevertheless, studies in both the United States and Britain have shown that huge numbers of postwar couples rejected those ancient family values, left their parents and other kin in the cities, and raced to pursue the emerging suburban family lifestyle.

A NEW FAMILY POLICY: THE G.I. BILL

The economic engine driving that innovative suburban lifestyle was a unique federal program. In the late 1940s,

> though unintended, the government had . . . adopted a family policy by making it possible for the generation of World War II veterans to form families of a distinctly autonomous sort. The federal government was doing . . . what their kin networks otherwise would have had to do[, i.e.,] help with an education and with the expenses of setting up a household.[68]

First of all, every veteran was entitled to a college education (tuition, books, fees) paid for by the government. If married, he got extra money to help support his wife and children. Second, every veteran was entitled to a home mortgage at very low interest rates. The new federal policy was called the G.I. Bill. It directed billions of federal dollars toward veterans' educations and home mortgages—its two pillars.

The G.I. Bill finally accomplished what most Americans had yearned for since the start of the industrial era. By making the nonconnected family style readily accessible to far greater numbers of couples than ever before, federal programs crystallized a fresh understanding of its availability for everyone.[69] It evolved from being a style of living limited merely to the fortunate few (albeit frequently on a temporary basis) to the kind of life actually experienced by the many on a permanent basis. And by the mid-1950s, the "many" included men who had never served in World War II. In 1955, for example, in Levittown, New Jersey, a $100 down payment could reserve a lot with a house to be built on it.[70] To qualify, the husband had to have an annual income exceeding $5,500. And because the U.S.

median family income at that time was around $5,000, growing numbers of *non*-World War II veterans had the money to afford the "idyllic" suburban lifestyle.

WOMEN'S CONTINUED DISADVANTAGE

By the late 1940s and throughout the 1950s, family in the United States was gripped by an internal contradiction. On the one hand, citizens had indeed repaired the damage of the 18th-century extended family. They did so by inventing a new family style that was largely free from kin obligations and oppression. Moreover, the federal government had assisted them significantly in their efforts. National programs enacted during the Great Depression (especially social security), followed by the postwar G.I. Bill, marked the last rites of an ancient style of family.

On the other hand, the new family style was itself severely damaged. Men and boys enjoyed a great deal more freedom, independence, and autonomy than did women and girls. Clearly, the revolution that had begun 200 years earlier was incomplete. In terms of principle 1, as described in Chapter 1, the task of balancing autonomy with responsibility remained unfinished. Nevertheless, women's interests (principle 2) were at least on the table— they had become a matter of national discussion, albeit quite limited. Furthermore, the notion that the government, acting in lieu of blood kin, has a role to play in the well-being of ordinary households (principle 5) was also a matter of public discussion.

The subsequent history of the last half of the 20th century is in part a record of women and men continuing the family revolution that began in the late 18th century. Government's role in the revolution is a significant piece of the debate. Chapter 3 picks up the next phase of the revolution in the post-World War II suburbs.

3

A CONTINUING REVOLUTION: THE 1950s TO THE PRESENT

◆◆◆ ——————————————————————————

In her 1946 study of post-World War II college women, sociologist Mirra Komarovsky concluded that although distressed over the prospects, virtually all of them expected eventually to give up the role of postcollege "career girl" for that of "married homemaker." [1] During the 1950s, hardly anyone would have said out loud that she or he was part of the historic struggle to balance gender autonomy with family responsibility. Instead, most simply ignored the imbalance and the damage it might be causing for women, men, and children alike. Thus, in one sense, we might say that during the 1950s, the family revolution was put on hold. But in another very real sense, it was not. The same kinds of discontents that spawned the revolution in the first place remained and actually became more intense.

SEPARATE, UNEQUAL, AND DISCONTENT

In *The Organization Man,* William H. Whyte's well-known study of a postwar Chicago suburb, he describes the nuclear family's neighbors as a "foster family. . . . What unites them most are the concerns of parenthood, and this preoccupation with children is a potent factor in keeping marriages on keel." [2] Whyte adds a local clergyman's observation that apart from their children and their "foster family," many postwar suburban husbands and wives had little in common, and thus might otherwise have sought divorce. This same theme of women and men living in divergent worlds but bound together by their children permeates yet another classic study of 1950s suburbia. Anthropologists John R. Seeley, R. Alexander Sim, and Elizabeth W. Loosley vividly portray the "culture of suburban life" in a place they call Crestwood Heights.[3] The resident women had been socialized in the same climate of egalitarian ideals as their husbands. Moreover, both mothers and fathers worked very hard to instill egalitarianism in both their sons and their daughters, and they insisted that the schools and other parts of the community minimize gender differences as much as possible.

Notwithstanding their shared commitment to gender equity, women knew very well that they were not genuinely equal with men, and they were keenly aware that neither their husbands nor the larger society viewed them as equal.[4] It was perfectly obvious to these wives that society prized occupational achievement more than parenting. Achievement supplied not merely money, but high levels of prestige, status, and self-esteem. The upshot was that no matter how successful women might be in their "careers" as wives, mothers, and community volunteers, they lived in a world that was totally different from, and subordinate to, the one in which their husbands lived.[5] Their unequal status left many of them profoundly frustrated and deeply disappointed.

Nevertheless, despite what Seeley et al. call these women's "considerable dissatisfaction within marriage," as well as the "absence of a deeply felt emotional unity," and despite the presence of "considerable conflict," the majority of Crestwood families "function fairly effectively." [6] "Effectively" simply meant that, like the couples in Whyte's study, they did not divorce. The "presence of children necessarily curtails the highly individualistic activities of both husband and wife . . . [and thus] entails very real sacrifices for the persons involved." [7] In effect, children became the glue that held together marriages that would otherwise have come apart.

AN EXPANDED MOTHER ROLE

It was the woman's job to tend to this glue, and thus to her marriage.[8] That meant that the 19th-century mother role described in Chapter 2 was considerably expanded. It became more comprehensive, first, because the average distance between the man's city workplace and the suburban home-place was now considerably greater than it was before. Owing to the fact that fathers had to commute more miles, they had less time to spend with their children. Second, many suburban fathers had taken up "careers," not merely "jobs." [9] Having a job meant being away from home some 8 hours per day, whereas a career implied being away from home many more hours per day, as well as traveling on business for any number of days or weeks at a time, including weekends. To be sure, child development experts had insisted for decades that fathers must be actively involved in the daily lives of their children—particularly as role models for their boys. Hence, it was thought regrettable that postwar suburban fathers had such limited time for their children. Nevertheless, that situation was defined as yet one more challenge for the resourceful mother. Experts gave her advice on how to meet that fresh challenge and thereby increase still further both the scope and significance of the unique role of Good Mother.

Experts added another facet to that role by informing mothers that kin, including grandparents, might possibly have *harmful* influences on their children. Grandparents were likely to "interfere with efforts to create the non-repressive environment required for the children's proper psychological development." [10] The result was that the suburban mother believed she had to assume comprehensive responsibility for child rearing for at least three reasons: First, she was better at it than anybody else; second, her husband was devoting himself to their family's material needs; and third, she had to protect her children from the potentially negative inputs of kin and other outsiders.

Furthermore, while the husband/father busily pursued his occupational achievements in a marketplace geographically removed from his family, the community became the stage on which the wife/mother's achievements were displayed. Her "career" demanded a willingness to supervise community activities for children and also to volunteer her time to myriad other organizations that aimed to benefit the community's general welfare. As one Crestwood wife/mother reported, "I'm on the go all the time now. Busiest woman in the community. I'm in everything—Home and School, National Council of Women, Community Chest—oh, you couldn't list them all. . . . For years I went to every school board meeting. It is awfully important to have an active community spirit." [11]

There seems little doubt that besides being the key player in the everyday success of her own family, the active wife/mother was also vital in maintaining community cohesion, solidarity, and effectiveness. To be sure, many suburban men participated in the evenings and on weekends in both children's and broader community activities. Nevertheless, such activities invariably remained secondary to their occupational careers. [12] But for women, the community *was* their career. And they pursued it with the same levels of energy, intelligence, and diligence that their husbands applied to their marketplace endeavors.

"Quiet Desperation"

At the time, several researchers remarked on what seemed to them a bizarre turn of events. Freedom to love had been a principal force driving the married pair from the authority and control of the extended family. "Being in love" was why post-World War II persons got married in record numbers. The 1950s were called the "Golden Age" of the nonconnected nuclear family lifestyle. [13] It was celebrated by almost everyone and reached the pinnacle of its success. Nevertheless, a significant number of married couples, like those in Crestwood Heights, were content to live without love, in a state, said one researcher, of "quiet desperation." [14] Whatever their discontents regarding the post-World War II nonconnected family style, most citizens tolerated its flaws and lived with their unease, at least through the 1950s. Post-World War II women (and men to a degree) were quite willing to sacrifice their own interests, including love, for the sake of their children, because they believed it was the right thing to do. At the same time, a tiny handful of critics were trying to focus attention on the damaged character of the suburban lifestyle—particularly its inattention to women's interests.

A "MASSIVE FAILURE"

Among those critics was the distinguished anthropologist Margaret Mead. Mead had won international acclaim for her studies of gender among nondeveloped societies of the mid-20th century. Those societies had kept the extended family lifestyle—the same style that prevailed in Western societies prior to the industrial era. And when Mead compared the extended style to "this [suburban] style of family organization," she viewed it as a "massive failure." [15] Mead used such provocative language because she believed that the very framework, or structure, of the nuclear family was itself inherently flawed. In Mead's view, the nuclear family was a failure, first, because it was nonconnected, or what another sociologist of the time called "isolated." [16] As Mead saw it, two isolated adults were simply not enough to take care of each other and their children. Her model for success was the extended family style she had studied in nondeveloped societies.

The second reason Mead viewed the nuclear family as a failure was that people had tried to correct its basic flaw by creating a strategy that simply ignored the defect. The strategy was to divide rigidly the roles of women and men. Virtually everything the extended family had done of a material nature was now funneled into the role of husband-father. Almost everything else was the responsibility of the wife-mother. Although it might have seemed efficient to design the nonconnected family that way, the strategy failed to remedy the basic fact of its structural—that is, situational—inadequacy. Sharply divided gender roles did nothing to increase the available person-power. Furthermore, Mead believed that the design was unfair to women and deprived the larger society of the contributions they could make via their own talents and abilities. She added that rigid gender roles kept men from developing into full human beings and cheated children in the bargain.

Mead was convinced that the emerging postindustrial era demanded that this flawed family structure be put right. She argued that the fundamental step in facing this reality would be to acknowledge gender inequity as the warp and woof of the 1950s nuclear family. By arguing in this manner, Mead anticipated principle 2 as described in Chapter 1. If the future is to be better than the past, said Mead, there must be a "growing disregard for sex as a basic mode of differentiation." [17] Accordingly, she proposed a family policy that was radical (as defined in Chapter 1—radical in the sense of "taking things by the roots"). In her case, going to the root of things meant basing new designs on an up-to-date version of the extended family. She suggested, for instance, that a man and woman with children might belong to a larger social network that would share with the parents both the burdens and the joys of child rearing. She said that such social networks should consist of various combinations of genders, ages, and sizes. These networks, she believed, would facilitate "companionship for work, play, and stable living."

Social Protections

Mead also anticipated policy principle 1 as described in Chapter 1. She argued that, whatever their shape, new family designs must be socially responsible. As society made the transition from the 1950s nuclear family style to more adequate designs, care must be taken, she said, to guard against harm coming to children and adults because of the process. Mead was, in effect, anticipating the fallout from what I have referred to in Chapter 1 as manufactured risk, namely, adults making lifestyle choices that could have negative outcomes for themselves and/or their children. She warned her readers that as they made changes in family styles, they must put in place "social protections for both men and women [and children] during the transition stages in the development of new styles of behavior." Her hope was that people would design families that would enable women as well as men to respond to the "demands . . . made on them for citizenship, economic contribution, and creativity." She added, "We are so urgently in need of every form of creative imagination to meet the [national and global] challenges already before us." [18] As Mead saw it, the design of new family styles must mesh individual freedom with a sense of responsibility for something larger than oneself.

AN "IMPOVERISHED EXPERIENCE"

Another critic of the time agreed with Mead that the fading of the extended family style held certain negative consequences for parents and children alike. Psychologist Frederick Stoller observed that the rise of suburbia meant the "elimination of the extended family as an effective source of [help and] values." He added that the absence of kin inputs "created a vacuum not necessarily filled by the increased influence of the parents." As he saw it, "The increasing isolation and independence of the conjugal family has resulted in an impoverished experience, thus placing an almost impossible burden on the family members." He complained about the fact that many parents "have set themselves up as expert child-rearers," and he believed that the "movement toward the isolated family may well be incompatible with a richer investment in family experience. It places enormous burdens upon the parents who must assume an expertise in the art of childrearing which is not realistic for anyone." [19] Like Mead, Stoller concluded that the nuclear family is simply too small for children's own good and, for that matter, too small for the parents' own good. Keep in mind that for Stoller, "too small" equaled two parents. Thus, recent dramatic trends toward solo parenting mean that increasing numbers of households are now even smaller than "too small."

Intimate Networks

Stoller, like Mead, proposed a policy solution that involved the design of an up-to-date version of the extended family style. He advocated connectedness among households not linked by blood—the "development of particular kinds of relationships and arrangements *between families,* i.e., intimate networks." [20] Such networks would be similar to those referred to in Chapter 2 as fictive kin. In Stoller's view, each intimate network, or fictive kin grouping, would consist of a small number of households sharing certain pivotal beliefs and practices. They would, for example, have relinquished what he called the "supreme illusion" that their parenting requires no external inputs. That is, they would accept the notion that friends are in fact requisite to help them become more effective parents. By precept and example, friends might assist one another in their mutual quest to enrich their children's lives. Adults would meet on a regular and frequent basis to share their feelings and experiences about parenting and, very frequently, parenting's connections to couples' marital relationships. Furthermore, group members might also establish an ongoing exchange of services and goods, including (but not limited to) child care, car rides, domestic chores, furniture, and household gadgets. Like Mead, Stoller believed that an intimate network of this sort would be preferable to seeking help from professional counselors in solving family problems.

Stoller acknowledged that some critics might protest that his modest policy suggestions represented a threat to the independence and autonomy of the nonconnected lifestyle. He responded that intimate networks would by no means diminish privacy, or the independence and autonomy it signifies. Each network, he believed, would establish its own comfort level of both sharing and exchanges beyond which it was not likely to move, apart from group consensus to that effect. As a result, some networks would tend to develop much lower, and others much higher, degrees of household permeability than others. In any case, he believed that the household network would encourage a "diversity of experience, a moving between privacy and sharing." [21]

Furthermore, Stoller asserted that the network's *spatial* features were just as significant as its social dimensions. He argued that balancing privacy with sharing requires that individuals call into question previously accepted and largely unchallenged standards of "architecture and urban planning." [22] He critiqued the suburban spatial arrangements that so strongly symbolized the ideal of nonconnectedness and so effectively facilitated it. Stoller was especially concerned that the typical suburb lacked common spaces where household members could venture forth from their own turf and gather on shared territory that belonged to, and thus symbolized, "all of us." He noted, moreover, that some designers and planners of his day were just as critical as he was of suburban housing and neighborhoods, and for reasons similar to his. Stoller speculated that perhaps designers and planners, together with social advocates like him, might together embark on a "fruitful and exciting exploration" to address their shared anxieties regarding families and neighborhoods. [23]

A "MAJOR PROBLEM"

Yet another influential social scientist of the time, Robert Nisbet, made the same point as Mead and Stoller. The nuclear family is a "major problem," he said, because it is simply too small to do everything society expects it to do.[24] And like Mead and Stoller, he too believed that households should reach beyond themselves to other households, and thus try to invent an up-to-date version of the extended family style that would blend responsibility with freedom. He was quite radical, or posttraditional, in stating that "there is no single type of family, anymore than there is a single type of religion, that is essential to personal security and collective prosperity." [25]

FEMINISM REVIVED

After women finally won the right to vote in 1920, the U.S. feminist movement slumped into dormancy.[26] However, in the early 1960s, a number of women concluded that they had suffered in silence long enough, and so they revived the feminist movement. Their aim was to achieve John Stuart Mill's objective of women's genuine equity with men in both the occupational and the personal realms (see Chapter 2). Initially, the movement was referred to as the "women's liberation movement," a label that signified its emphasis on freedoms, rights, and independence. At first, very little was said about duties and responsibilities. Obligations were rarely mentioned, because almost all feminists (female and male) believed that men would understand the fairness and the justice of women's interests. Because it was obviously the right thing to do, it was assumed that husbands would participate with wives in furthering women's labor force participation. Among other things, that meant doing routine household chores, learning to cook, and, most of all, becoming highly involved and effective parents.

The idea was that the husband would become a Good Father (yet remain a Good Provider), just as the wife would become a Good Provider (yet remain a Good Mother).[27] Moreover, both would play their interchangeable roles within the context of the nonconnected household style. However, men's response to the call for role interchangeability was less than overwhelming. Men failed to involve themselves in the domestic realm to the same degree as women. Compared with men, women remained disadvantaged in the marketplace.[28] Although feminists had been counting on men to behave in a "responsible" manner—a manner that would balance women's freedoms—it did not turn out that way. The genders were not able to identify and implement an equitable balance of *in*dependence with *inter*dependence. At the same time, few people paid any attention to the arguments of Mead, Stoller, Nisbet, and others, that a responsible transformation of household gender roles required the participation of external support networks of some kind.

Government Participation

External reinforcement emerged, however, in the form of several government initiatives aimed at furthering the interests of women from all social classes. They were, like social security and the G.I. Bill, examples of government benefits for all citizens—not just the poor. The 1964 Civil Rights Act, for example, prohibited discrimination on the basis of race and *gender*. A few years later, the federal government enacted specific statutes requiring the public and private sectors to take "affirmative action" to provide women and minorities with greater educational and occupational opportunities.[29] Third, in the late 1960s and early 1970s, several states, followed by the federal government, made abortion a woman's right. Next, California, followed by most other states, passed no-fault divorce laws, making the marriage termination process much simpler and less onerous than it was before.

Finally, in 1972, the U.S. Congress passed the Equal Rights Amendment (ERA) to the U.S. Constitution and sent it to the states for their required approval. (Later in this chapter, I explain how that approval was thwarted.) Versions of the ERA had been submitted to every session of Congress since 1923, and the wording that the 1972 Congress ultimately passed had in fact been hammered out in the 1940s.[30] Following is the entire text of the amendment:

> *Section 1.* Equality of rights under the law shall not be denied or abridged by the United States or by any state on account of sex.
>
> *Section 2.* The Congress shall have the power to enforce, by appropriate legislation, the provisions of this article.
>
> *Section 3.* This amendment shall take effect two years after the date of ratification.

In a very real sense, history was repeating itself during the 1960s and 1970s. Some 200 years earlier, in the mid-18th century, critics were explicitly calling for nuclear family freedoms.[31] By the mid-20th century, critics were calling overtly for women's freedom and equality. Male-female relationships had been changing gradually throughout the industrial era, and especially since the 1920s. But in the 1960s and 1970s, some critics called for the profound transformations advocated by Mill, Mead, and many others.

CONFRONTING THE SEXUAL DOUBLE STANDARD

Feminists of the 1960s insisted that women must have the same freedoms, rights, and privileges as men in every realm of society, including the sexual. The 1920s had expanded the range of permissible premarital sexual expression and had redefined the link between those behaviors and love and marriage (see Chapter 2). Although the range of culturally permissible sexual practices fell short of actual intercourse, it was certainly not uncommon during the 1950s for engaged couples several weeks shy of their wedding day to "do it." [32]

However, the 1960s advocates for the second sexual revolution aimed to eliminate the double standard altogether.[33] By asserting that coitus as well as all other sexual behaviors were perfectly acceptable at any time between consenting adults who were acting honestly and responsibly, 1960s and 1970s women and men completely disentangled sexual expression from any necessary link with love, engagement, or marriage. Women demanded sexual equality by asserting their rights to enjoy any and all forms of sexual pleasure in the situations and times of their choosing. They rejected the old Dating Game in favor of the freedom to be whole sexual beings without tarnishing their reputations or their value on the "marriage market." The reinvention of sexuality was supported by advances in contraceptive technology, especially the birth control pill.

Unfortunately, men's responses to women's initiatives in the sexual realm were as tepid as they were in the domestic and occupational realms. In particular, men tended to presume that the disappearance of the double standard signaled the formal end of their ancient responsibility to negotiate honestly and honorably with women regarding sexual behaviors.[34] Prior to the Dating Game, a woman could say no because "we're not married." During the Game, she could say no because "we're not yet engaged." However, after the Game's protections evaporated, many men assumed that women's sexual assertiveness and openness had cost women any and all rights ever to say no. For large numbers of men, the sexual freedoms swirling around them were heady indeed. They could enjoy spontaneous and passionate sex without fretting about pregnancies or unwanted attachments. What's more, they didn't even have to pay for it! The outcome, not surprisingly, was that the historic sexual exploitation of women continued, although in disguised forms, and often with greater guile.[35]

LOVE IN THE LATE 20th CENTURY

Love as Emotional Intimacy

As part of the solution to the impasse described above, many women, and some men, advocated the insertion of emotional closeness into cross-gender relationships.[36] We might call this the "intimacy revolution." The result is that among growing numbers of persons, love has gradually taken on an added dimension only dimly perceived by Jane Austen's characters. Love now means being a "best friend" to one's partner. Being a "best friend" transports us far beyond the 19th- and early-20th-century idea of leisure-time companion. It carries us eons past the slick 1950s slogan, "The family that plays together stays together." Love now demands that one be a trusted intimate—a confidante with whom a partner can unmask the secrets and anxieties of her or his innermost being. However, unlike visiting a priest or a "shrink," emptying one's soul is a two-way street. Merely being a good listener is not enough, because that fails to make the listener vulnerable. Accordingly, "a best friend proves that he or she can be trusted with my secrets by sharing his or hers as fully as I do."

The experience of emotional intimacy is rich indeed. Nevertheless, it seems that throughout most of the industrial era it was largely circumscribed by gender. Historian Nancy F. Cott suggests that because women and men existed in two vastly different worlds—hers the domestic, his the market-place—it was extremely difficult for the genders to bridge their spheres and become genuine confidantes.[37] Women, according to Cott, were much better at being one another's confidantes than they were at getting close to men. Not only were women and men worlds apart in terms of their everyday work, they were seen as vastly different creatures, and thus simply unable to cross over into each others' inner souls.

However, in recent decades, women have been crossing into the male domain of the marketplace. Many advocates believe that men and women are more alike by virtue of being human than they are unlike owing to gender. Consequently, because their spheres increasingly intersect and because their fundamental sameness is becoming increasingly apparent, the dimension of emotional intimacy ("not being afraid to tell you who I am") is being added to our understanding of love. To love someone is to have a "soul mate"—that is, a person with whom one is emotionally vulnerable and thus to whom one is profoundly connected.

In 1965, social scientist Lee Rainwater concluded that married "couples speak of sexual relations as the central fact and expression of marriage, as the base from which grows most of what is important about marriage and family." [38] However, he made this observation prior to the redefinitions of sexuality and love just described. Sex has now become detached from marriage. It is freely available in a wide range of settings and is no longer viewed as having any unique connection with marriage. Moreover, the intimacy revolution means that having a soul mate is just as vital as having a sexual partner. Once again, that may occur either within or outside of marriage. Hence, if Rainwater were writing now, he would likely say that *both* sexuality *and* emotional intimacy are the "central fact and expression" (or essence) of the contemporary "relationship."

In effect, sex has been forced to share its center-stage role with emotional intimacy. Many persons, and women in particular, appear to embrace the fundamental notion that, ideally, one and the same partner should be both lover and confidante. Most people are convinced that sexual intercourse is enhanced by emotional intimacy, and vice versa. As a result, whatever the reasons many women and some men may in the past have honored monogamy, today at least part of its relevance emerges from the sense that "this is my soul mate, and I am loath to do anything that could conceivably poison the well of our shared emotional richness."

Accordingly, emotional intimacy may be one factor helping to reinforce the permanence of some contemporary relationships. In the past, stability was externally imposed because there were virtually no legal means to divorce, or because women had no economic means for independent survival, or for the sake of children, or for religious reasons, or owing to the stigma of divorce. Today, however, stability is much less likely to be imposed than to be freely chosen. And it is more likely to be chosen if the couple shares what each partner considers to be a reasonable amount of emotional closeness. High levels of intense sexual gratification can be gotten with a fresh partner literally overnight. By contrast, the nurturance and cultivation of emotional intimacy require a substantial investment of time, energy, and effort. Consequently, like a rare and delicate flower, once intimacy blooms it is highly prized.

Unfortunately, intimacy is also quite susceptible to withering. When an individual is no longer emotionally close to the person who used to be her or his best friend, she or he experiences a deep loss and feels pain mixed with a profound sense of emptiness. Hence, it follows that just as intimacy strongly binds a couple, its perceived decline on the part of one or both partners becomes an exceptionally potent factor in unbinding them. A loss of intimacy gradually corrodes what social scientist Charles Horton Cooley has called a sense of "we-ness," namely, feelings of bonding to and solidarity with one's partner.[39] Over time, one or both partners may come to feel that life without intimacy is mere existence. As a result, they may terminate their relationship. Each partner is then free to seek another person with whom she or he can try to forge bonds of intimacy. The former partners' quests for personal independence are expressed by their freedom to leave one relationship and to form another.

Love as Caring for Oneself

Underlying that freedom is yet another salient feature of contemporary love. In the past, according to social scientist Ann Swidler, women expressed their love in the form of duty toward others: "I love you; therefore I'm obliged to take care of you."[40] For example, alongside caring for her children, the most vital obligation for the 1950s wife was the construction of a home environment that "restored the husband's spirits after the proverbial hard day at the office."[41]

But, says Swidler, love may also be an assertion of individualism: "I love myself; therefore I'm obliged to take care of myself." Historically, men had the opportunity to express both facets of love. They could love their families by taking care of their wives and children. But they could also love themselves by, among other things, pursuing occupational achievement. Today, large numbers of women are appropriating for themselves the ancient ideal that "I'm obliged to love myself *as much as* I love my neighbor" (e.g., partner, children). A woman's commitment to love herself includes, as Mead argued, the obligation to develop her full human potential—to be all that she can be. Her full human potential includes participation in profound levels of emotional intimacy. And it may also include the sort of labor force participation that assures economic autonomy, or self-sufficiency.

English professor Louise DeSalvo has described how she came face-to-face with the obligation to love herself. She records in her memoirs that when she was 25 years old and mother to an infant, her husband (a resident M.D.) informed her that he was about to split because he had fallen in love with a nurse. DeSalvo writes:

> What he did spurred me to growth, to finding what *I* wanted. I now wanted a career. And my own money. And access to the public world. . . . I wanted to . . . engage in serious, important intellectual discussions about literature. I never wanted to depend on a man again. And, I realized, that if men might leave you even if you do everything you're supposed to, then you might as well do whatever you want.[42]

Self-Sufficiency

DeSalvo's conclusions reflect a theme sounded by a number of 1960s and 1970s feminists. They argued that a woman should aim for more than mere labor force participation. On top of that, she should aim at eventually becoming economically self-sufficient.[43] Loving herself, and thus taking care of herself, had a "bottom-line" component: It meant that, if need be, she would at length be able to meet her own economic needs, apart from a man. Self-sufficiency also implied that if she chose to bring a child into her life, she would be able to provide for that child's economic and emotional needs as well.[44] At the same time, being a self-sufficient woman in no way excludes the idea of maintaining an ongoing, committed relationship.

Ironically enough, the 1996 Welfare Reform Act may be having the unintended consequence of reigniting interest in the feminist objective of self-sufficiency.[45] Until recently, poor mothers (black, white, Latina) have been able to subsist apart from men's economic inputs, largely because of government subsidies such as Aid to Families with Dependent Children ("welfare" in the form of cash payments), food stamps, low-cost housing, and Medicaid. As the first two of those supports are slowly being downsized (and the future of the latter two is uncertain), poor mothers are being informed that they must ready themselves to function effectively in the information age. The message is, "You must eventually become able to support yourself and your children on your own."[46] There is nothing in the Welfare Reform Act that requires a woman to get and stay married. Instead, a massive federal and state effort is now under way to oblige poor mothers to take care of themselves and their own children, without making a husband's presence part of the agenda. Marriage, although praised in principle, is quietly relegated to a back burner.

This current strategy stands in stark contrast to the federal "income maintenance" experiments of the late 1960s and early 1970s.[47] Their overarching policy objective was to provide poor, *coresident* married couples with enough cash for them to remain stable. Proponents of those programs, mostly economists, reasoned that many couples who were too poor to make it on their own were splitting up because federal rules required the husband to exit the household before the mother could get AFDC dollars. As the economists saw it, the mothers perceived AFDC as their ticket to household survival. Hence, the logic behind the income maintenance experiments was deceptively simple—if couples had sufficient cash to live on, they would not split up.

What actually emerged from the experiments was totally unexpected and quite astonishing to the economists. Within the same neighborhoods, it turned out that couples receiving the additional government dollars were *more* likely to split up than were couples who were *not* getting an infusion of extra cash. That unintended outcome was one factor that helped put a speedy end to those experiments. In retrospect, some sociologists conjectured that giving cash to a household served to highlight the man's redundancy in the eyes of the woman. The man was supposed to have been the household's chief provider, thereby earning prestige, respect, status, and esteem. His failure to provide was likely to have undermined the couple's love and bonding.[48] Hence, the couple's previously fragile love, combined with the influx of dollars suddenly making the man's presence gratuitous, contributed to his leaving the household.

In similar manner, the full range of consequences that might emerge from the 1996 Welfare Reform Act is currently unclear. However, one could infer, without being totally outrageous, that through these new policies the government is unofficially throwing its considerable weight behind a norm that endorses women's economic self-sufficiency. The objective of this latest attempt at welfare "reform," as sold to the general public, was to penalize poor women who were allegedly sponging off of taxpayers, relying on others to support them and their illegitimate children. Accordingly, there seems little doubt that many of those women and their children are likely to suffer considerable pain during the years ahead.[49]

Nevertheless, the subtle latent consequence may be that the norm "A woman should be able to take care of her family apart from a man" may be infusing American culture unnoticed via the back door. Is it believable that economic conservatives find themselves in the incredibly ironic position of inadvertently promoting a feminist agenda item? Will welfare reform accomplish what feminist ideology could not? Sociologist Kenneth Fox suggests that very often we tend to "cast [poor solo mothers] entirely as victims and fail to recognize their aspirations to be independent and self-supporting." In his view, many white and minority women are plunged into poverty as a "result of their own struggles to escape dependence on marriage for economic support." Hence, instead of seeing them as victims, he believes it is "far more appropriate to consider these . . . women [who are] supporting their children on their own, as a potential labor force with tremendous energy and determination." [50] In contrast to the earlier income maintenance programs (as well as to the G.I. Bill, which provided subsidies for veterans' wives and children in the 1950s), welfare reform simply disregards the historic theme of the wife's dependence on her husband. Not only that, the belief that children need two parents, although still honored as the ideal, is having to share center stage with the notion that one parent may be sufficient. The message is that a lone parent should be able to "make it" if she or he works hard enough and has sufficient backup resources in the form of education, job training, transportation, and child-care services.[51]

Cohabitation: Love Without a License

Thus far, we have seen that two significant components have been added to our late-20th-century reinventions of love—emotional intimacy and caring for oneself. A third component, however, involves subtraction instead of addition. Until very recently, persons in love who wanted to share the same residence required official permission in the form of a marriage license. To live together openly apart from marriage was perceived by kin, friends, and community as "living in sin." Such obscene behavior was regarded as shameful and as a blatant disregard of both law and custom. Nevertheless, in the past couple of decades, growing numbers of heterosexuals in Western societies have been redefining love to include the right *not* to marry, yet to draw on many of its benefits. To their shared love (including sex, companionship, and emotional intimacy), they add the material economies of coresidence ("Two can live as cheaply as one"). In addition, growing numbers of those cohabitor households also include children.[52]

Furthermore, the research literature reveals that when it comes to everyday matters such as housework, employment concerns, sexual behaviors, decision making, and parenting, cohabitors behave in ways that are virtually indistinguishable from the behaviors of both homosexual couples and married couples.[53] However, unlike same-sex couples, cross-sex couples do in fact have the right to marry. They simply choose not to exercise it, at least for the time being. A large number of cohabitors are divorced from previous partners or are separated from their current spouses. The majority of cohabitors (divorced or never married) eventually (re)marry—either their current partners or someone else.

Nevertheless, alongside the tendency of most cohabitors to marry, researchers take note of a smaller number of cohabitors that they label *long-term*. Those are couples who have lived together for a number of years without obtaining a marriage license. In her research, sociologist Marion C. Willetts defines long-term cohabitors as heterosexual couples identified by a national study who had been sharing the same household uninterruptedly for at least 4 years—between 1987 and 1991.[54] A number of couples in the study had probably been together longer than that.

Domestic Partnership

Interest in long-term cohabitation has increased in recent years with the advent of "domestic partnership" ordinances, which have been passed by several cities around the United States.[55] Those statutes allow cohabiting couples (same-sex or cross-sex) to go to their city clerk, pay a fee, and register as "domestic partners." Some cities (e.g., San Francisco, Chicago, New York), in their role as employers, grant the partners of their cohabiting employees the same fringe benefits they grant to the spouses of married employees. Several major corporations—including but not limited to the Gap, Levi-Strauss, Ben & Jerry's, Disney, Time Warner, and Apple Computer—as well as the Democratic National Committee also have equal-treatment policies concerning their cohabiting employees. One report says that among *Fortune* 1000 companies, half have some type of domestic partnership provisions for their workers.[56] Carrying the matter a step further, the city of San Francisco is proposing to amplify its current domestic partner statute. The city's aim is "to require the companies with which it does business" to have the same types of equal-treatment policies for all of their own coupled employees that the city now has for its workers.[57] The rationale for this new statute is analogous to what governments already do in requiring their contractors to use hiring practices that are nondiscriminatory toward minorities and women.

The Wedding as a Ritual of Transformation

An intriguing question is why cross-sex cohabitors—especially if they enjoy the tangible benefits of domestic partnership—would bother marrying at all. That issue is a variation on the question that some gay and lesbian advocates put to homosexuals: If you already share love and commitment, and if you have domestic partner benefits, why bother with "legal marriage"? Those advocates see little point in fighting for something that doesn't seem to be working too well among many straight couples.[58]

One reason most heterosexuals in the United States continue to seek legal marriage is the ritual character of the wedding ceremony. On the basis of her research, anthropologist Pamela Freese uses the term *ritual* to describe North American weddings.[59] In any culture, a ritual is part of a public observance in which an official of some kind follows a clearly prescribed formula that is believed to bring about significant transformations that could occur in no other way. For example, placing "holy" water on an infant's head (i.e., baptism) is believed to remove her "original sin," thereby transforming her forever and fitting her for heaven. Or when a Roman Catholic priest pronounces certain Latin phrases over ordinary bread and water, they are thereby transformed into the actual body and blood of Jesus.

Likewise, a public wedding ceremony is a ritual in the sense that it is believed to transform the couple from what they previously were into an entity that is "totally other"—a wholly different and distinctive reality. At the time of their wedding, their kin and friends, along with the state and often the church or synagogue, bestow on the couple a type of approval, honor, and esteem that is unique and obtainable by no other discernible means. What is more, that esteem follows them beyond the wedding, because whenever they happen to make known their marital status, strangers immediately accord them the respect appropriately due that position.

Ever since the early-19th-century novels of Jane Austen (as cited in Chapter 2), persons in the West have been reinventing love to a remarkable degree. Waller, Goode, and other mid-20th-century social scientists have echoed what literary figures had long described (and ordinary citizens knew), namely, that marriage can readily exist quite apart from love.[60] Now we are demonstrating that love, coresidence, and parenting can exist quite apart from marriage. Today, hardly anyone blinks an eye when a couple, straight or gay, exercises a right that until recently was forbidden both by law and by powerful custom—they choose to "move in" together, to publicly "live in sin." On the other hand, at least in the United States, most citizens continue to perceive marriage as a *unique* social status that accords its participants an enviable degree of approval, prestige, and esteem. As a result, the status of "being married" is eventually sought by most heterosexuals, and now also by a growing number of homosexuals.

Love and License Among Cohabiting Same-Sex Couples

Although the general public supports the idea of gay civil rights—especially with regard to jobs and housing—it has thus far resisted the idea that homosexuals should have the freedom to choose marriage. President Clinton's 1996 endorsement of the "Defense of Marriage Act," placing the federal government on record as strongly discouraging homosexual unions, is viewed as one factor that supported his reelection bid.[61] There are several complex reasons most citizens feel uneasy about same-sex marriage. One of these is the perceived affront of such marriage to the uniqueness of heterosexual marriage. A second is its allegedly negative consequences for children. Regarding the first reason, advocates (both heterosexual and homosexual) for same-sex marriage call into question the prevailing cultural belief that all persons would ipso facto be better off if they were heterosexually married. Instead, they affirm the strange-sounding idea that some citizens are actually better off being married to persons of the same sex. As for the second reason, researchers have tended to conclude that the children of same-sex parents are in fact no worse off and no better off than the children of straight parents.[62]

In view of the public's uneasiness about same-sex marriage and parenting, some advocates are working very hard to challenge the strongly held belief that marriage is "for straights only." They see their struggle as part of the ongoing reinvention of love that has been occurring in Western societies for many centuries. More than 100 years ago, the young lover of Irish poet and playwright Oscar Wilde, Lord Alfred Bruce Douglas, called it "the Love that dare not speak its name." [63] In contrast to that dark silence, in 1997 a major media event occurred when actress Ellen DeGeneres "came out" as a lesbian on her own prime-time TV show, *Ellen*. Some 40 million viewers watched the coming-out episode of the show, and "thousands of people [straight, gay, and lesbian] celebrated at private and public parties," while an "organization called Americans for the Truth about Homosexuality protested in front of ABC's Washington news bureau." [64] Sociologist Kristin Esterberg was quoted as observing that this media event was "important . . . because Ellen is such a mainstream character. Television is really where a lot of people get their ideas about other people, so having Ellen come out is very important." [65]

Although the glare of national publicity is quite new for same-sex unions, such unions themselves are not new. Historian John Boswell has reported that nonformal same-sex "marriages," along with ceremonies to celebrate them publicly, have existed in Western societies since Greco-

Roman times. They also took place in premodern Japan and China, among Native Americans before the Europeans arrived, among "many African tribes well into the twentieth century," and in parts of the Middle East, Southeast Asia, Russia, other parts of Asia, and South America.[66]

Although many people—past and present—would prefer to ignore the reality of same-sex unions, today's advocates want to talk about the simple yet profound idea that gay and lesbian couples love each other in precisely the same ways as straight couples. In November 1996, ABC Television broadcast an hour-long documentary about four committed couples—two lesbian and two gay. Repeatedly, the couples made the seemingly unassailable point that heterosexual couples have been making for well over 200 years: We love each other; why shouldn't we get married? The couples ranged in age from their late 20s to their late 40s. All had been cohabiting for several years before making the decision to seek formal approval of their unions. However, because they could not get legitimation from the state, they sought and received endorsement from their places of worship, and the program included footage of their "commitment ceremonies." [67] One of the lesbian couples had been together in a committed union long enough to have had a baby boy via artificial insemination. *New York Times* TV critic Walter Goodman observed that "what comes through is how conventional these couples are in their affections and their hopes. Even if law and custom withhold the word 'marriage,' they still seek to make a home together, to be a family." [68]

The striking similarities between the three younger couples and younger heterosexual couples planning wedding festivities were plain from the reactions of the couples' parents. Although the parents inevitably expressed certain misgivings, they nonetheless firmly supported the couples' freedom to choose: "After all," said one father, "they have the right to be happy." As for the older lesbian couple, the striking similarities with the dominant culture were also apparent in the positive reactions of the adult (straight) children of their prior heterosexual unions. As far as was noted in the program, the only kin who spoke against the older couple's freedom to love was a sister of one of the women, who was described as a religious cultural conservative.

Interviews with several family members of all four couples revealed that whatever initial doubts they might have had about these unions, they had finally become persuaded that the unions were the "right thing to do." The reasons they gave were similar—now their child, or their mother, would finally have a "best friend" with whom she or he could share her or his life. The "sharing," as reported by the couples themselves, included both companionship and emotional intimacy, as well as an already demonstrated commitment to sexual monogamy. The younger lesbian couple already shared their own child, and both younger male couples said that parenting was an option.

Whether same-sex marriage will eventually, if ever, gain the same degree of formal recognition as cross-sex marriage is not at all clear. For example, in mid-1997, the Hawaii State Legislature attempted to "head off the issue of homosexual marriages" by passing a bill under which "any two adults who cannot legally marry will have inheritance rights, the right to own joint property and the right to share medical insurance." [69] And in late 1998, "Hawaii voters gave the legislature authorization to overturn a court ruling and ban same-sex marriages, while Alaskans voted 2-1 in favor of a constitutional amendment that defines marriage as a union between one man and one woman." [70] But at the same time those events took place, the Vermont State Supreme Court agreed to hear the case of a "gay male couple seeking the right to marry." [71] However, even if same-sex marriage were to become officially recognized in one particular state, several other states, as well as the federal government, have announced that they would refuse to regard such couples as formally married. Consequently, it appears inevitable that the issue of same-sex marriage must one day be resolved by the U.S. Supreme Court.

In any event, as these legal and political struggles continue for many years to come, advocates for same-sex marriage are using the media and other venues to make their case. They argue that their freedom to love is fundamentally a civil liberty—they have the human right to be treated in the same manner as straight citizens. Gays and lesbians claim for themselves the powerful cultural norm that people in love should have the freedom to design and build their own life together. That being the case, it appears that growing numbers of same-sex couples are likely to form and also go public with their "committed unions," even as the political struggles continue, and no matter what their outcomes. Advocates hope that as straight citizens become exposed to same-sex unions and discover how similar they are to their own relationships, they will gradually come to accept them as simply one more thread making up our richly textured society.[72]

The Culmination of Changes in Love:
The Erotic Friendship

Boswell reminds us that "language is a frail medium for [capturing the] powerful and overwhelming emotions" of love. That is so because the feelings we glibly call love are "profound, urgent, and ubiquitous" at the same time that they are "jumbled, shifting, and imprecise." [73] Nevertheless, we have no alternative but to use language to try as best we can to communicate what love might imply in posttraditional society.

Consider, for example, the problems faced by the members of the kibbutzim as they groped for the appropriate words to capture their social expressions of love. The kibbutzim were agricultural communities first established in Palestine (now Israel) in the early 1900s.[74] These close-knit communities agonized over what sorts of words might convey love within the unique social context their founders created. "From the very beginning," reports anthropologist Melford E. Spiro, "the terms, 'marriage,' 'husband,' 'wife,' were abandoned because of their invidious connotations." In place of those conventional labels, kibbutz members spoke instead of the "couple." That meant a man and a woman in love, and whose commitment to one another was recognized and legitimated by their entire community. Because they are publicly known to be "in love," says Spiro, the couple is allowed to have their own room. In contrast, two people who are "merely lovers" (i.e., sexual partners) would not request a room and would not "be given one were they to request it." [75]

The Generic Essence of the Erotic Friendship

Spiro adds that being a couple fulfills "one *generic* and crucial function—the satisfaction of a need for intimacy." Intimacy consists of sexual gratification and also "psychological security (friendship, comradeship, succor)." [76] In the discussion earlier in this chapter, we saw that the contemporary "relationship" contains these same "generic" features. Lerke Gravenhorst is a German sociologist who has also wrestled with language that might possibly capture something of the character of what it means to be a "couple" in posttraditional societies. As she sees it, to be "in love" can be apprehended by the curious-sounding term *erotic friendship*.[77]

Erotic in this context does not refer principally to sensual pleasures in and of themselves. Instead, it captures my earlier reference to the continuing significance of monogamy in contemporary society, that is, the professed ideal of commitment to one sexual partner at a time. *Erotic* designates the boundary around the couple: It indicates that they have freely chosen to limit their experience of sensuous pleasures to one another, to the one with whom they are "in love."

Next, Gravenhorst unites her description of erotic with *friendship*, by which she means far more than leisure-time companionship, although that is surely included. More to the point, she is principally concerned with evincing the contemporary ideal that one's lover should at the same time be one's confidante. Conjoining *erotic* with *friendship* pushes to the fore a social reality that, as we have seen, has become increasingly prominent throughout the past three decades. In today's posttraditional world, most people (heterosexual and homosexual) hope to fall in love and to fashion relationships based on two foundational elements: First is the relationship's sexual boundary, and second is the relationship's dynamic essence or core, its emotional intimacy. To use the metaphor of the organic cell, one could say that the relationship's nucleus is emotional intermingling, whereas its lining is the norm of sexual exclusivity.

Gravenhorst acknowledges that she writes from a feminist perspective, that she is concerned with women's interests. In her view, the mingling of lover with confidante—the sharing of emotional and sensual pleasures within an established boundary—is an issue that most women care very deeply about. She says that her aim as a feminist is to reinvent the idea of family, making it a place where women's interests are as significant as those of both men and children. Importantly, asserting the equivalence of women's, men's, and children's interests makes the reinvention of family much more than simply a woman's issue. It then becomes, more broadly, a *human* issue. Emotional connectedness within the context of sexual exclusivity is arguably vital to both genders, not just to women.

Terms such as *love, loving, romance, being in love, sleeping with, seeing, dating, boyfriend/girlfriend, relationship, living with, married to, going with, coupled,* and *committed to* tend to be vague and often bewildering because, as Boswell observes, they tend to gloss over what actually bonds the dyad.[78] Accordingly, the merit of Gravenhorst's language, though unfamiliar and awkward, is that it pinpoints what Spiro calls the "generic" essence of being in love. In pharmaceuticals, a generic drug is a single biochemical formula that may be marketed under several different brand names. The generic essence of being in love is the committed sexual partnership united with emotional interpenetration. If that is the essence of being in love, it follows that the couple can be either heterosexual or homosexual. There is absolutely no distinction at all between cross-sex and same-sex couples when it comes to having a partner who is both lover and confidante at the same time. Consequently, erotic friendships may take the form of a variety of "brands," including straight and gay couples.

Adding Features

Once a couple has formed an erotic friendship, they are then free to add to the generic essence of their relationship as many or as few additional interests and goals as they wish. Shared consumption is one example of an interest—that is, an "optional feature"—that any erotic friendship might add. This feature includes buying gifts for one another and spending money together on goods, leisure activities, vacations, and so on. If one or both partners has a child, either residing with the partner or elsewhere, the couple then find themselves sharing a second feature, namely, certain aspects of parenting, including spending time with and money on the child.

If, after a while, the couple move in together, their economic interdependence escalates considerably. That feature also carries with it a shift in how others view the couple, and thus how they view themselves. They are now presumed to be somewhat more serious and committed than if they were merely "boyfriend" and "girlfriend." Their cohabitation may signal to kin and friends that they are edging toward either marriage or a public commitment ceremony. And indeed, many erotic friends (whether cohabiting or not) choose to add the optional feature of marriage or a public ceremony, followed by the added option of children. They may, of course, have already been parenting together for some years. On the other hand, rather than add marriage, some cohabiting couples opt either to end their erotic friendship altogether or merely to subtract cohabiting from their erotic friendship by returning to separate residences.

In any case, each of these optional features, separately or in some combination, may or may not be added to the generic essence of the couple's relationship—that is, their erotic friendship. The mix of emotional intimacy with sexual exclusivity is the foundation on which they might choose to erect a great deal more or hardly anything at all, or perhaps something in between. Today's erotic friendship represents the current development of the more than 200-year-old quest for freedom and choice in love relationships. Ideally speaking, an individual enters an erotic friendship without constraint in order to seek and give highly prized gratifications. Hence, he or she is correspondingly at liberty, regardless of added features, to exit at any time if the rewards dip too low and the costs rise too high. That much freedom returns us once again to policy point 1 as described in Chapter 1—the issue of balancing independence with responsibility.

THE COUNTERREVOLUTION AGAINST NEW VIEWS OF SEX, LOVE, AND MARRIAGE

Recall that Margaret Mead warned about placing so much emphasis on our freedoms that we overlook our obligations. The erotic friendship, and all the liberties it implies, represents a "radically new style of behavior." [79] Such manufactured risk, Mead predicted, "may engender counterrevolutions that may be ideological or religious." Her idea of counterrevolution is the same as what Giddens calls "fundamentalism." [80] The term *fundamentalist* describes a rigid set of mind: It is tradition defended in the traditional way. It implies a reluctance to engage in dialogue concerning old traditions and a refusal to discuss the possibility of creating new ones. Mead predicted that whether religious or secular, the counterrevolution might "refocus attention on the home, limit sexual freedom, curtail the individual development of women, and subordinate the creative capacities of the individual adult to the needs of the group for docile parents, workers, and citizens." [81]

"Kids First"

There is little doubt that Mead forecast the future with remarkable accuracy. A counterrevolution has indeed been mounted against the traditions of freedom and independence that have been expanding for 200 years and that have accelerated over the past 30. The 1960s ideal of justice and equality for women has been replaced by the slick media slogan "Kids First." Cleverly, the counterrevolutionary strategy is not meant to put down women in any way. Instead, the basic game plan is to elevate children's interests above all other concerns. For example, social scientist Amitai Etzioni writes that "between 1960 and 1990 American society allowed children to be devalued, while the golden call of 'making it' was put on a high pedestal." He adds that during this period, new values became widely accepted: "the right of women to find themselves, to discover their identities, and to follow their careers the way men do." [82] Although Etzioni takes great pains to state that the "women's rights movement" is not totally to blame for the devaluing of children, he asserts that it may be one of the causes. He goes on to say, somewhat sardonically, that women are "obviously entitled to all the same rights men are, including the pursuit of greed." [83] His solution to children's problems begins with both parents paying more attention to their children and less to careers and consumerism. Intriguingly, Etzioni feels compelled to assure us that his ideas are "not an indirect way of suggesting that mothers should stay home." [84]

Perhaps not, but what he and like-minded critics do is to elevate, albeit very subtly, the goodness of children's well-being to a plane beyond the goodness of women's well-being. In preparation for takeoff, the flight attendant tells us that if an oxygen mask appears, "Put yours on first, then assist your child." On initial hearing, that instruction appears remarkably selfish: If there's a way to get air, shouldn't children have the first chance? However, the obvious message is that taking care of oneself is the chief means of doing the right thing by one's child. That message is the foundation on which the revolution in love and family has rested for 200 years. The counterrevolution challenges that belief, principally at the expense of women. It is futile to speculate whether today's counterrevolution would be any less strident if citizens had heeded Mead's call for "socially responsible protections" in the form of organized support networks. Most people ignored her call and presumed instead that profound transformations in love and gender relationships could be achieved within the context of the nonconnected household. Many people were and are convinced that a strongly committed couple, by working very hard, can have it all: a satisfying erotic friendship, occupational achievement for both genders, and rewarding parenthood.[85]

"Cultural Decay"

Alongside the "Kids First" slogan, today's counterrevolutionaries argue that contemporary reinventions of love, relationships, and families are symptoms of a festering decay in American culture.[86] Professor Robert H. Bork is a well-known proponent of this point of view. In a review of Bork's recent book, *Slouching Towards Gomorrah*, David Denby observes that "in Bork's America, good values and good ideas produce good behavior; bad values and bad ideas produce bad behavior. . . . For Bork, there is no economy or class structure: there is merely 'culture.' " [87] Culture conveys values, beliefs, and norms regarding what is appropriate and inappropriate, good and bad, right and wrong, worthy and unworthy, desirable and undesirable. In recent decades, according to Bork, American culture has been permeated with too many undesirable ideas, including the redefinitions of sex, love, and marriage just described. Ralph Reed is a nationally known cultural conservative who shares Bork's point of view. Reed is also a *religious* cultural conservative, and is the former director of the Christian Coalition, a national political action organization.[88] Reed is now writing a book in which he says that his aim is to achieve "a thoroughly Judeo-Christian culture." [89]

Not only do cultural conservatives describe recent revolutionary changes in sex, love, marriage, and parenting as cultural decay, they also want to stop the decline by ending the revolution.[90] The steps they want to take to do so include, but are not limited to, the following: They want to pass legislation that would severely restrict the right to divorce. They also want to make certain that, whatever the implications, every child should have two resident parents during her or his entire first 18 years. And especially during the child's early life, they want the mother to retain the role of chief parent. They want to place legal restrictions on children's exposure to sexuality (e.g., in the public schools, through the media, and on the World Wide Web). And they take a dim view of unmarried childbearing, regardless of the woman's age or economic circumstances. They want to limit a woman's right to choose abortion, and they vigorously oppose any efforts to grant homosexuals the right to legal marriage.

Cultural conservatives sound their alarm by uniting a fear of cultural decay with the "Kids First" slogan. Their reasoning is that as the culture has declined, there has been a corresponding drop in children's well-being. They contend that children are suffering because adults are selfishly pursuing their own individualistic interests with regard to personal relationships, occupational achievement, and consumption patterns.

Restricting Divorce

No-fault divorce laws, which make the termination of marriages relatively uncomplicated, have become a prime target of cultural conservatives. They believe that "easy divorce" enables parents to ignore their children's well-being by subjecting them to the disadvantages of a one-parent household. Cultural conservatives believe that one way to cut back on the numbers of lone parents is by making divorce more difficult. In 1997, for instance, the Louisiana State Legislature passed a "new and more binding . . . marriage contract . . . that would permit divorce only in narrow circumstances such as adultery, abuse, abandonment, a lengthy marital separation or imprisonment." [91]

The *New York Times* story on the contract adds that "the bill is the first legislative success in a nationwide movement led by conservative Christians and pro-family activists to rewrite or repeal no-fault divorce laws, which they say have helped lead to escalating divorce rates and the disintegration of families." [92] Cultural conservatives believe that making divorce virtually inaccessible would cause adults to behave more responsibly toward children. Adults, they say, would be forced to realize that they should not have children unless they are determined to stay together. The "new" Louisiana law is, of course, the same type of restrictive statute that virtually all states had prior to the 1970s. It is a prime example of what Mead meant by *counterrevolution.* What the cultural conservatives have been able to do is to require Louisiana to turn back the social clock.[93]

The Fate of the Equal Rights Amendment

Cultural conservatives' success in Louisiana is merely one bit of evidence that they are now a potent political force.[94] Most observers agree that their political clout began to crystallize around their opposition to the Equal Rights Amendment. Indeed, it can be said that the first shot of the counterrevolution was fired at that time. After the 1972 Congress passed the ERA, 22 states quickly ratified it, followed by 8 states in 1973, 3 in 1974, 1 in 1975, and 1 in 1977. However, the amendment was never ratified by the final 3 states needed, and the ERA eventually expired. The person credited with leading the charge against the ERA was a lawyer named Phyllis Schlafly.[95] She organized a national grassroots movement to defeat the ERA by proclaiming a simple but compelling message: The ERA "would take away the marvelous legal rights of a woman to be a full-time wife and mother in the house supported by her husband." [96]

The second event that helped crystallize the counterrevolution was the 1973 U.S. Supreme Court decision that allowed women the right to choose abortion.[97] Cultural conservatives viewed both abortion rights and the ERA as symptomatic of the "cultural decline" that they believed was already apparent in the 1970s. Divorce rates were beginning to rise, the numbers of children living in solo-parent households were thus increasing, and more and more mothers were entering the paid labor force. Cultural conservatives viewed the rising tide of self-fulfillment, or individualism, as a major force corroding American culture and its families. During the 1970s, researcher Daniel Yankelovich conducted several national surveys documenting the spread of individualism, especially among women. He found that by 1980 "the search for self-fulfillment is . . . an authentic grass-roots phenomenon involving . . . perhaps as many as 80 percent of all adult Americans. . . . [Citizens are] taking big risks in pursuit of new conceptions of the good life." [98] Thus it is no coincidence that those were the same years in which cultural conservatives emerged as a significant political force in the United States. In their view, citizens' risk taking in the pursuit of self-fulfillment was and is having deleterious effects on the institution of marriage and family, on children, and indeed on the entire culture.

The 1980 White House Conference on Families

The counterrevolution received a huge boost from an event that, ironically enough, many observers believed would actually further the family revolution begun two centuries earlier. Jimmy Carter, himself a "born again" Christian, became president in 1977, and he viewed the alleged worsening plight of children with considerable alarm. Hence, he authorized the 1980 White House Conference on Families, the aim of which was to assist families at all social class levels.[99] However, most cultural conservatives were leery of the conference's government organizers, who, among other things, altered its title. Originally, it was to have been a conference on *"The American Family,"* but the organizers changed it to a conference on "American *Families"* in order to convey a " 'neutral' model rather than the traditional husband-wife-children model." [100]

The 1980 White House conference (analyst Gilbert Steiner has called it "star-crossed") stands as a watershed in the development of U.S. policy struggles over families. The conference added significantly to the political strength of the cultural conservatives,[101] and in the years following, conservatives not only further honed their ideas about family policy, they continued to increase their political influence. The conference united a wide range of cultural conservative groups around their shared opposition to its government organizers, whom they viewed as proponents of "liberal" family policies and programs. The bedrock proposition uniting that array of cultural conservative groups was that "right-minded [family] policy should reinforce traditional American patterns, not abide deviations that smack of irresponsibility." [102]

Steiner reports that the cultural conservatives of the early 1980s left no doubt whatsoever as to what they meant by "right-minded policy." Their overriding policy goal was "the stability of marriages." [103] And today that objective remains unchanged. The ultimate aim of cultural conservatives is to facilitate the intact, heterosexual marriage with children.[104] The chief solution to the problems of today's children and families, they believe, would be for Americans to recapture what the conservatives describe as a "marriage-culture." [105] In their view, the nuclear family style seems to be the only mechanism able to stem the surging tide of alleged moral break-down, social disintegration, cultural decay, and suffering children. Accord-ingly, their vision of the desirable state of society includes an increase in the numbers of heterosexual men and women getting and staying legally married—at least until all their children have left their care.

CONCLUSION

In this chapter I have traced contemporary developments in the 200-year-old family revolution, picking the story up in the suburbs of the 1950s. For many American women, those were hardly the best of times. Although men and boys were experiencing many of the freedoms promised by the non-connected family style, women and girls were subject to most of its burdens. The 1960s saw efforts to correct that damage—the continuing imbalance favoring women's obligations over their independence. Margaret Mead cautioned that the quest to achieve gender equity should include the "radi-cal" policy of designing up-to-date versions of the extended family.

While her radical strategy was being ignored, women and men were carrying out profound transformations in their gender relationships. Women were and are seeking the full range of freedoms already enjoyed by men—freedoms promised by the nonconnected family style. At the same time, homosexuals were and are seeking the same range of freedoms already enjoyed by heterosexuals. Curiously enough, recent policy initiatives by economic conservatives aimed at disadvantaged women may have the unintended effect of contributing significantly to the ongoing gender revolution.

As Mead predicted, a counterrevolution has been launched by cultural conservatives—some of whom are secular and some of whom are religious. Cultural conservatives fail to engage in a dialogue concerning how to construct innovative ways to continue the revolution in gender and family patterns. Instead, they propose, at best, to halt the revolution where it is or, at worst, to reverse it—to recapture the past. Their principal strategy is seemingly unassailable: "Children," they say, "are the helpless and hapless victims of adult freedoms. Why shouldn't adults be prepared to sacrifice on their behalf?" Although they do not target women directly, it is nonetheless women who would bear the brunt of the conservatives' policy initiatives. It is women, far more than men, who would be called upon to sacrifice their independence.

Intriguingly enough, a handful of people are currently trying a novel approach to managing family life in the information age. The approach is not conservative, nor does it fit easily under any other label. These persons are testing a few of the ideas suggested by Mead, Stoller, and others regarding support networks and fictive kin. Their nonideological goal is simply to help families cope with today's unique stresses and strains. They are especially concerned with providing the best environment possible for children. Their strategy is known as cohousing, and that is the theme of Chapter 4.

4

COHOUSING AS
FAMILY REFORM

◆◆◆————————————————————————

A rchitect Dorit Fromm tells us that the beliefs and values that eventually gave rise to what is now known as cohousing were spawned in Denmark in the mid-1960s. However, the actual label of *cohousing* itself did not appear until 20 years later.[1] That term was coined by two American architects, Kathryn McCamant and Charles Durrett, who, in the late 1980s, were in Denmark studying collaborative communities. The Danes who created the initial collaborative, or cohousing, communities were "unhappy with living in the city or isolated in suburban one-family houses that 'destroy the landscape and the soul,' and they agreed it was best to live close to each other in housing designed with their needs in mind." [2] Initially, they were merely a small group of friends struggling to figure out how to fulfill their needs and implement their ideals at the same time. They were soon influenced by a 1967 essay titled "Children Should Have a Hundred Parents," in which a Danish cohousing advocate argues that children should have a special place in the creation of a collaborative community.[3]

On both sides of the Atlantic, cohousing may be found in densely populated urban regions as well as in areas that are less densely populated.[4] For example, a recent *New York Times* article reported on a cohousing neighborhood planned for an area not far from New York City. Featured in the article were Michael and Gail Sklaroff, who were part of the group planning the community, which is to be called Cantine's Island. As the couple watched their children swim in a creek located on the land for the soon-to-be-built community, Michael Sklaroff told the reporter, "We're not trying to escape the city." He added, "We'd been interested in cohousing for a long time when we heard a radio interview about a group starting up in Saugerties. At first we started going to meetings informally. Then we got more involved and became permanent members." [5]

REFORMING THE NONCONNECTED LIFESTYLE

Hence, when I say that cohousing is an attempt to reform family, I refer principally to the two features identified by its Danish founders and also sought by ordinary people like the Sklaroffs. First, it is *collaborative*, meaning that adults living in nearby households reach across their boundaries and, to one degree or another, try to help each other out. Second, children are a vital component of neighbors helping neighbors. In effect, cohousing was and is an example of the "radical" arrangements advocated by Mead, Stoller, and Nisbet, as discussed in Chapter 3. Like those Americans, a few Danish citizens concluded that the nonconnected family style is inadequate to fulfill their needs and implement their ideals. Accordingly, family reform means "taking things by the roots." In this case, the roots are up-to-date versions of the extended family style. Reform implies experimenting with contemporary arrangements that express household connectedness. Reform means that connectedness should be one segment of a comprehensive thrust aimed at addressing the many needs of today's adults and children—needs stemming from "manufactured risk" and "external risk" (see Chapter 1).

Cohousing advocates would concur with cultural conservatives (whose views are discussed in Chapter 3) that those needs are considerable. However, unlike conservatives, they are flexible regarding the internal composition of particular households within the community. If a household contains a couple, they may be married, cross-sex cohabitors, same-sex cohabitors, or just friends. At the same time, a household may contain only one adult of any age, and he or she may reside there with or without children. In short, the households in cohousing mirror those in contemporary society. Each household is governed by freedom, flexibility, and change. Cohousing advocates do not attempt to roll back the hard-won liberties of the past 200 years. They accept the reality of manufactured risk, as described in Chapter 1. They are not counterrevolutionaries or fundamentalists, but neither are they genuine revolutionaries. They are not intent on pushing ahead with the long-term revolution in family and gender patterns. Instead, their objective is much simpler—to provide a buffer zone around each household to cushion it against the shocks of living in what Giddens calls a "runaway world": "Their intention is to strengthen the family by creating supportive social networks, and by sharing certain daily tasks." [6]

By no means, however, do cohousing advocates view social connectedness as a panacea, or cure-all, for what ails today's families. In no way, for instance, does cohousing repudiate the idea of government programs (e.g., social security or a safety net for poor households) described in prior chapters. Nevertheless, keep in mind that cohousing was conceived in societies that possess the most extensive government programs in the world. Besides Denmark, these include Sweden, Holland, Germany, Austria, France, Belgium, and Switzerland, as well as Canada.[7] It is plain, in other words, that some citizens in those societies feel the need to add the dimension of social connectedness to existing government programs.

SPATIAL DESIGN AND SOCIAL CONNECTEDNESS

Recall from Chapter 3 that Stoller complained about the spatial as well as the social features of post-World War II suburbia. Its spatial features, he argued, symbolized and reinforced household isolation. Accordingly, he would have strongly endorsed the sorts of spatial features planned for the Cantine's Island cohousing community mentioned above. Those features symbolize and reinforce social connectedness. Hence, as used here, the idea of family reform includes both social *and* spatial connectedness. The Danish founders of cohousing saw the two dimensions as inseparable. Placing the two together is what makes cohousing unique. Cohousing is significantly different from what many Americans already experience in the form of social support networks.

Support Networks

More than a century ago, the pioneering French sociologist Emile Durkheim demonstrated that suicide tended to be more common among persons who were less embedded within social networks.[8] Ever since that time, social scientists have studied the many ways in which social embeddedness enhances personal well-being. *Embeddedness* refers to participation in various kinds of social support networks. In the case of households, these networks may be friendship groups that provide emotional support or friends that exchange services such as child care and transportation. Support groups may consist of friends who do leisure activities together or they may be made up of acquaintances who belong to particular churches, synagogues, or clubs. Their benefits are obvious: Researchers have found that socially embedded adults and their children are able to cope more effectively with the many stresses and strains of contemporary life than are persons who live outside of support networks.[9] Social support networks are a kind of halfway step on the road to cohousing. Thus far, however, only a tiny fraction of the people who participate in support groups have gone on to form cohousing communities.

Cohousing combines the privacy and autonomy of the nonconnected style with some of the most desirable features of the preindustrial, extended family style. The buildings in a cohousing development are typically sited close by one another. Each building may contain one private dwelling unit or several attached private dwelling units. Parking is relegated to the perimeter of the neighborhood, leaving only walkways and bicycle paths within the community itself. Houses typically have front porches and are set close to the walkways. Consequently, persons who are strolling or biking about the neighborhood experience frequent opportunities to talk to and hang out with others relaxing on their porches. The land on which the neighborhood is sited belongs to all its members. Furthermore, every cohousing community contains a jointly owned building called *the commons.*

The commons is a building with a large room and a series of several smaller rooms that may serve a variety of purposes. The commons building is a potent material symbol of the group's sense of "we-ness." It sharply distinguishes the community from the typical nonconnected neighborhood. Aside from being used for socializing ("hanging out") and for spontaneous parties, birthday and anniversary celebrations, and other special occasions (such as the group's founding), the commons can also serve as a dining room—a place to share meals on either a regular or an ad hoc basis. A kitchen is built within the commons to facilitate the members' work in preparing food (and cleaning up) together. The commons is also a place for shared child care and other children's activities. And, importantly, it is the location for the group's formal sessions of participatory group decision making. In short, a distinctive spatial environment is the physical setting for the uncommon social relationships found in a cohousing community.

SOUND NEIGHBORHOODS AND HEALTHY FAMILIES

For many years, studies of poor families have highlighted what everyone knows—namely, that healthy families, sound housing, and safe neighborhoods are indivisible from one another.[10] A recent national study explains why some children achieve at higher levels than others, and also why some experience greater well-being. The authors conclude that

> prosperous and well-functioning communities and neighborhoods appear to have important positive effects on children's attainments. Our findings suggest that growing up in those neighborhoods with the greatest concentration of social problems and the worst economic deficits has a particularly deleterious effect on children's outcomes.[11]

This research demonstrates that children who are surrounded by advantaged social and spatial arrangements do better in life than children who are not so fortunate.

Nevertheless, aside from that commonsense fact, family policy and family research have failed to make the social-spatial intersection a central issue.[12] It is curious that most researchers have tried to understand families apart from their spatial environments—the housing and the neighborhoods in which they dwell. Taking physical spaces for granted, however, was not a failing of early-20th-century social scientists. Many of them paid careful attention to the crucial linkages between social life and the physical design features and spatial layouts of neighborhoods and communities.[13] Accordingly, when I refer to cohousing as family reform, I mean it in the complete sense envisioned by cohousing's Danish founders. The health of adults, children, and families is fostered by the *interweaving* of social with spatial features.[14]

Exhibit 4.1 is a diagram of a proposed cohousing neighborhood. It displays the physical placement of such cohousing features as parking, private household dwelling units, and the commons building. This particular cohousing neighborhood was proposed by several researchers to local officials who operated the site on behalf of the U.S. Department of Housing and Urban Development (HUD). The site had, for many years, consisted of several dozen nonconnected households made up of poor African American lone mothers and their children. The researchers' proposal was aimed at shifting interested volunteer households from a nonconnected to a connected lifestyle. Although at first local officials supported the project, after a time they withdrew their support, and the proposal was never translated into reality.[15] I describe the reasons for the failure of this proposal in Chapter 7, where I also consider some of the political implications of living in a connected neighborhood.

BALANCING FREEDOM WITH CONNECTEDNESS

Collaborative communities of one sort or another have been around for thousands of years. Perhaps the most striking fact about them is that most have not survived for very long. But equally significant is the fact that people have never given up trying to build long-lasting collaborative communities.[16] Even though skeptics say such communities are unrealistic, some individuals try afresh anyhow, hoping that this time around, they will somehow be able to make it work. Researchers report that from ancient times to the present, the single biggest problem facing collaborative communities has always been how to manage the inevitable tension between individual freedoms and group responsibility.[17] Collaborative communities' inability to resolve that tension is the core explanation for why most of them have tended to be short-lived. One social scientist has expressed the tension in terms of six different, but overlapping, issues:

♦ How to get the work done, but without coercion
♦ How to ensure that decisions are made, but to everyone's satisfaction

Exhibit 4.1 Proposed renovation of a HUD nonconnected neighborhood into two adjacent cohousing groups, each with its own commons house.

79

- How to build close, fulfilling relationships, but without [undue] exclusiveness
- How to choose and socialize new members
- How to include a degree of autonomy, individual uniqueness, and even deviance
- How to ensure agreement and shared perception around community functioning and values[18]

Chapter 2 showed that the extended family lifestyle broke apart because younger members sought the freedoms of cities, the opportunities of industry, and the freedom to choose their own spouses. They very much wanted the privacy, independence, and autonomy of the nuclear family style. Chapter 3 showed that, in its turn, the nuclear family style has now fallen on hard times, in part because women are seeking the freedoms and opportunities that were once solely the province of men. Balancing the competing forces of freedom and responsibility is no less a challenge to cohousing neighborhoods. Despite the arduous nature of the incessant struggle to reconcile these two opposing forces, each cohousing community must somehow reconcile them. That is the absolute requirement to ensure the community's ongoingness.

THE STRUGGLES OF GROUP DECISION MAKING

In order to keep on balancing freedom with responsibility, a cohousing neighborhood must give painstaking attention to each of the issues listed above. In particular, the community members must figure out how to make group decisions that everyone can live with. The process of designing and implementing cohousing is no simple matter. The decision-making struggles of each new cohousing group are comparable to those experienced by the first Danish cohousing group in the late 1960s. The members of that community, reports Fromm, spent several years participating in the grueling process of creating both their spatial and their social connectedness. The Danes got architects to participate with them in creating the spatial features of their community, including the shared spaces common to all households. Members also took part in designing the external features of the private residences of each household, as well as in designing their roadways, parking areas, and landscaping. Finally, they took bids from contractors to decide who would do the actual construction of their community.

Those early years were also taken up with hammering out the broad objectives that would shape the overall character of their proposed neighborhood. The next step was to derive from those objectives the more specific norms that might govern the day-to-day life of the community. Fromm reports that during those early years, "ideological questions as well as site preferences caused some members to [break off and] form a new group." [19] Finally, in October 1972, 27 families from the original group moved into their community, which they called Saettedammen.[20] As far as I can tell, the Cantine's Island project, mentioned at the beginning of this chapter, seems to emulate the spirit of Saettedammen. The members themselves are designing both the spatial and the social features of their own community, although they have hired architects to assist them and contractors to build it. Their hope is that their considerable outlay of energy and effort (along with money) will result in a healthier environment for themselves and for their children.[21] By means is cohousing an idyllic, conflict-free environment. As the Danish example shows, cohousing is marked by nonstop decision making, tortuous negotiations, and sometimes by conflicts that turn out to be nonnegotiable.

Fromm observes that one of the very first U.S. collaborative neighborhoods was very much like Saettedammen.[22] The Santa Rosa (California) Creek Commons got started in 1977 with 10 persons each making a $5,000 down payment on the land for their projected community. A year later, each person had to contribute an additional $2,500, and more was required later on. And as far as investing time and energy is concerned, between 1977 and 1982, when the members finally moved into their housing, the group held 135 meetings.[23] Like the members of Saettedammen, Santa Rosa members spent innumerable hours developing the broad guidelines and principles for their community, as well as its specific norms. Once those guidelines and norms were in place, persons wanting to join had to agree to abide by them before the community would approve their membership. Most of the original members had previously been part of the Society of Friends (Quakers). Thus, they wanted the community's guidelines to reflect their own views of what life should be like: They wanted a place where "people of different ages, backgrounds, religions, and cultures could live together. They were not particularly well off, but felt that . . . by combining their talents and resources" they could devise and maintain a supportive environment for adults and children alike.[24]

Alongside their debates regarding the community's social connectedness, they too had to work with architects and designers in order to plan the community's physical and spatial layout. Financing was a major obstacle, because at that time public and private lending agencies in the United States had no familiarity whatsoever with the concept of cohousing. In particular, lending officials found it inconceivable for the "developer and the consumer to be one and the same." [25] As one consultant to the Santa Rosa group put it, "It was . . . successful . . . because of the people. . . . I don't know if you can ever reproduce the people and the motivation they had to persevere." [26]

Their perseverance never ceased, even after they had moved into their neighborhood. For example, each member was expected to attend monthly meetings, and also to contribute no fewer than 8 hours per month serving on committees and/or doing work in the community. There was a committee for each of the following areas: building and grounds, garden and landscaping, membership and marketing, social activities, parents' support group, education, finance, community room, and time and management. In addition, there were two committees on children's activities.[27] Several Santa Rosa members confided to Fromm that they spent many more than 8 hours a month doing the things that needed to be done in order for the community to thrive. "By joining," they told her, "every individual becomes a member of a community that has set a certain standard and quality of participation. It's a very subtle peer pressure that says if you join . . . you not only give a minimum of 8 hours per month, but you also meet the needs as they come along." [28]

Furthermore, when important issues arise in a collaborative community, the group as a whole must meet many times a month in order to address them. All too often, those meetings can be quite time-consuming. The matter of lengthy meetings is particularly salient for Santa Rosa, in contrast to Saettedammen. In the latter, as well as in most cohousing neighborhoods, issues are resolved by a majority vote. But in Santa Rosa (reflecting many members' Quaker heritage), total group consensus is required for resolution of every issue. As in any democratic setting, some issues are never fully resolved. The best the group can do is hope to develop a solution that works for a while, knowing full well that later on they will have to meet again to revisit the same issue. Chapter 1 notes that the fourth principle of an innovative family policy is "dialogic democracy." Plainly, cohousing communities like Santa Rosa are grounded in that principle. Dialogue is embedded in the day-to-day life of the community. Adults (and sometimes youth) get to participate in, and help shape, the decision making that affects their everyday lives.[29] Cohousing is a virtual "laboratory of democracy"—a theme that I elaborate in Chapters 6 and 7.

ISSUES THAT MAY UNITE OR DIVIDE A COHOUSING NEIGHBORHOOD

Children

Despite, or perhaps because of, the fact that children's well-being is one of the principal themes of cohousing, it turns out that in Santa Rosa "children are . . . one of the main sources of [recurring community] conflict." [30] On the one side, most Santa Rosa members care deeply about all of the community's children, and want very much to participate in the lives of "all our children." For instance, one Santa Rosa father told Fromm, " 'The neighbors had a daughter the same age as mine, and they were like sisters.' Children can knock on a neighbor's doors and be welcomed. When they have a problem, they have a choice of people to turn to for assistance." [31] Fromm goes on to say that "neighbors help out with child care and baby-sitting. One member took care of an 8-year-old in the afternoon while her father, a single parent, worked. 'I watch her when she comes home from school, and if I'm busy, the neighbors take turns keeping an eye.' Older children are available to baby-sit for the youngest." [32]

On the other side, some members are not at all prepared for the "radical" idea that every adult has a certain degree of responsibility for "all our children." Those members feel annoyed by the behaviors of certain children and complain that the birth parents are not doing enough to keep their own children in line. And when those members themselves try to keep the children in line, some of the birth parents feel that those members have exceeded neighborhood guidelines, and thus intruded on the parents' "natural" parental rights. The upshot is that disagreements regarding children's behaviors often have to be resolved by one of the "committees on children." If that fails to resolve the dispute, it then has to be brought to the community's monthly meeting. One member became so frustrated over the community's inability to resolve disagreements over children that she eventually moved out of Santa Rosa: "Everyone has a different idea on how to bring up their children. You can imagine that some people are very allergic to forms of behavior that don't bother other people." [33] In short, commitment to the well-being of "all our children" can be a powerful force uniting the community, and thus contributing to its ongoingness. But, by the same token, if conflicts over children's behaviors are not resolved in a manner that is satisfactory to most members, then that becomes an equally potent force threatening the neighborhood's stability.

Political or Social Agenda

The same potential to unite or divide the community exists when members decide to adopt a social agenda and/or political ideology.[34] Just as they were committed to the well-being of children, the Scandinavians who first experimented with cohousing were equally committed to the well-being of the natural environment. Likewise, as they planned the physical features of their community, some Santa Rosa members argued strongly for making it as friendly as possible to its natural surroundings. Among other things, that meant the use of energy-efficient designs. One of those designs was an atrium greenhouse that also served as the "common solar collector for the surrounding units, complete with a system of operable fans and vents." [35]

Cohousing advocates on both sides of the Atlantic believe strongly that cohousing is an obvious place to design the types of features that promote ecological sustainability. A Cambridge, Massachusetts, cohousing neighborhood that was completed in 1998 received a lot of national attention because it was fitted with state-of-the-art technologies aimed at conserving natural resources.[36] The suburban lifestyle has been severely criticized, not only because of its social limitations (as discussed in Chapter 3), but because it is extraordinarily unfriendly to the natural environment.[37] In 1996, Australian social scientist Graham Meltzer studied 18 of the 22 occupied cohousing communities in North America. His aim was to discover whether or not members had designed spatial features that are ecologically friendly. He found that cohousing "facilitates the sharing of resources and reduced household consumption. . . . It provides a physical and social milieu which nurtures stewardship and an awareness of the consequences of one's actions for others . . . and for the environment." [38] Incidentally, Anthony Giddens argues that ecological concerns are integral to his new politics of the radical center.[39]

In short, like attitudes toward the rearing of children, levels of commitment to the sociopolitical ideal of sustainability, or the "green" agenda, can either contribute to or detract from a collaborative community's solidarity and ongoingness. When members coalesce around strategies to promote a given ideology, such as a shared green agenda, that has a singular impact on their sense of "we-ness"—their esprit de corps. But if that does not happen, such ideologies hold enormous potential for driving wedges between group members, thereby threatening their neighborhood's ongoingness.

Dyadic Intimacy Versus the Primary Group

Most cohousing advocates aim to cultivate friendship groups within their communities. However, like attitudes toward child rearing and political agendas, friendship groups can either build up or weaken a community's solidarity. One of Fromm's respondents described the character of the friendship network within her cohousing community: "Sometimes I feel that we've found another way to live where it doesn't have to be . . . lonely. It's a feeling . . . that we've become an extended family, part of each other. . . . It's just a feeling of real joy and belonging—we're living the difference." [40] Plainly, such powerful feelings hold considerable potential to bond group members together, thereby helping to ensure the community's ongoingness.

Another way to describe a friendship group is to call it a "primary" group. A primary group is marked by we-feelings, or a sense of we-ness.[41] We-ness implies belonging to something that is bigger and more important than oneself. A person who belongs to a primary group is convinced that he or she matters to others in the group, that they genuinely care about what happens to him or her. By the same token, the other members of the group matter to that individual; he or she cares about what happens to them. The flip side of belonging to a we-group is that it helps to reinforce the individual's sense of me-ness, or identity—"Who I am." It also reinforces a person's self-concept—"The fact that I matter to others proves I'm a worthy person."

Although belonging to a primary group is indeed a rich experience, couples who live in cohousing must also face the issue of how to balance group intimacy with their own dyadic intimacy. Failing that, their own erotic friendship may be threatened or the community's ongoingness may be at risk, or perhaps both may be imperiled. As I have discussed in Chapter 3, dyadic love is now being reinvented. Today, emotional intimacy between partners is an essential component of their relationship's generic essence. We seek a confidante—a soul mate. We want to share strong dyadic we-feelings with that person—feelings that supply security and identity and that reinforce our self-concept. At the same time, we seek transcendence via that person. By belonging to him or her, we become part of something larger than ourselves, namely, a dyad. That being the case, why would a couple in love want or need a community primary group? Wouldn't joining up be a signal that one or both partners need more, or deeper, emotional intimacy than the other is capable of providing? If they are in love, why would they want to supplement their two-person "primary relationship" with a multiperson "primary group"? Why open up the boundaries of their relationship in that fashion? What would be the consequences of doing so?

During the late 1940s and early 1950s, British sociologist Elizabeth Bott asked similar kinds of questions.[42] She studied a number of urban marriages in order to describe their "degree of connectedness" with their surrounding social networks, which included friends, neighbors, and relatives. She wanted to know how many and what kinds of activities each spouse did with persons in his or her network. And she wanted to discover the consequences of those outside influences on their marriages. Bott found that the more extensively the wives and husbands were connected with persons belonging to their networks, the less involved, or connected, they were with one another. By contrast, spouses who had less extensive network connections were more involved, or connected, with one another. And in the late 1950s, social scientist Lee Rainwater came up with similar conclusions among a sample of urban Americans. Furthermore, Rainwater added that couples who had *fewer* outsider connections, and thus greater involvement with each other, tended to report *higher* levels of marital satisfaction.[43] Couples with *more* outsider connections, and thus less involvement with each other, tended to report *lower* levels of marital satisfaction.

These earlier investigations imply that a couple's participating in a primary group located in cohousing might possibly drain time and energy from their cultivating emotional intimacy with each other. The primary group is, after all, a source of emotional satisfaction from persons of the same or opposite gender. As a result, someone may experience so much emotional intimacy with outsiders that she or he has little energy or inclination to pursue it with her or his partner. That would not make a great deal of difference as long as the partner does not object. But if he or she does protest, then for obvious reasons the balance of the couple's public-private involvements would need to be renegotiated. The result for some couples might be a lessening of primary group involvement. Some might even decide to move out of the collaborative neighborhood. But on the other hand, one or both partners may not wish to lessen their primary group involvement, much less leave the neighborhood. Although doing that may protect the neighborhood, what about their own relationship?

One way to approach these sorts of puzzling matters is to acknowledge that the contemporary expectation for profound dyadic emotional intimacy may perhaps be yet another instance of asking "too much" from at least some of today's couples. It could be that a certain number of couples (especially the male partners) may have gone about as far as they can in the quest for each other's inner souls. If that realization dawns on a couple who live, say, outside of cohousing, the partners may seek professional help in order to open up greater "communication" between them. If that doesn't work, and one or both partners remain emotionally deprived, they might very well split up. Hence, it could be in the self-interest of some of those emotionally deprived couples to participate in a cohousing neighborhood. If they have no other complaints about each other, and thus might stay together if their needs for emotional intimacy were met, the neighborhood might be a resource that could maintain their stability. For those couples, opening up the "friendship" segment of their relationship, permitting partners to experience emotional intimacy with outsiders, might possibly have advantageous results.

At the same time, other couples might feel that they are the best of soul mates. They do indeed experience a profound degree of shared emotional intimacy. Nevertheless, they are keenly aware that it never stands still— either their intimacy deepens or it declines. Accordingly, some of those soul mates might regard participation in their community as a potential stimulus toward even greater dyadic closeness. Both members of a couple, for example, might view their neighborhood as a place to cultivate additional intimate friendships that facilitate shared openness and mutual self-disclosure.[44] The richness gained from those types of friendships could then be brought back and shared with one's unique friend. Consequently, allowing the boundaries of their erotic friendship to become more permeable might possibly enrich their relationship. For them, connectedness with outsiders could enhance their internal bonding.

In short, like attitudes toward child rearing and particular sociopolitical agendas, the primary group experience has enormous potential to unite the community or to weaken it. Each of these three matters illustrates the inevitable tension between the desire of the household to be free from external controls and the need for community solidarity. There are no pat answers or ready-made formulas that cohousing neighborhoods can call on to solve these constantly recurring dilemmas. Each neighborhood must try to negotiate these and other matters on a case-by-case basis as they emerge. And, as I said earlier, the tension between freedom and connectedness is not unique to cohousing neighborhoods. Historical examples of collaborative communities show that they experienced that very same tension. However, compared with cohousing, the principal distinction was that most of the historic communities devised rigid, and often controversial, formulas to try to manage that tension.

HISTORIC STRUGGLES OVER THE FREEDOM-CONNECTEDNESS TENSION

The Shakers

To take an example of such a rigid formula, several mid-19th-century American collaborative communities met the "problem of tension between the nuclear family and the community by doing away with all heterosexual relationships." [45] Among the best known of these 19th-century communities was that of the United Society of Believers, or the Shakers. The Shakers emulated the three-point formula that the Roman Catholic Church had used for centuries among its many communities of monks and nuns. First of all, the Shakers enforced celibacy among members. They could neither have sex nor marry. The Shakers concurred with the Catholic communities that "two-person intimacy poses a potential threat to group cohesiveness unless it is somehow controlled or regulated by the group." [46] Second, members of the Shakers had to renounce all control over their private property. Aside from personal belongings, they had to renounce the right to have material things. Third, they had to conform to strict rules imposed by the group.

Nevertheless, the Shakers diverged sharply from Catholic communities in the ways they organized their social and spatial arrangements regarding women and men. Shakers of both genders typically resided in the same buildings. Each building housed from 30 to 90 members, and the group in a given building was known as a "family." Men and women slept in separate rooms, and, although they had meals in the same dining hall, they ate at different tables. The daily tasks of men and women around the community were also quite distinct. Furthermore, the genders had very little informal contact, except during the "union hour." At the designated time, "a group of 'sisters' would enter a room in which a number of 'brothers' were present and spend an hour conversing as couples. . . . All in all, it does seem to have been a successful device in providing the minimal amount of sexual contact tolerable in an essentially celibate community." [47]

At religious services, women and men danced in the same room, but were never allowed to touch. Their dancing frequently became quite exuberant, and visitors came from miles around to see it. It was those visitors who coined the label "Shakers" after witnessing the members' uninhibited bodily movements. The Shakers were an example of celibate men and women who, having "renounced the flesh," lived together in a community that functioned as a means of satisfying their fundamental human need for deep primary relationships. Persons who were freed from the commitments of dyadic love and parental involvement were thereby unfettered to make extensive investments of time and energy in their community. In short, the Shakers resolved the freedom-connectedness tension by making extensive group obligations far more important than any kind of individual freedoms.

The Oneida Community

Because most 19th-century collaborative communities found celibacy unworkable, a few adopted a drastically different formula. Nevertheless, the new formula was aimed at precisely the same problem of minimizing tension between the nuclear family and its community. The practice was called "free love, including group marriage, in which every member was expected to have intimate sexual relations with all others." [48] Although the strategies of celibacy and free love are totally opposite in practice, their outcome is identical—that is, every community member has equal potential to develop the same type of primary relationship with every other member. The best known of these free love groups was the Oneida community.

The founder and driving force behind the Oneida group was the charismatic clergyman John Humphrey Noyes. He was "critical of monogamy because he saw it as . . . encouraging exclusivity and selfishness. . . . 'The heart should be free [said Noyes] to love all the true and the worthy.' " [49] Noyes argued that free love reduces the likelihood of possessiveness, jealousy, and strife, which often accompany a couple's relationship. And by minimizing the significance of dyadic love, he argued, one could maximize the chances for community success and survival.

Noyes, however, never permitted free love to equal promiscuity. He and his followers strictly controlled and carefully regulated sexual relations among members. They were never allowed to become licentious, any more than they were permitted to be monogamous. The Oneida community was particularly systematic in specifying who could have sex with whom and when. Oneida also managed the community reproduction of children through prevention of unwanted pregnancies by "requiring a form of contraception known as male continence, involving the muscular control of ejaculation." [50] The plan was that the man should stimulate the woman until she experienced orgasm, at which point he would withdraw, apart from any orgasm of his own.

Children were viewed as belonging to the entire Oneida community as well as to their birth parents—they were "all our children." Hence, adults who had no offspring were required to participate actively in the upbringing of community children. And adults with natural offspring were expected to pay attention to other community children as well. Noyes and his followers believed that linkages between parents and their natural children were as much a threat to community bonding as was marriage: "It was exclusive [parent-child] attachments that Oneida wished to soft-pedal in favor of ties to the whole group as a family." [51] For example, Pierrepont Noyes (son of John Humphrey Noyes) wrote what one observer called a "charming portrait of the impact of the Oneida system as seen by the child." It was quite obvious, Kanter has noted, that the group did nothing to "change the playful world of children." [52] But at the same time, the younger Noyes was keenly aware of the community's "religious teachings [and] even while sometimes distressed by separation from his mother, he still accepted the group life of the whole as the focus of his existence." [53]

In short, the Oneida strategy for managing the inevitable tension between household and community differed sharply from that of the Roman Catholic communities and the Shakers. Oneida had its own means for defusing the emotionally charged nature of dyadic love and parenting. But precisely like the Catholics and the Shakers, Oneida group members owned everything in common and held no private property. And analogous to Catholic communities, final authority was vested in a single person whose pronouncements were indisputable. For the Oneida group that meant the masterful John Humphrey Noyes. In short, like the members of Catholic communities and like the Shakers, Oneida members too believed that their own best interests emerged from serving their group. Freedom and independence were nonissues.

The Kibbutzim of the 1940s and 1950s

In the 20th century, the post-World War II Israeli kibbutzim invented a different (yet similar) formula for managing the inevitable tensions between individual freedoms and group responsibility. Based on his research into those agricultural communities, anthropologist Melford Spiro has reported that what is referred to in Chapter 3 as the erotic friendship was an explicit and unmistakable feature of the post-World War II kibbutz.[54] Marriage in the formal and everyday senses that kibbutz members had known it in Europe (from which many of them had migrated) was not encouraged. Furthermore, at that time individual couples' children did not reside with their birth parents, nor were parents ultimately responsible for their offspring's economic or emotional well-being. The children lived in dormitories, were cared for by nurses, and were supported by the labors of the kibbutz as a whole.

Nevertheless, parents and their offspring visited with each other regularly and maintained powerful emotional bonds. They "comprised a distinct and recognizable social [primary] group" both in their own eyes and in the eyes of the entire kibbutz.[55] Between the ages of 5 and 6, children moved from the kindergarten dormitory to the primary school dormitory. This transition was crucial for many reasons, not least of which was that "it introduce[d] them into social responsibility and work." [56] At that time, each child was assigned specific duties, requiring about an hour per day. Obligations might include cleaning their own living space, classrooms, and dining hall, as well as helping out with the school's landscaping, vegetable garden, or poultry run. After grade 6 and around age 12, they entered high school and moved to yet another dormitory. At this critical juncture, the children become an actual part of the productive—that is, bottom-line—agricultural labors of the community. They spent several hours each day working alongside adults and were expected to take on gradually both the identity and the role of "contributing member" to the success of the community's agricultural enterprise.

In that regard, the "single most important ideal" of a kibbutz was the "moral value of labor." [57] Arduous and diligent physical work was, of course, essential to the success of those struggling agricultural enterprises. But kibbutz members also felt that their shared physical labor possessed a mystic quality that contributed to their spiritual well-being. Individual liberty was a second fiercely held postulate. Nonetheless, in terms of relative priority, kibbutz members believed that the "interests of the individual must be subordinate to the interests of the group." [58] Put another way, at the same time they highly valued "private initiative," they held unswervingly to the goal of making every member feel a powerful sense of "responsibility to their kibbutz." [59] In short, although drastically different from groups such as the Shakers and the members of the Oneida community, the post-World War II kibbutzim shared with them the same general formula for managing the freedom-connectedness tension, and that was to declare unequivocally that the interests of the group take precedence over those of any single individual.

North American Communes of the 1960s and 1970s

If the Shakers, the Oneida group, and the kibbutzim resolved the freedom-connectedness tension by placing group obligations above individual freedoms, the North American communes of several decades ago were diametrically opposite—180 degrees different. Most communes elevated personal freedoms far above group interests. Indeed, among many communes, it was hard to identify any group interests at all.[60] By and large, most commune members sought to "drop out" of, and thus retreat from, society. A central theme of the counterculture of that time is captured by the expression "Do your own thing." The themes of responsibility and obligation—central to each of the communities discussed above, including cohousing—were noticeably missing from the counterculture.[61]

Furthermore, commune members objected strenuously to virtually every feature of mid-20th-century marriage. They were suspicious of marriage in ways that stretched far beyond the feelings expressed by the Shakers, the Oneida group, or the kibbutzim. For instance, several commune members told social scientist Benjamin Zablocki their views of marriage: "Marriage is institutionalized neurosis"; "Marriage is a trap, an artificial commitment toward a limited life-style"; "It's unnecessary bondage that limits people's creative, intellectual, and community growth"; "I don't think much of my parents' marriage." [62] The hostile feelings of those counterculture youth were in large part a reaction to what they perceived as the stultifying post-World War II nuclear family lifestyle in which they had grown up.[63] Today, one rarely hears the sort of bitterness and vitriol toward marriage expressed by Zablocki's respondents and verified by most other studies of 1960s and 1970s communes.[64] Those kinds of acerbic reactions are now much less typical because most Americans have deliberately shifted away from the most onerous and oppressive features of the 1950s family style.

But commune members, in fierce reaction to that rigid lifestyle, simply ignored the matter of group responsibility altogether.[65] As a result, unlike the Shakers, the Oneida group, or the kibbutzim, counterculture youth frequently failed to develop any formula for managing sexuality, dyadic love, and parenting.[66] Consequently, over time, most of their groups simply fell apart.

Spatial Features

Alongside these and other important social differences between communes and cohousing, there are acute spatial distinctions as well. Zablocki notes that for members of 1960s communes, "a collective household [was] deemed essential." [67] *Collective* meant that every group member lived under one roof, with very little personal privacy. Living together in a large building of some kind symbolized one of the commune members' most vital ideals—the quest for what they called "spiritual communion." Unfortunately, says sociologist Philip Selznick, "communion is psychic unity." It is not social unity, and a functioning community requires social unity to survive. Social unity emerges out of a "range of activities and associations. . . . The commune is an inherently unstable social form. If it desires more stability, the commune must become a community." [68] But in order to survive as a community, the commune needed to construct means of balancing responsibilities to the group with individual freedoms. And few, if any, communes were able to do that.

Plainly, cohousing differs drastically from the ways of life of the Shakers, the Oneida group, and the kibbutzim. In each of those cases, the group managed the tension between personal freedoms and group responsibility by placing *group interests* on a much higher plane than individual freedoms. On the other side, most communes of several decades ago faced the tension unsuccessfully by placing *personal freedoms* far above any sense of group responsibility and group solidarity. But in contrast to each of those previous cases, cohousing struggles mightily to place *household freedoms* and *group responsibility* on the same plane. Cohousing has neither pat answers nor ready-made formulas. Instead, at both the formal and informal levels, it has to rely on a never-ending series of tortuous efforts to solve problems and to negotiate disagreements—first, among members and, second, between members and the cohousing group as a whole.

FREEDOM AND CONNECTEDNESS IN TODAY'S "COMMUNITY AS COMMODITY"

Although no one would confuse today's cohousing with yesterday's communes, one might easily confuse cohousing with what political scientist Dennis Judd calls today's "community as commodity." [69] This type of housing development bears a certain superficial resemblance to cohousing, especially in its spatial features.[70] In fact, however, it differs markedly from cohousing in several ways, which I describe below.

Community as commodity refers to a particular type of housing development that the building industry has recently been marketing to American consumers. As noted in Chapter 3, in the 1920s, and again after World War II, the building industry convinced consumers that the American Dream includes a single-family, detached house, protected from outsiders by as much grass as possible. However, as Judd notes, by the 1960s "this version of the suburban dream began to yield lower returns." [71] Because land was getting so expensive, developers concluded they would have to build higher-density housing in order to continue making money. Hence, in 1961 the industry successfully lobbied the Federal Housing Authority (FHA) to begin "to insure loans for condominiums in multiunit buildings." [72] In order to protect the value of the property (and thus the loans), the FHA stated that it would not insure a loan until after the builder had drawn up, and gotten FHA approval for, a strict set of community guidelines. The guidelines must guarantee that the owners will not be allowed to do anything that might threaten property values. Once the bylaws were approved, they could not be changed "without a unanimous vote of the members." [73] Persons who bought units automatically became members of the "home owners association" and were thus rigidly bound by its "restrictive covenants."

The Common-Interest Development

Later on, in order to increase its sales further, the building industry added a new spin to those covenants. By the early 1980s, it changed the public's perception of the covenants by playing down their restrictive character. Covenants are now marketed as devices for what the industry calls "common-interest developments" (CIDs). To avoid the guidelines' being perceived as limiting choices, the industry now touts them as the basis for expanding personal freedoms. High-pressure salespersons convince gullible buyers that the covenants contribute to a "sense of community." Allegedly, the "community" comes into being merely because persons happen to share the same leisure interests. They might, for example, be retired persons, or adults over age 19, or persons who like golf, tennis, shuffleboard, boating, fishing, hiking, cycling, or whatever. For example, an ad in a national magazine for a development called Las Campanas Santa Fe informs readers, "This remarkable community comes complete with all the amenities your lifestyle demands including a Jack Nicklaus designed golf course." [74]

Judd reports that "the number of CIDs, which include New Towns, cooperative apartments, condominiums, and single-family houses constructed by a single developer, exploded from about 1,000 in the early 1960s to well over 80,000 by 1984. . . . In Florida . . . by 1990 condos outnumbered single-family dwellings." He predicts that by the "next century CIDs in some form will have become the principal form of new home ownership in most metropolitan areas." [75]

Needless to say, CIDs differ dramatically from cohousing. Nevertheless, CIDs sometimes use the label of cohousing, even though they have virtually nothing in common with, say, Santa Rosa Creek Commons or Cantine's Island. Although CIDs have the "accoutrements of community: a name [e.g., Las Campanas], a community center, a school, a recreational center," they are little more than an aggregation of households. [76] They are merely nonconnected households that happen to reside within specialized types of housing developments. Although governed by sets of minimal regulations, their aim is not to establish collaborative communities. For example, their goals do not include the creation of primary groups aimed at enriching the lives of adults. Nor do they intend to create settings in which adults can participate in the lives of "all our children." Nor do they intend to take on any sociopolitical objective such as sustainability. Few CID residents would resonate to the feelings expressed by one of Fromm's respondents: "For me, this [cohousing] is a real way of living. It is not a matter of portioning off a part of myself but living in a whole way, both giving and taking." [77] In short, CIDs pay virtually no attention to collaborative living as defined throughout this chapter. And although they give lip service to

the ideals of community, they very much prefer the liberties of the nonconnected lifestyle.

The Fortress Mentality

A number of urban planners believe that recently CIDs have taken a
disturbing and potentially ugly turn. Judd calls this trend "CIDs as For-
tress." [78] In the Middle Ages, immense walls were constructed around many
European cities to keep out the unwanted rabble, who were perceived as
threats to the safety of the citizens. Today, clever marketers play on citizens'
fears of crime and violence by touting their CIDs as the "new walled
cities." [79] Security becomes a principal selling point. At the very least,
gaining entrance to such a development requires passing a security guard
or the use of a computer-coded ID card to open a locked gate.

In addition, high walls and other barriers are frequently erected to keep
out all unapproved persons. According to Judd, "Leisure World, a California retirement community, is surrounded by 6-foot walls topped with
barbed wire. Quayside, a planned community . . . blends the atmosphere
of a . . . small town of the 1920s with the latest in high-tech security: laser
beams sweep the perimeters . . . and television cameras continuously monitor the living and recreation areas." He adds that in the Los Angeles area,
gated communities "are rapidly replacing all other kinds of development." [80]
A number of urban planners argue that the spatial design of the gated
housing development dramatically symbolizes the determination of the
"haves" to maintain a lifestyle wholly separate and distinct from the "have-
nots." All too often, *have-nots* becomes a code word for African Americans.[81] Analyst Thomas Friedman worries about "trusting a country where
the rich live behind high walls and tinted windows. That is a place that is
not prospering as one country. That is a place where the rich not only say,
'I don't want you to see how I live,' but 'I don't want to see how you
live.' " [82]

Adults-Only Developments

Still another peculiar type of CID is the adults-only development. This
is a housing area whose members declare unequivocally that they want little

or no involvement at all in the lives of "other people's children." For example, in early 1997, the national media gave a lot of attention to the case of an Arizona retirement community (Superstition Heights) that had a rule against any household's having a permanent resident under age 19. A 16-year-old had moved in with her grandmother because her own mother was dying of cancer, and thus was no longer able to care for her. The Superstition Heights association sought to evict the girl, but the state's attorney general ruled that she could stay.[83] In a separate incident, a 16-year-old boy fled his physically abusive father to seek refuge with his grandparents, who lived in a different Arizona adults-only development. That association also tried to evict the offending child, but there again the state intervened on his behalf.[84] Adults-only developments represent an extreme version of how to connect adults with children. For the residents of these communities, the connection means that each household in the area pays attention to its own relatives. Grandchildren, nieces, and nephews are welcome to visit, but if a visiting child is not related by blood to the resident adult, both are suspect. And in any event, no youngster is allowed to reside there on a permanent basis.

CONCLUSION

Although cohousing was conceived and born in the late 1960s, it was *not* designed as a means to further the long-term revolution in gender and family patterns. Instead, it was and is perceived in much more modest terms. It is simply a practical strategy intended to reform some of the shortcomings of the 1950s family style—especially its social and spatial isolation. Cohousing advocates believe that both adults and children should become part of social support networks located within their own spatial settings. Households in cohousing communities maintain their *in*dependence while they struggle to achieve and maintain a sense of *inter*dependence. Cohousing neighborhoods vary in the degrees to which they try to balance freedom with responsibility. Some want to hold community obligations to a minimum, whereas others aim to expand cross-household responsibilities. For all concerned, the balancing act is a constant struggle. Examples of issues that contribute to the struggle include neighbors' involvement in the rearing of the community's children and the potential tension between dyadic intimacy and community connectedness.

Cohousing is quite distinct from a number of historic and contemporary efforts to "build community." It is, for instance, highly pragmatic and nonideological. Nor do its advocates attempt to package and sell "community" as a commodity. If its advocates tend to feel strongly about any overarching cause, it is a concern for the ecological environment. Most cohousing communities are designed in ways that are intended to expedite sustainable development. And although their residents would no doubt strongly agree with the statement "Men and women should get equal pay for equal work," women's interests in general are not part of the social and political agendas of most cohousing communities.

And that is precisely the point. Aside from sustainability, cohousing holds little in the way of a social or political agenda. Its advocates have little or no interest in reinventing public policy in general or family policy in particular. To be sure, many of their activities are compatible with several of the principles of an innovative family policy described in Chapter 1. These include a balance of freedom with responsibility and participation in dialogic, or democratic, decision making. Moreover, cohousing communities accept the reality of manufactured risk in contemporary society and do all they can to buffer its consequences for children and adults alike. Nevertheless, cohousing advocates do not perceive themselves to be in the forefront of the ongoing gender and family revolution. For that, we must shift from the present to the future. We must go to Part II for a discussion of the New Everyday Life.

PART II

INVENTING THE FUTURE BY COMPLETING THE REVOLUTION

5

EMPOWERING WOMEN: BALANCING THE PRIVATE AND PUBLIC SPHERES

♦♦♦ ─────────────────────────────

Part I described the family revolution that began in earnest some 200 years ago. At first, couples simply wished to free themselves from unwanted kin authority and control. This freedom implied several things, but most of all it meant the right to marry the "one I love." At the same time, it meant the couple's right to pursue their own economic well-being, even if that meant a degree of material hardship and emotional distress for their parents and other kin.

As the 19th century wore on, it became increasingly clear that most men were profiting from the new lifestyle a great deal more than were most women. Consequently, the family revolution added a further objective. Just as nuclear families sought and obtained independence from their extended families, women sought emancipation from men. *Emancipation* does not mean the absence of meaningful social and psychological ties; rather, it refers to the capability to control one's own destiny. By that measure, most women today remain in a subordinate position to most men. The specific indicators of that subordination include, but are not limited to, income, job status, and political office.[1] To be sure, since the 1960s there have been substantial gains for women in all three realms. Nevertheless, women tend to earn less than men who have the same educational levels. Women are underrepresented in many professions and in the higher ranks of business, colleges and universities, and all branches of government. And if we look inside the household, we find that most women continue to exercise less influence than most men over a wide range of vital matters (an issue that I discuss further later in this chapter). Plainly, the 200-year-old family revolution is incomplete.

While pondering how to keep the revolution going, we must realize that every Western nation is now caught up in the "New World Order." [2] We are sailing through uncharted waters on our way from the industrial age to the posttraditional, information age. Among other things, this new age means that it is becoming increasingly difficult for any man to assume that he will be able to fulfill his culturally prescribed role of "Good Provider." [3] Analyst Hugh Heclo shows that "structural economic changes are undermining the older idea of [men's] secure" lifetime employment.[4] Woven into the fabric of the post-World War II family lifestyle was the motif that throughout his lifetime the male breadwinner would be able to work consistently for a decent wage. But since the 1970s, the presumption of a predictable occupational trajectory throughout a man's life course has grown increasingly untenable.[5] Throughout the West, men can no longer expect the kind of job stability and security—including steady increases in wages and benefits—enjoyed by their fathers and grandfathers.

The upshot is this: At any social class level, a contemporary woman who expects to rely on a man to provide for her and her children has far less certainty than her mother or grandmother once had that such expectations will be met in a consistent manner. In practical terms, today's uncertainties mean that "every married woman is a potential single mother and every child is a potential member of a one-parent family." [6] With that assertion, Heclo says two things about posttraditional society that most of us already know: First, no marriage (or any relationship) can presume the level of security and stability that existed under the umbrella of the 1950s family style; second, no job can be safe and secure in the way many jobs were during the post-World War II period. What I have referred to in Chapter 1 as "external risk" has spread widely throughout the class structure.

In an article written just after the passage of the 1996 Welfare Reform Act, analyst Ellen Willis notes that "if the welfare state is in deep trouble," the reasons can be traced to the convulsive economic, political, and social forces surrounding everyone, not just the poor. She adds that "feminism, sexual freedom, and market forces have destabilized a family structure based on male dominance and female dependence, yet we haven't found satisfying alternatives." [7] In short, what I have referred to in Chapter 1 as "manufactured risk" pervades every level of society. Thus, according to Willis, concentrating principally on the plight of the poor is not only "condescending but increasingly inaccurate." The effects of worldwide economic restructuring are "creeping up the class ladder" from blue-collar workers to upper-middle-class professionals. As a result, "no one's way of life or standard of living is secure." [8] The malaise once confined to the poor has now diffused upward to economically advantaged children and adults.

Cohousing is a buffer against the inevitable disturbances experienced by adults and children alike as we shift from an industrial to a postindustrial society. It was invented as a means of absorbing some of the shocks caused by the ongoing family revolution. Cohousing is a way to restore certain valued traditions from the agricultural era without sacrificing equally valued traditions constructed during the industrial period. However, few if any of its advocates view cohousing as a mechanism for advancing the family revolution. Instead, they see it merely as a way to lessen some of the revolution's unsettling consequences.

UTOPIAN REALISM

Part II of this book is about completing the revolution. It explores the slippery "terrain that usually remains untrod due to social scientists' self-imposed exile—the regions between what is and what might be." [9] My aim is to describe the kind of family policy that, in the emerging information age, might advance the revolution.

It has been said that any policy statement is a vision of the future.[10] Policy is a conception of how we want things to be. We believe that if we can make certain things happen, people will be better off than they are right now. In the early 1960s, for example, President Kennedy gave the nation and the world a vision of the future when he stated, "We shall put

a man on the moon by the end of the decade." Once that broad vision
became official U.S. policy, hundreds of specific technical programs were
put in place to try to achieve it. Kennedy's vision is an example of what
Anthony Giddens calls "utopian realism." [11] The policy vision described in
Part II is also a case of utopian realism: *utopian* because it is lofty and idealistic and *realistic* because it has its basis in existing research and theory—
our understandings about the ways in which society operates. It is realistic
because, like the moon shot, it could happen if people want it to happen—it
is not mere fantasy. The policy vision laid out in this and the following
chapters belongs to what some call "futures studies." [12] The basic assumption of futures studies is that "not everything that will exist has existed or
does exist." [13] Finally, the same question that Giddens asks about his
general social policy applies to family policy in particular: "What other
possibility is there?" [14] If the family policy vision proposed here is not
put in place, then what is the alternative vision for continuing the family
revolution?

GENDER INTERCHANGEABILITY

Analyst Gilbert Steiner has observed that following World War II, the
Scandinavian countries (Sweden, Denmark, and Norway) explicitly developed an unambiguous family policy objective, and they have never vacil-
lated in their support of it. That policy objective was "equality for women . . .
[meaning] a formal recognition that all family functions except carrying a
fetus and nursing an infant can be performed by either men or women." [15]
Realizing full well the monumental scope of their first goal, the Scandinavians made their corollary policy objective the "protection of children." [16]
The Scandinavians hoped to achieve gender equity through male and female
"interchangeability." They hoped that women and men alike would be able
to choose freely from an identical menu of life-course options, both in the
workplace and in the homeplace.[17] If women were no longer locked into
household obligations, and if men were no longer locked out, then women
should be able, reasoned the advocates, to achieve autonomy, or economic
self-sufficiency (see Chapter 3). Autonomy, they believed, is the surest road
to gender equity. Embedded in these efforts to enhance gender equity was
the strong expectation that many men would quickly comprehend, and

eagerly embrace, the morality of gender equity. Advocates optimistically predicted, for example, that men would make meaningful changes in their own domestic and parenting responsibilities. To help achieve gender interchangeability, the Scandinavian governments established a wide range of programs. Those included, but were not limited to, extensive day-care facilities and paid workforce leaves for men and women.[18] No other nation in the world has equaled the Scandinavian nations in the scope of national programs aimed at women's interests and gender interchangeability.

Equal-Partner Marriage: An Unrealized Vision

Underlying the Scandinavian policies and programs was a model that came to be known as the *equal-partner marriage.* In the late 1960s and 1970s, it was heralded on both sides of the Atlantic as a notable step beyond the flawed family lifestyle inherited from the 1950s.[19] Its foundation, as well as its driving energy, was gender interchangeability—the idea that both men and women should participate fully in both the marketplace and the homeplace. Advocates for the equal-partner marriage believed that the shift away from entrenched gender stereotypes would benefit children substantially. For one thing, children would get greater nurturing and more varied role modeling from men than they had received in the past. Second, children would be inspired by, and would accept as desirable, women's occupational achievements.

The levels of gender equity currently enjoyed by most Scandinavian women are indeed greater than those experienced by most North American women. For example, women make up almost a third of the members of the Scandinavian parliaments, and a woman has served as Norwegian prime minister. Furthermore, the number of Scandinavian women who are local political officials is "steadily rising." [20] Nevertheless, there as here, women tend to be overrepresented on "boards of culture, education, and social and health care." At the same time, women tend to be underrepresented on political bodies that control finances and make final program decisions. For that reason, Scandinavian social scientists Lisa Horelli and Kirsti Vespa quip that "where there are women, there is little money and little power. Where there is money and power, there are no women." [21] In other words, in spite of a national commitment to gender equity, and in spite of generous government programs calculated to achieve it, Scandinavian women have not yet fully escaped their historic subordination to men.

Horelli and Vespa report that Scandinavian women experience inequity not solely in the public sphere, but in the private realm as well: "The Scandinavian welfare states have not been able to stop women's double load of managing both work and home." [22] Women there, as here, continue to be the chief householders as well as the chief parents. Although Scandinavian men participate more fully than North American men in both housework and parenting, relatively little genuine role interchangeability exists on either side of the Atlantic.[23] For a century and a half, feminists on both sides of the Atlantic have argued that women's emancipation rests on three crucial dimensions: First, a woman must be well educated; second, she must have unimpeded access to the labor market; and third, she must be able to earn income sufficient to support herself and any children for which she is responsible. Since the 1960s, women have made remarkable strides in all three dimensions, and there is no doubt they will continue to do so. Nevertheless, given the fact that gender equity still eludes us, is there anything else we can do to expedite the achievement of that goal? Can we "peer into the future and talk together about the society [we] hope to build"? [24]

A NORDIC FEMINIST VISION

A 1979 conference of more than 100 persons did indeed peer into the future. Meeting in Sweden, the conference participants sketched the outlines of what they call "a Nordic Feminist Vision." [25] They acknowledge that their policy objective is an instance of utopian realism.[26] Though idealistic, they believe it to be potentially workable. Their long-term policy objective is the empowerment of women. They believe that the more women are empowered, the more likely they are eventually to attain equity with men. They concur that women's empowerment demands the three legs of education, occupation, and income. Furthermore, they contend that empowerment requires a fourth leg, which will transform a shaky stool into a sturdy chair. That fourth leg consists of bringing the private lives of women and men into greater balance with the public sphere. The fourth leg redefines both the spatial and the social environment of the household.

The New Everyday Life

Calling their vision the *New Everyday Life* (NEL), advocates propose to construct collaborative communities whose explicit social and political vision is to enhance women's empowerment. They call the establishment of NEL an "all-win" situation, in which "men, women, children, youth, and the elderly" alike would benefit.[27] In effect, they propose to create cohousing neighborhoods with a political and social agenda that extends beyond the "green" issues described in Chapter 4. They contend that physical space is a woman's issue no matter what her social class.[28] They believe that gender discrimination is exacerbated by, among other things, the layout of suburban neighborhoods and the designs of suburban houses. For example, researcher Amy Wharton says that she, like most of us, has only recently become aware of gender discrimination by spatial design: "Like most [U.S.] sociologists interested in gender, work, and family I [*used to*] take the physical environment within which women and men act largely for granted." [29] Giddens admits that the ancient struggle between the genders continues unabated, and hopes for mitigating it in some fashion are not very high.[30] To do so would require "*a pact between the sexes.*" [31] Advocates believe that the NEL community is a place where a lifestyle alliance between the genders might indeed be constructed and could continue to evolve. It is a structural setting—a situation—in which the genders could perhaps learn to hammer out the details of an alliance that furthers their own interests as well as those of their children. Advocates suggest that apart from some type of situational innovation such as NEL, prospects for rapprochement between the genders appear disheartening.

A Cure for Isolation

For many decades, advocates of gender equity assumed that we could fashion equity and yet maintain the nonconnected family style. NEL supporters question that assumption. Under current circumstances, they say, most women and men feel compelled to devise "individual solutions to collective problems." [32] In accordance with the nonconnected style, couples believe they should be able to solve family problems on their own, typically apart from consulting other couples. They persist in their faith even though other couples face similar problems and could thus benefit by sharing their experiences across household boundaries. Accordingly, NEL advocates believe it is vital to "break the isolation of the nuclear family." [33]

Feminists from a previous era argued that women should end their isolation from paid work and become connected with the labor force. Similarly, today's NEL advocates argue that women should end their neighborhood isolation and become connected with other women and men within a collaborative community. The fundamental issue to consider is whether we have pushed the nonconnected style as far as we can in terms of its capacity to accommodate women's empowerment. The equal-partner arrangement stretches that style's elasticity to the breaking point. And if that style has run its course, what then? Does the next phase of the family revolution require that we try to fashion socially and spatially connected neighborhoods? Should we construct neighborhoods that aim at women's empowerment as well as the best interests of men and children?

Some feminists have expressed grave misgivings about what is known as *communitarianism*. [34] That ambiguous label means different things to different people. When it means a revival of family and social patterns that in any way undermine women's historic struggle for gender equity, it is unacceptable. [35] But when communitarianism means encouraging women to participate voluntarily in a community of "choice" such as NEL, then, says philosopher Marilyn Friedman, it is a positive idea. [36] Philosopher Amy Gutman agrees, and adds that the challenge for communitarians is to "creat[e] new . . . institutions rather than increas[e] the power of existing institutions or reviving old ones." [37] Responding to that challenge is what NEL is all about. But what would NEL neighborhoods of the future look like? How would they differ from the cohousing communities that already exist? What are some of their specific features that might enhance women's empowerment? In what ways would this connected lifestyle move significantly beyond the scope of the nonconnected lifestyle? And how would these neighborhoods of the future accommodate the six principles of a comprehensive family policy identified in Chapter 1?

WOMEN'S EMPOWERMENT

This section describes three goals that an NEL neighborhood might try to put in place. Each objective facilitates the all-encompassing objective of women's empowerment and equity. The first goal is to free women from violence and/or the threat of violence. The second goal is to enhance individual women's capabilities of negotiating with the men in their lives regarding everyday matters. These include, but are not limited to, employment, education, child care, and domestic chores. The third goal for bringing about women's empowerment is to enable the community to address certain interests of men. All three goals demand a much more intricate balance between the private and public spheres—between freedom and connectedness—than anything described in Chapter 4.

Sanctuary: The Specter of Violence

Recall that the sixth policy point described in Chapter 1 concerns men's violence against women. No matter how significant women's public achievements eventually become, it cannot be said that gender equity is anywhere near at hand until women feel free from everyday male violence. In recent years, hundreds of studies have documented the grim reality of men's physical and sexual aggression toward women. Curious as it sounds, the majority of male violence is in fact directed toward "the woman I love"— whether wife, cohabitor, or girlfriend. Furthermore, recent studies show that lesbian and gay couples likewise experience dyadic violence.[38] Many proposals have been offered to reduce and/or prevent dyadic aggression. However, most of these assume the nonconnected lifestyle. Empowering women effectively to counteract male aggression may require a different premise.

The new premise is that the boundaries of the household should be made sufficiently permeable so as to define force against women as a neighborhood issue.[39] It should not be a matter left principally to household discretion. The aim is not to meddle or intrude in an unwarranted fashion. Instead, the rationale is simply that aggression is all too often a reality that women and children cannot cope with on their own. It is yet another example of Robert Nisbet's assertion that society asks "too much" of the typical nonconnected household.[40] Consequently, NEL members would declare their community to be a "violence-free zone." They would state explicitly that aggression is not simply a domestic issue; rather, it is a community matter. Every member is responsible, as fully as possible, for trying to protect neighborhood women from physical and sexual abuse (I address the issue of aggression toward children in Chapter 6). Everyone shares the obligation to pay attention to the maltreatment of women. Community members would establish this objective and try to carry it out, fully aware that it makes the boundaries of the household much more permeable than they have been for a long time.

Historian Nancy Cott explains that in 18th-century Massachusetts, the Puritan doctrine "I am my brother's keeper" supplied a theological justification for, among other things, seeking to bridle the extremes of household violence.[41] However, by the late 19th century, the Second Wave ideal of household independence and freedom from kin control was becoming a status symbol sought by urban families wishing to be recognized as "middle-class." [42] Among other things, household privacy meant that husbands and wives sought to weave a curtain of secrecy around their own relationship. They wove the same curtain around relationships with their children. They wanted to shield their family from the prying eyes of kin and neighbors. Their relationship privacy included keeping household violence confidential from outsiders. However, working-class people, along with poor people, were frequently unable to shield domestic aggression from professional social workers. Historian Linda Gordon studied the case records of an actual immigrant family living in Boston between 1910 and 1916. Because the husband regularly beat his wife, the man's father finally intervened. The father "came to the house and gave his son 'a warning [to stop it] and a couple of slaps,' after which he improved for a while." Later on, "the father extracted from [his son] a pledge not to beat his wife for two years!" [43]

Today, however, especially in middle-class suburbia, that type of intervention (by relative or friend), if it exists at all, is much rarer than it was among early-20th-century immigrants. In contemporary society, domestic violence—men against women, mothers or fathers against children, siblings against each other—is viewed as "private family business." Although family members are free to strike one another, neighbors, relatives, police, and social workers hope they can keep their aggression modest and moderate. But when a woman comes to work with black eyes, bruises, or welts, or goes to the hospital emergency room with broken bones, officials may be forced to react because her partner has gone "too far." At that point, officials may step in, and her partner may be arrested and/or required to get therapy to curb his violence. Gordon reports that professional social workers began in the late 1800s to get involved in domestic violence. They were perceived as a substitute for the historic role of kin and community in trying to keep household aggression in check. However, then and now professionals typically get involved only after the fact—they react once the aggression has become extreme enough to command official attention.

Anthropologist Barbara Smuts reports that in a present-day rural community in the Central American nation of Belize, "a man will sometimes beat his wife if he becomes jealous or suspects her of infidelity." [44] That is, of course, the precise scenario that has been played out in most cultures since the dawn of recorded history. And it continues today in developed and nondeveloped societies alike. However, Smuts adds that in this particular community, "women live near their female relatives." As a result, when a man beats his wife, "onlookers run to tell her female kin. Their arrival on the scene, combined with the presence of other glaring women, usually shames the man enough to stop his aggression." [45] Smuts, like Gordon, reminds us that sometimes kin and neighbors can and do act to protect women against male aggression. Smuts's own research has been on physical and sexual aggression among primates such as monkeys, chimpanzees, and orangutans. [46] She has found that female primates who forge social bonds and community alliances to protect themselves and their young are much less vulnerable to male aggression than are females lacking those alliances.

A "Different Future"

Smuts believes that human females likewise require the help of other adults to deal effectively with male aggression. She contends that male violence demands a structural, or situational, solution in the form of inno-vative social arrangements. In all too many cases, says Smuts, violence is not something the nonconnected woman can cope with by herself. Signifi-cant reductions in male violence against women depend, she argues, on the "uniquely human ability to envision a future different from anything that has gone before." [47]

By declaring itself to be a violence-free zone, the NEL neighborhood would fulfill Smuts's vision of a "different future." Households would embrace the concept that their boundaries should be permeable enough to allow community participation in the matter of male aggression toward women. The embracement of this objective is both symbolic and real. It is symbolic because by endorsing it, each household puts itself on record as being willing to relinquish some of its privacy in the interests of all the members of the community as a whole. But it is also quite real because it supplies a structural strategy for addressing the typically hidden traumas of men's violence. This strategy clearly empowers the woman. She is no longer alone in facing either the threat of violence or actual violence.

The reality that the woman is not alone is signified by the spatial contours of the NEL neighborhood. The spatial construction of suburbia, which symbolizes household independence and privacy, inadvertently spawned the ideal setting for violence against women and children. In sharp contrast, the spatial contours of an NEL community—including the com-mon areas where people simply "hang out"—would symbolize a commit-ment to the goal of minimizing male aggression. The physical spaces would advertise the community members' shared values, beliefs, and objectives regarding male violence. Hence, spatial connectedness becomes integral to the social ideal of a violence-free zone.

Furthermore, the fact that women themselves participate in the creation of both the spatial and the social features of their community speaks to the issue of their empowerment. Today, the question is typically phrased, How can society *protect* women from male aggression? The insinuation is that because women are "weak," they require defense from powerful forces beyond themselves. By contrast, the NEL community would raise a different question: How can a woman get her own empowerment? How can she herself get strong enough to resist male aggression? The answer, of course, is that she herself creates the conditions of her own safety. And those conditions are spatial as well as social.

A Safe Place

The term *violence-free* implies the absence of something, namely, aggression. And although it is true that violence would be subtracted from the community, it is equally appropriate to conceive of the matter in a more nuanced light. Why not think of the NEL community as a place where *safety* is added in? During the Middle Ages, if a man pursued by the sheriff got to the altar of a church and held on to it, the priest declared that he had "sanctuary." As long as he held on, the sheriff could not arrest him, and for a poor man at that time, arrest was tantamount to being hanged, even if he was innocent. Sanctuary implied a "safe place"—a means of providing a minimal degree of justice for poor people. Today, many of us are familiar with the "safe place" symbol sometimes displayed by certain public buildings. The symbol assures a woman that once she enters the building, she is free from the onslaughts of her man. Sanctuary requires the presence of a third party—a person or persons who are authorized to guarantee the woman's safety. Hence the NEL community would be a sanctuary—a place where safety is publicly added to a woman's life in ways that are well beyond the scope of the nonconnected style.

To be sure, this "public" approach to a "private" family matter could be perceived by some critics as extraordinarily threatening to the social order. For example, the 1970s marked the beginning of national attention to the issue of aggression closeted by the privacy of the nonconnected household.[48] Consequently, as part of a response to growing public concern over domestic violence, bills were introduced into both houses of Congress in 1980 (S-1843 and HR-2977) to fund the construction of "safe places." Those would have been buildings, or shelters, staffed by support personnel. The shelters, which would have been sited within nonconnected neighborhoods across the nation, would have been places to which women and their children could flee in order to escape male aggression. Congress, however, rejected these bills, in large part because of pressure from religious cultural conservatives. Opponents argued successfully that the shelters would become "anti-family indoctrination centers" and would "encourage disinte-gration of the family." [49]

Practical Considerations

Clearly, an NEL community declaring itself to be a sanctuary would find it quite difficult to implement its lofty ideal. Once the assertion is made that "our community is a safe place," how would members actually make it work on a day-to-day basis? In particular, how would members avoid becoming nosy, meddlesome, or authoritarian? How would a household make its boundaries permeable enough so that aggression can be monitored as a genuine community concern and at the same time retain its desired degree of privacy and autonomy? Recall from Chapter 4 that most cohousing community members spend numerous hours engaged in group decision making. If a future NEL neighborhood declares itself a sanctuary, its members should expect to spend many additional hours trying to grapple with this complex matter.

For example, imagine a scenario in which the husband and wife in household B want the community to participate with them in stopping the husband's aggression. In practical terms, how would the members actually respond? Next, assume a much more complex scenario stemming from differing viewpoints, either between households or between a wife and husband. For example, members of household A may believe that the man in household B is acting in a violent manner toward his wife. But because neither the wife nor the husband in household B perceives his behavior as violent, they do not wish household A or any other household to get involved. Consequently, what, if anything, would the community do? Furthermore, what if the wife in household B does want community involvement, but her husband does not? What then would household A and the other households do?

Recall from Chapter 1 that as long as dialogue continues, male violence is less likely to erupt. The minimum pact that NEL households would have to forge with one another is that any hint of household aggression must, *at the very least,* be fully discussed by the community. As long as there is community dialogue, the hope is that a resolution satisfactory to all parties involved could somehow be achieved. Their firm commitment to ongoing dialogue would surely be requisite to every NEL neighborhood, just as it is now to most cohousing communities. The difference, of course, is that in NEL situations, there is likely to be a great deal more for the neighborhood to struggle with.

Nonviolent Couple Decision Making: A Level Playing Field

Researchers have studied couples' decision making for many decades.[50] For a long time, only married couples were examined, but recently cohabiting couples (cross-sex and same-sex) have also come under scrutiny.[51] These studies have rarely targeted violence and aggression. Instead, researchers have considered how couples negotiate the everyday matters of life—things such as child care, employment, consumption, domestic chores, and time spent with friends and kin. Underlying this research has been the assumption of the nonconnected lifestyle. However, as Chapter 4 has shown, the typical cohousing community is already based on the premise of a relative degree of connectedness across households. Recall that in cohousing, the overlap of couple decision making with neighborhood decision making begins long before there is an identifiable community. Members meet for many months—perhaps several years—to resolve the details of obtaining land and designing their shared physical spaces.

Although conflicts over such matters are agonizing enough even when a couple attempts to build or renovate a house, in that situation only two persons are involved. In a collaborative setting, couples must reach beyond themselves to take part in tortuous multiperson negotiations aimed at designing community spaces and devising neighborhood norms. Recall, moreover, that once a collaborative community is in place, its households must engage in a never-ending process of balancing neighborhood interests with their own. Community members are continuously involved in group problem solving. In trying to "ensure that decisions are made, but to everyone's satisfaction," the cohousing community becomes a virtual laboratory of democracy.[52]

Figuring Out Everyday Matters

Furthermore, as noted above, in an NEL community couples would take a crucial step toward making household boundaries significantly more permeable than they are in the typical cohousing situation. The NEL community takes that additional step by making "outsiders" an integral part of the couple's dialogue aimed at avoiding violence. The rationale for doing so is that sanctuary contributes to women's empowerment. But beyond that, women's empowerment might also be enhanced in another pivotal manner: by allowing NEL community members to participate with the couple in negotiating everyday household issues. This is the realm of *non-violent* arguments, disagreements, conflicts, disputes, or battles. The rationale for taking the radical step of allowing the community to participate in couple decision making is that it helps to make the playing field on which the genders negotiate somewhat more level. (I define *radical* here as in Chapter 1, as "going to the root of things.") Bear in mind that as alien as it sounds to us, wives living within the connected family style of the agricultural age could routinely look to their kin for "support in case of marital conflict, and advice in case of serious incompatibility." [53] It has only been since the advent of the nonconnected family style that women have lost that kind of external reinforcement.

Dyadic Power

For several decades, couple decision making was frequently labeled the study of "power." [54] Not surprisingly, husbands were consistently found to have more power than wives. Much has been written regarding the ways in which a woman might somehow achieve a greater balance of power with the man in her life. Virtually all of the proposals have assumed the nonconnected lifestyle. However, as we have just learned, that style may be inadequate for addressing the specific issue of male violence toward women. Hence, the next question becomes, Is that style equally deficient for addressing the matter of women's power when it comes to deciding such everyday matters as employment, parenting, and consumption?

Implied in the discussion of the erotic friendship in Chapter 3 was the idea that both partners are willing and able to negotiate effectively. *Effectively* refers to the capability of each partner to get the other partner to behave in ways that both consider important, right, and fair.[55] Within the post-World War II family style, husbands were typically more effective than wives for any number of reasons, not least of which was women's isolation from paid labor. Even though wives were frequently distressed by their situation, there was not a great deal they could do about it.[56] By contrast, love as we know it today is not typically marked by those forms of external compulsion and passive acquiescence.[57] The erotic friendship is characterized by never-ending streams of decision making in the forms of problem solving, conflict, and negotiation.[58] It is through those processes that couples struggle to achieve both partners' well-being, as well as attend to their children's interests. These often excruciating processes are like the mixture within a heated crucible, from which is extracted the ever-shifting balance of dyadic freedom and responsibility.

Nevertheless, the fundamental problem confronting women as they seek to negotiate that never-settled symmetry is that the playing field between the genders is not yet level.[59] Accordingly, many women continue to find that their own interests receive lower priority than the interests of both their husbands (or cohabitors, or boyfriends) and their children. In particular, women tend to place themselves at significant disadvantage by willingly assuming greater responsibility than men for children's well-being. To avoid sacrificing children's interests, women are inclined to forfeit their own.

As she negotiates with her partner, the nonconnected woman may or may not have friends or kin to whom she can turn for advice on resolving those conflicts. Whether or not she does, she is ultimately on her own while negotiating conflicts with her man. Very likely, most couples today (cross-sex and same-sex) would, most of the time, prefer to deal privately with the prickly issues that face them. Nevertheless, an NEL neighborhood would, as one of its guiding principles, construct the norm that couples would be able to seek out the help of a person or persons from other households. Couples could invite trusted neighbors, with whom they have become friends, to participate with them in the resolution of difficult challenges. The upshot is that a woman would no longer find herself negotiating in isolation with her man.

The Friend as Mediator

In an NEL setting, a couple would be doing their decision making in concert with a neighbor(s) that is (are) more than a mere "audience." Instead, the neighbor(s) would operate more like a mediator.[60] As difficult as it may be, the mediator would seek to be as evenhanded as possible and to work with the couple apart from arbitrarily siding with one partner or the other. He or she or they would labor together with the couple to try to figure out what appears to be the most appealing and reasonable choice or set of choices for the woman, or man, or couple to make. At the very least, the neighbor(s) can serve as a sounding board off which the couple might bounce potentially innovative solutions. The neighbor(s) might also serve as an outlet through which the partners can vent the anger, frustration, and hostility they feel toward each other.

Besides helping to construct a creative solution, trusted neighbors may also be able to help implement the solution. Let's say, for instance, that a woman in the NEL community seeks paid labor and/or greater involvement in her current occupation. However, her male partner feels that he is at a crucial point in his own career trajectory. As a result, he lets her know that he is currently unable to do the additional amount of shared parenting and/or housework required to promote her aims. Hence, she brings in trusted neighbors to help them figure out what to do—to help the couple satisfactorily resolve their serious and potentially divisive conflict. After carefully listening to both partners, the neighbors suggest that several community members are available to be responsible for the couple's children while both parents are working. Neighborhood assistance may also be available for their housework.[61]

The Neighborhood as Resource

Previous studies have frequently used the term *resource* to help explain the basis of marital power.[62] Typically, a husband has been said to have more decision-making power than his nonemployed wife because he has income, whereas she does not. Income has been identified as the prime resource fortifying that husband's power. By the same token, employed wives, because they have gained the resource of income, have been found to have more power than nonemployed wives. At the same time, the fact of having a paid job has been considered a resource in and of itself, even apart from the income the job generates. Education has also been identified as a resource: The more years of schooling a woman has, the more power she tends to have. In similar fashion, we might consider the NEL neighborhood as an additional resource. Being part of an NEL community would enable the woman to negotiate more effectively with her man than would otherwise be the case. Neighborhood friends would help make the playing field between the genders somewhat less uneven. That is so because trusted neighbors would operate on two levels—dialogue and execution. First, they would try to assist the couple in devising a solution that each partner feels is satisfactory. Second, they would work together with the couple in actually trying to implement the solution's day-to-day details.[63]

The Interests of Men:
A Pact Between the Genders

Thus far, we have learned that the NEL community might contribute to women's empowerment, first of all, by declaring itself to be a safe place. Second, it might expedite women's empowerment by opening up the boundaries of couple decision making regarding the everyday matters of life. Third, women's empowerment is enhanced when attention is paid to men's interests—when an alliance is established between the genders.[64]

The NEL neighborhood would be a "win-win" situation, say its advocates, because the interests of women, men, and children would be brought into some sort of balance. Nevertheless, men are currently the dominant status group throughout the larger society. The structure of an NEL community would almost surely imply some degree of threat to existing male privilege. For one thing, men living in nonconnected households don't have to tolerate "outside interference" in their couple decision making. The equal-partner arrangement faltered because, among other reasons, most men found it too costly.[65] It is too much of a threat to male interests. If that is so, why would men voluntarily participate in a social and spatial structure that is not only far more demanding than the nonconnected style, but also more costly to their historic prerogatives?

Ever since women's interests became part of the family revolution in the mid-19th century, women have struggled against male privilege. Women (and their male allies) have pushed against those privileges, and men have reluctantly given up some ground. The gender struggle is analogous to the racial struggle. Blacks (and their white allies) have pushed against the privileges of whites, and they too have reluctantly given up some ground. The more allies blacks have, the more successful they are likely to be. Similarly, women have sought to enlist as many men as possible in the struggle for gender equity. By and large, the appeal for men to change their historic behaviors has been made on the basis of the interests of women and children. Men have been urged to facilitate women's interests because it is moral, right, and fair—it is good for women. Likewise, men have been told that it is good for children to have men participate more fully in their lives. By comparison, much less has been said about men's interests.

In the past, when the matter of a man's self-interest was raised, he was informed that his own life would be richer and more satisfying if he would stimulate his partner to "be all that she could be." Likewise, he was told that his own existence would be richer if he became profoundly involved in his children's lives. Available evidence suggests that a certain number of men (especially among the better educated) agreed in principle with that message.[66] They conceded that it is surely in a man's own best interest for him to confront his "undisclosed self" through greater engagement in the lives of women and children. The matter of greater male engagement is analogous to aggression, and also to women's effectiveness in dyadic decision making. Everyone is against the first and in favor of the second. Likewise, everyone is in favor of greater male engagement in the lives of women and children. But where are the structural, or situational, means for men to achieve greater engagement in women's and children's lives? Giddens, along with many others, believes that one reason for limited male engagement is the traditional definition of paid work and its integral link with male identity.

The Rise of Productivism

According to Giddens, the industrial age gave rise to

> productivism . . . an ethos in which "work," as paid employment, has been separated out in a clear-cut way from other domains of life. Work becomes a standard-bearer of moral meaning—it defines whether or not individuals feel worthwhile or socially valued; and the motivation to work is autonomous. Why one wishes, or feels compelled, to work is defined in terms of what work itself is—the need to work has its own inner dynamic.[67]

Giddens adds that productivism sometimes turns paid work into an addiction—a "driving emotional or motivational force which is unmastered by the individual." [68]

Today, it is not uncommon to hear younger persons of both genders announce, "I want a good job, *and* I want a life at the same time." In effect, they are expressing a message that many advocates have been speaking for many decades. And that is that although economic self-sufficiency is a nonnegotiable requirement for every woman and man, it is just as essential for every person to enjoy a range of other experiences as well.[69] For example, if a man's erotic friend is a woman, his human potential is fully developed to the extent that he furthers the development of her human potential. In short, "The more I love her, the more I love myself." (Needless to say, the same principle would apply to a same-sex erotic friendship.) Similarly, the man's human potential is fully developed to the extent he furthers the human development of the children in his life. In other words, "The more I love them, the more I love myself."

But if one is addicted to paid work, trying to enjoy other kinds of rich human experiences can be both strenuous and stressful. Today, some men resist the notion that their moral worth is determined principally by their marketplace success. They say they would prefer to spend more time with their partners and children. And they add that they would be willing to do more chores around the house. In effect, they profess to want more of an equal-partner arrangement. Nevertheless, because productivism "still survives as the dominant ethos," it is extraordinarily difficult for any man to wean himself from that addiction and pay close attention to women and children, even if it is in his own self-interest to do so.[70]

It is vital to note that some of today's women are just as resolute as some men in the pursuit of occupational achievement and success. In her 1998 commencement address to the women graduates of Barnard College, Joyce Purnick told how she got to be the metropolitan editor of the *New York Times*. She began as a clerk, and by the time she had worked her way up to the position of editor, it was too late for her to have children. She advised the graduates, "You *cannot have it all.* . . . All along the way, you make choices." Although she acknowledged that she regretted not having children, she stated:

> I am absolutely convinced I would not be the metro editor of the *Times* if I had had a family. . . . There is no way, in an all-consuming profession like journalism, that a woman with children can devote as much time and energy as a man can. . . . I am the first woman to run the largest department at *The New York Times*, not only because I am qualified . . . but because the course of my career allowed me to *become* qualified and stay competitive.[71]

In Purnick's view, it is virtually impossible for women to compete effectively with men in the marketplace, because men seldom "have" children in the comprehensive sense that most women do. If, however, a man were to "have" children in that sense, he would risk losing his competitive edge compared to most other men and some women. Hence, most men perceive it to be in their own self-interest to have children, but not genuinely to *have* them. Compared to women, most men can "have it all," or at least a great deal more than most women. But as Purnick says from her own experience, and also from observing many other highly motivated career women around the nation, "With rare exceptions—in nearly all competitive professions—women who have children get off the track and lose ground." [72] Hence, what would it take for some men to give up their competitive edge in order to further the interests of women and of children?

A Fresh Look at Paid Work

Part of the answer to that thorny question lies with the already shifting nature of paid work in the information age. One of those changes has to do with the sheer numbers of jobs that are evaporating in an increasingly high-tech global environment.[73] As it becomes ever more efficient for companies to design technology to do what humans once did, critics wonder what kinds of paid jobs many persons might be able to get. Certain fast-food restaurants, for instance, have already begun testing technologies that may eliminate the smiling minimum-wage person behind the counter. Instead, the customer would insert cash, credit card, or ATM card into a user-friendly device (not unlike today's sleekly designed soft-drink machine or gasoline pump) and immediately receive the order. And certain supermarkets are testing mechanisms that allow purchasers to scan their own groceries, thus reducing the numbers of checkout clerks needed. Consequently, getting any kind of job, much less a good one, is likely to become increasingly problematic, especially for persons who are not well educated and/or who are not conversant with high-tech gadgets. Thus, what are the implications of more and more people around the globe competing for relatively fewer jobs? How will men and women gain a sense of moral worth if many types of paid work become less available?

A Fresh Look at Productivity

But rethinking paid work also involves something far more significant than the potential decline of paid jobs, as vital as that is. Giddens argues that we ought to move away from our preoccupation with productivism and target productivity instead.[74] Productivity is easily understood when it comes to the economic realm. It is measured by the ratio between the investment (money and time) and its payoff. For example, if last month it took a worker 2 hours to make 80 widgets, but this month it takes him only an hour, his boss might conclude that the worker has become more productive. However, if in his haste the worker has made defective widgets that are then returned by the customer, his boss no longer views him as being productive. Clearly, productivity implies a dimension of quality as well as quantity.

The role of quality in productivity becomes infinitely more complex when we ponder additional examples. Let's say, for instance, that novelist A writes three books in 5 years. Each one sells hundreds of thousands of copies, and each is made into a popular Hollywood movie. Despite the critical judgment that the novels lack literary quality, novelist A has been quite productive in a quantitative sense. By comparison, novelist B writes only one book in 10 years. Despite the fact that it sells only a few thousand copies and could never be squeezed down to the length of the typical film, its literary quality is universally judged to be very high. Although B has not been as productive as A in a quantitative sense, B has been much more productive in a qualitative sense.

Noneconomic Productivity

The reality that productivity possesses compelling nontangible dimensions leads Giddens to conclude that "there is no reason why it [productivity] should not be extended to non-economic areas." [75] In short, a person can be productive in ways other than money, goods, or tangible services. For decades, feminists and other humanists preceded Giddens in saying that we should apply the notions of productivity and moral worth to realms beyond paid labor. Parenting is a chief example of noneconomic productivity. Virtually all parents, regardless of ideology, fervently hope that their "investments" in their children will be productive in terms of producing "high-quality" children. Besides the obvious infusion of money, parental investments also include time, talents, and energy. Nevertheless, the definition of *high-quality children* remains elusive; evaluation of the quality of children typically resides in the eyes of the parents. For example, parents who are religious conservatives and parents who are feminists likely hold vastly different views as to what constitutes a high-quality child. [76]

Depicting a high-quality child is exceedingly more difficult than describing a novel of high quality. That is one reason there are almost no monetary rewards for parenting. Although virtually everyone believes that being a productive parent should be rewarded, citizens cannot agree on what *productive* means. And among those who believe in rewarding parents, many remain unconvinced that the rewards should be monetary. [77] And among those who do believe the rewards should be monetary, there is no agreement as to what dollar figure should be assigned to parental productivity. Perhaps the closest proxy we have for the monetary worth of parenting is found in the salaries paid to "dog pound keepers" compared with the salaries of nursery school teachers. National data show that the average annual salaries of pet workers are greater than those of persons who take care of preschool children.[78] Even if the government subsidized the salaries of nursery school teachers, making them equal with kennel workers, the problem of how to describe a high-quality child still remains. Until and unless that puzzle is solved, it will be very difficult to pay productive nursery workers more money than nonproductive nursery workers. Obviously, the same problem would apply if the government were to consider a policy by which "productive" parents would be rewarded according to the "quality" of their own children.

Productivity and Moral Worth

In Western culture, and increasingly throughout the world, moral worth is assigned to productivity. Thus far, productivity has been limited to economic endeavors and rewarded monetarily. Up to this point, there has been no way to assess validly the productivity of domestic activities such as parenting. Hence, there has been no satisfactory way to reward those activities, either monetarily or by nontangible means. As a result, moral worth is not assigned to the production of high-quality children in the same way it is now assigned to being a success at one's job. And because it has been impossible to disengage male identity from the moral worth of productive labor, it is not surprising that many men have avoided becoming genuinely engaged in parenting.

By comparison to most men, the identity of most women has, so far at least, been less interwoven with the moral worth of productive economic labor. As a result, it is not uncommon for a woman to leave paid labor in order to devote herself (full-time or part-time) to her child for the infant's first few years of life. Caring for her child may supply her with enormous amounts of intrinsic rewards, and despite her occupational sacrifice, the woman is convinced she is doing the "right thing." Furthermore, her husband, relatives, friends, and neighbors, as well as her church or synagogue, may continually reinforce her with a powerful sense of esteem and approval. Nevertheless, as meaningful as those kinds of rewards are, society does not accord to her the same sense of moral worth that it does, say, to a woman such as Joyce Purnick.

The NEL as a Zone of Productivity

For decades, the mystery has been how to fasten the same sense of moral worth to noneconomic productivity that is now the unique domain of economic productivity. Solving the mystery would seem to be the only way to get men as involved in child care as women are. So far, advocates pleading that society should affix moral worth to noneconomic productivity have assumed the situation of the nonconnected lifestyle. However, asking the isolated household to make noneconomic productivity appealing to men may be yet another instance of asking it to do "too much." Just as it is "structurally challenged" when it comes to aggression, and also to women's effectiveness in decision making, the isolated household appears to be severely limited in this third sense as well. Accordingly, just as it declares itself to be a zone of safety, the NEL community would also declare itself to be a *zone of productivity*. The community would aim to be a place that creates and rewards a person's nontangible productivity, regardless of his or her gender or age.

Doing so would accomplish several things. To begin with, it would address men's interests because it would supply a source of moral worth other than the marketplace. Simultaneously, as some men became more involved in community productivity, some women would gain the option to become more involved in marketplace productivity. Those dual sets of options imply a third path toward women's empowerment, aside from the two discussed above. A woman becomes empowered because she participates in creating sanctuary, and because the community participates in the couple's decision making, and also because she participates in creating a zone of productivity.

But how would a connected lifestyle succeed where the nonconnected lifestyle has so far failed? Can Giddens's optimistic view of productivity ever be made a reality? "Productivity stands opposed to compulsiveness and to dependency, not only in work but in other areas, including personal life. There is a close tie between autonomy and productivity. A productive life is one well lived, but it is also one in which an individual is able to relate to others as an independent being, having a developed sense of self-esteem."[79]

Children's Capital

Perhaps the most vital realm of community productivity lies in the creation of children's *social capital* and also children's *human capital*.[80] I shall leave the definitions of both terms, and also the means by which they are produced, for Chapter 6.[81] For now, let us say that the NEL community would, first of all, offer an explicit definition of *high-quality children*. Such children would be those who possess optimum amounts of both social and human capital. Second, advocates would argue that the structure of the NEL neighborhood enables it to produce both types of capital much more efficiently and effectively than can the typical isolated household. Third, that type of productivity must be assessed and suitably rewarded. Men or women who are judged to be effective in producing both types of children's capital should be compensated, although not necessarily with money. They would, for example, deserve status, esteem, and influence within the community for being so highly productive.[82] Indeed, the NEL community would argue that the degree of moral worth affixed to this type of productivity should be just as great as that currently attached to economic productivity.

Group Influences on Creating and Maintaining Norms

Plainly, the NEL agenda requires the invention and maintenance of a whole new set of radical norms. (Again, I use *radical* here in the sense noted in Chapter 1—that of "going to the root of things.") That is the case for aggression, for couple decision making, and surely for productivity. Bear in mind that new cultural norms are rarely if ever established by individuals or households operating in isolation. Innovative norms come about instead through groups of persons acting together, such as an NEL neighborhood. The reasons a multiperson group is able to generate new norms are straightforward: First of all, groups legitimate, or endorse, innovative behaviors ("I'm not the only one behaving in this 'odd' manner—my friends are doing it too, so it must be okay"). Second, not only do groups make new norms seem like the right thing to do, a number of persons are available to reinforce and legitimate innovative behaviors. Someone who actually conforms to group norms is rewarded and approved by a range of members who are important to him or her. But someone who fails to conform to group norms is denied rewards and is potentially exposed to group disapproval.[83] In the case of an NEL community, the fresh norms have to do with aggression, dyadic decision making, and nontangible productivity.

The significance of shared physical spaces in reinforcing group norms cannot be overestimated. The common spaces of an NEL neighborhood visually symbolize the commitment of group members to one another and to their collective goals. Their proximate, tangible spaces make their elusive social goals seem more in evidence. Their spaces embody their goal of women's empowerment as well as the three modes of achieving it. On a more pragmatic note, the spaces site people near one another so they can more easily keep on encouraging members who might otherwise be tempted to slack off. Whether it is a matter of resisting aggression, involving others in couple decision making, or being productive in terms of children's social and human capital, members are close by to bolster one another and to offer suggestions on more effective ways to accomplish group objectives.

The Social Context of Gender Flexibility

The degree to which 21st-century men might actually participate in producing children's capital, is, of course, open to question. Much would depend on the NEL community's effectiveness in constructing and reinforcing the perception that the moral worth of producing children's capital is just as significant as producing economic capital. Keep in mind that a man or woman choosing to excel in the production of children's capital would by no means relinquish his or her economic self-sufficiency. Recall that this has been defined as the capability to provide for oneself and one's child(ren).[84]

But the big question for both genders is, How far beyond the level of self-sufficiency does one wish to travel? Keep in mind that many highly motivated, and talented, occupational achievers of either gender, such as Joyce Purnick, are not driven principally by a need to pile up more dollars. Instead, they are impelled chiefly by the essence of the work itself. Because the responsibility and the challenge supply extraordinary amounts of stimulation and profound intrinsic satisfactions, they keep on pursuing their work, and thus reap more of its satisfactions. Admittedly, some successful persons are driven by the pursuit of money. Having accumulated a million dollars is not sufficient to keep them from chasing a million more. However, not all men are driven by either the need to achieve or the accumulation of wealth. Once they feel capable of being self-sufficient, they might prefer instead to seek self-esteem and moral worth in alternative realms. Nevertheless, by the mere accident of their gender, males are under intense social pressure to keep on striving for increasingly greater levels of occupational achievement and/or money. Currently, there seems to be no compelling structurally based alternative to the role of "productive male worker" and to the sense of moral worth it supplies.

However, the NEL community would offer men flexibility at different points throughout their life course. Men seeking an alternative basis for moral worth might be able to find it in the NEL neighborhood. The community would provide them with an opportunity to develop a sense of moral worth and self-esteem in a setting other than the marketplace. Even though the society around them might not at first endorse it, the community would aim to establish and reinforce the notion that producing children's capital is just as worthy as producing financial capital. By the same token, men who are occupationally driven would by no means be excluded. They would be welcomed, and their contributions to the neighborhood (intangible and perhaps tangible) could be a matter for negotiation. Furthermore, men change over time. At one point in his life course, a man may wish to concentrate on labor force productivity. However, at another point, he may wish to concentrate on producing children's capital. The NEL neighborhood provides a setting that would allow him at any given point in time to concentrate on either type of productivity—or, if he chooses, to try his hand at both at the same time.

Needless to say, that kind of life-course flexibility would apply equally to women. Women who choose to be high-flying achievers would be welcome. And if they elect to bear children, community participation in parenting would make it less likely that they would suffer the kinds of occupational setbacks described by Ms. Purnick. Correspondingly, women who are less occupationally driven would also be free to develop a sense of community-sanctioned moral worth via the production of children's capital. Moreover, the neighborhood would offer women the same opportunity as men to focus on occupational productivity at one point in time and on the productivity of children's capital at another, or perhaps to try to focus on both at the same time.

That sort of lifelong gender flexibility is what feminists of the 1960s and 1970s had in mind when they envisioned the equal-partner marriage. Unfortunately, the isolated household style has so far been able to support only limited gender versatility.[85] By contrast, the NEL neighborhood would propose a structural mechanism for achieving what has thus far largely eluded us. Its flexibility could be an important inducement for some men to participate. At the same time, its situationally based gender flexibility could be a vital element in facilitating the long-term objective of women's empowerment.

CONCLUSION

Part II of this book is about inventing the future as we complete the family revolution. To do one implies the other. This chapter has proposed a vision for the future that is based squarely on the goal of completing the revolution—that is, achieving gender equity. Empowering women, I have argued, implies making the boundaries of the household relatively more permeable to community inputs. That means achieving a greater degree of symmetry between the public and the private spheres than currently exists. Apart from increased symmetry, the household remains isolated and thus "structurally challenged"—challenged in the sense that, by itself, the household is severely limited in terms of facilitating gender equity.

Completing the revolution means that Part II is about designing a family policy that addresses the six principles identified in Chapter 1. In this chapter I have considered all six points except positive welfare. For instance, the New Everyday Life community seeks to "repair damaged solidarities" (principle 1). It struggles to balance responsibility for the group with personal and household freedoms. A prime example of that struggle overlaps with the ways in which the NEL community would address principle 6. Specifically, it would seek to create sanctuary—a violence-free zone where women might live apart from the threat and/or reality of men's violence.

An additional policy principle addressed by the NEL community lies in its creation of a win-win situation—one that pays special attention to women's interests yet at the same time attends carefully to the interests of men and children (principle 2). A pivotal way that comes about is in the construction of a zone of productivity. That means a place where the production of children's capital might generate a source of moral worth for both genders equivalent to the moral worth now gained solely from economic productivity. Furthermore, like cohousing communities in general, the NEL neighborhood would aim to foster group dialogue and democracy (principle 4). However, involving the community in couples' own decision making would be a unique feature that distinguishes it from cohousing. That feature and the creation of sanctuary are two strategies aimed at expediting the empowerment of women (principle 3). A third strategy would be to pay careful attention to men's interests in the manner just described.

The NEL is an example of Giddens's utopian realism. It is a vision of the future that, although idealistic, is said to be realistic at the same time. *Realistic* simply means that the vision has a basis in existing theory and research. It is not mere fantasy. If, however, the vision is said to be unworkable, then Giddens's question remains: "What other possibility is there?"[86] What other means exist for completing the family revolution? Whatever the answer, an essential element in completing the revolution lies in the creation of an egalitarian environment for children. Feminists have always hoped to construct a milieu for the next generation that is far more friendly to gender equity than the current one. And the creation of that kind of environment is the topic of Chapter 6.

6

EMPOWERING CHILDREN AND YOUTH: MAKING PARENTING PUBLIC

◆◆◆──

Part II of this book is about completing the family revolution begun some 200 years ago. Chapter 5 showed how the NEL community might reinvent adult relationships in order to facilitate gender equity, thus advancing the revolution. But family obviously includes children as well as adults. What kinds of changes might we propose for parent-child relationships? And for child-child relationships? How would those changes promote the family revolution? Would those changes be as radical—in the sense of going to the root of things—as the changes envisioned for adult relationships?

In Chapter 4, I noted that today's cohousing communities do not imply radical changes in children's behavior. Instead, the neighborhood is seen as a buffer between children's lives and the unpredictability of contemporary adult behaviors. No matter what changes (e.g., personal, occupational) might occur in parents' lives, the cohousing community may operate as a source of stability and security for children. Because NEL generally subsumes cohousing, those same principles are found in an NEL neighborhood.[1] However, in addition, NEL takes a significant step beyond cohousing. The NEL vision for children is a case of "utopian realism," just as it is for adults. It is both a lofty ideal and a realistic possibility at the same time. The vision has its basis in existing theory (our ideas about how society works) and research. Furthermore, the vision for adults and the vision for children may be seen as the threads of a fine handwoven carpet. The threads, or visions, crisscross and complement one another. Together, they make a complete whole; apart, they do not. Chapter 5, for instance, showed that in order to address men's interests and to empower women, the community must figure out how to attach considerable moral worth to the production of children's capital. Thus, making life better for women, and for men, implies that at the same time, life is made better for children too.

For women, empowerment means living on a more equal footing with men. But what does it mean to "empower" children? And how does children's empowerment fit with the broader issue of the family revolution? What is the connection between children's empowerment and gender equity?

CHILDREN IN NONINDUSTRIAL SETTINGS

Chapter 2 noted that although 19th-century families migrated from rural to urban areas in pursuit of economic opportunity, many found poverty instead. The upshot was that large numbers of urban mothers and children labored many hours a day alongside husbands and fathers—only now their "fields" were sweatshops and unsafe factories. It seemed perfectly reasonable that industrial-age children should contribute to their families' economic survival. They had, after all, been doing precisely that for thousands of years throughout the previous agricultural era. Many children in many parts of the world had little choice but to toil alongside their parents in the never-ending tasks of subsistence agriculture.

But they did not toil only alongside their parents. Recall from Chapter 2 that many extended family households were typically sited nearby their blood kin. There is no doubt that, whenever possible, each nuclear family preferred to live by itself in its own household. Nevertheless, being close by made it easier for kin to help each other out in the performance of agricultural tasks. Indeed, "helping out" in every conceivable realm of life was the essence of the connected family lifestyle. Furthermore, depending on their ages and genders, children were required to help out too. For everyone, existence was perilous at best—life was "nasty, brutish, and short." In order for everyone in the extended family to survive, all members had to do what they could.

Even the small children, for example, could feed chickens and gather eggs. They could help plant seeds in and pull weeds from the family's garden. When the garden's vegetables grew ripe, they could help to pick and carry them. As they grew older, children of both genders learned to milk cows. Girls then began to participate with their mothers, other adult women, and older sisters in household chores. At the same time, boys began to participate with their fathers, other adult men, and older brothers in the performance of many different kinds of tasks, including the clearing of land, the care and feeding of livestock, the making and mending of fences, and the cultivation and harvest of crops. Recent studies of the experiences of slave children prior to emancipation provide a general picture of what most children did in the typical agricultural environment: Until around age 13, they were doing chores such as "hauling water, fetching wood, tending gardens, cleaning the yards, and feeding livestock." [2]

Importantly, slave children performed those kinds of tasks both for their masters and for the fictive kin networks of which they were a vital part. Recall from Chapter 2 that being a trustworthy member of a fictive kin network was essential for survival in the hostile and alien environment of the plantation. That reality applied to children no less than to adults. One of the most vital tasks that slave youngsters performed was the care of younger children while adults were toiling in the fields or in the master's house. Keep in mind that the youngsters were responsible not only for their blood siblings, but also for all the children that belonged to their fictive kin network. Sociologist William Corsaro observes that there is a "striking similarity" between the "communal child care" performed by older plantation youngsters and the child-care practices that occur now in many regions of contemporary rural Africa.[3] Where fictive kin exist today in those regions, older youngsters are fully expected to be responsible for "all our children," and not solely for their blood relations. Alongside their work, slave and free children alike found ample time to play. The slave children played games among themselves and frequently with the white children as well. They also explored, hunted, and fished. The fun of hunting and fishing was amplified by the fact that when they actually caught game or fish, they were contributing to their household's food supply.

Another study documents the experiences of children who, along with their parents, migrated from Europe and settled the Great Plains (Nebraska, Kansas, the Dakotas, and Oklahoma) of the United States in the years 1880 to around 1900.[4] Like children who had been part of agricultural communities for centuries past, they were a vital and indispensable part of their households' economic well-being. From their earliest days, these late-19th-century rural youngsters participated in chores in and around the house, and later on they (girls in particular) cared for younger children. As the children matured, they became necessary to their families' economic production. Indeed, historian Elliott West doubts that families and communities would have been able to survive, much less to prosper, apart from children's work.[5] However, as with all children, fun was very much a part of their lives. Games, exploration, hunting, and fishing provided a keen sense of excitement and satisfaction. And, as it had been in agricultural settings for centuries, any animals or fish they caught contributed to their families' food supplies.

Children's Productivity and Autonomy

Corsaro asserts that children in agricultural settings did not—and do not—necessarily consider their tasks to be irksome. In his view, "they felt a sense of autonomy, as well as pride for their contributions to the family." [6] *Autonomy* is simply another way of describing empowerment. *Sense of control* is yet one more label for the same thing. All three labels capture the fundamental idea that an "empowered person" is able to do what he or she wants to do, at the same time that other people accord him or her a sense of worth for doing it. Recall from prior chapters that, for today's woman, empowerment requires that she be economically self-sufficient. Being able to provide for herself (and any children she may have) gives her a sense of autonomy and control over her own life that she can get in no other way. It also earns her the esteem and respect of others and enables her to deal with men very differently than if she were not self-sufficient.

The productive work of children in agricultural settings empowered them in two senses—first, in the present and, second, for their anticipated future. First of all, because they were doing something "right now" that was highly significant in the lives of other children and adults, those persons rewarded them with esteem and prestige. Second, there was an obvious connection between doing their present tasks as well as they could and their future well-being. A boy who learned to be a good farmer could expect to survive (and perhaps prosper) later on as an adult. And a girl who learned to be a good farmer's wife could thereby position herself to make the very best match possible—that is, to marry the boy who seems most likely to become a successful farmer. In short, their contributions to their nuclear and extended families, and to their community, became the springboard to their current and future empowerment. And if there had been child development specialists around, they would have studied the complex processes whereby children in agricultural situations actually gained a sense of autonomy and control. The researchers would have detailed the ways in which children learned to take charge of their own lives, both in the present and for their anticipated future.

CHILDREN IN INDUSTRIAL SETTINGS

However, as noted in Chapter 2, child specialists did not surface until the late 19th and early 20th centuries. They were keenly aware of the fact that more and more children were living in urban areas, where they were not able to make the identical kinds of economic contributions that rural children had made. That is not to say that late-19th- and early-20th-century working-class urban children failed to make important economic contributions.[7] In fact, they did so by taking part-time jobs and giving some or perhaps all of their wages to their families. And when they were old enough, many dropped out of school in order to take full-time jobs and thus contribute even more money to their families. Unfortunately, many of the shops and factories in which children worked were unsafe and unhealthy. Social critics advocated for child labor laws, aimed first at raising the ages at which children could be employed and second at improving their working conditions. The emerging labor union movement strongly supported those laws and insisted that men's wages should be raised to compensate for the loss of their children's incomes.

Perhaps the most compelling reason to cut back, or perhaps eliminate, children's employment was the new industrial-age connection between children's lives and their future well-being. Instead of springing from their contributions to family and community, children's success in life was now seen as based in their academic achievement. Part-time employment might hinder children's school performance. And if they dropped out of school to work full-time, their long-term chances for economic well-being were clearly jeopardized. For these and a variety of other reasons, child specialists, parents, and politicians began to put a somewhat different spin on the ancient question of adult-child relationships.

For centuries, agricultural-age adults had asked, What can we do for our children? At the same time, they asked, What can our children do for us? The two questions were not contradictory. By learning to help out, children were in effect learning to take care of themselves. Today, industrial-age adults ask the first question, but tend to overlook the significance of the second. Most of us believe that by being good parents, good teachers, and good citizens, we thereby *help* children. And although that is no doubt true, the matter of *empowering* children to take charge of their own lives through service is less frequently considered. Over the past hundred years or so, there has been a subtle shift away from the ancient idea of children serving adults. The slick media slogan "Kids First" highlights that shift. Now we ask, What can parents, teachers, and society do *for* children? How can we *help* boys become Good Providers? How can we *help* girls become Good Wives and Good Mothers? Alongside those questions has come a great fear that adults might do the wrong things *to* children. If we do the wrong things, or if we fail to do enough of the right things, we fret that children are likely to suffer both now and in the future. More recently, there has been a growing anxiety about *protecting* children from forces external to the nuclear family, such as the media, drugs, and adult predators. And although all of these historically newer issues have given rise to obviously legitimate concerns, the more ancient issues of children's contributions and their resulting empowerment have been lost in the shuffle.

Children as Social Agents

Corsaro and a growing minority of other social scientists are trying to remedy that fault by viewing children as active agents of their present lives as well as of their future destinies.[8] Instead of viewing children merely as passive receptors of what adults do *to* them, these researchers want to find out what children do *for themselves,* as well as for the larger society. As social scientist Sylvia Blitzer sees it, we must learn to view children as "social agents." [9] In that light, it makes sense to ask, How do contemporary children and youth take charge of their own lives? How do they seek and gain empowerment, autonomy, and a sense of control?

One of the most obvious and important examples of youth invention is what sociologist James Coleman has called the "adolescent society." Following World War II, Coleman and other researchers studied the kinds of peer groups adolescents were constructing for themselves—especially in the new suburbia described in Chapter 3.[10] Their parents were perhaps the last generation of urban dwellers who, as adolescents, had been expected to contribute at least some of their wages to their families.[11] Once settled in the affluent suburbs, those parents focused totally on the matter of what they could do for their children. The idea that children could or should do something significant for their families seemed like a distant and unwelcome anachronism.

According to Coleman, as they were being freed from virtually all significant responsibilities to their nuclear households, youth created peer groups that supplied both fun and a sense of control over their own lives. The suburban adolescent "was dumped into a society of his peers, a society whose habitats are the halls and classrooms of the school, the teen-age canteens, the corner drugstore, the automobile, and numerous other gathering places." [12] Within the context of those physical spaces, adolescents naturally forged strong and fulfilling friendships. However, the world they invented was "far removed from [the] adult responsibilities" that their parents and teachers told them they must assume in the seemingly distant future.[13]

In short, post-World War II adolescents first of all constructed a social world that excluded adults to a much larger degree than had almost any generation before. Previously, children and youth had also constructed a life apart from adults—especially during play. Nevertheless, agricultural work had typically been a joint effort of children and adults. Second, although the postwar adolescents' new world gave them a sense of control, it was geared to the immediate present and often ran counter to parental beliefs about their children's current and long-term well-being. Compared with children and youth from earlier decades, there seemed to be little connection between empowering themselves as adolescents and their future empowerment as adults. To the contrary, parents worried that excessive peer group involvement could be detrimental to their children's future well-being.[14]

CHILDREN IN THE NEW EVERYDAY LIFE

The construction of the "adolescent society" occurred during the height of the industrial era. It gradually replaced the life that children and youth experienced during the agricultural era and the early industrial period. We are now entering the information age, or posttraditional society. Although no one expects adolescent peer groups to be displaced, the question can be raised as to whether the creative energies of children and youth can also be put to other kinds of social construction as well. More specifically, what is the position of children in the New Everyday Life? How could children and youth participate with adults so as to empower themselves in a manner that has positive implications for both the present and the new and uncertain future?

Sanctuary and Children

The first step in women's empowerment, as noted in Chapter 5, would be to create a "safe place"—a violence-free zone. That proposition holds just as strongly for children's empowerment. Children can have no sense of control or autonomy if they live under the threat and/or reality of adult aggression. Declaring a community to be a sanctuary for children means that all members of that community would state explicitly that violence is not simply a domestic issue. The viewpoint that the children in the community are "all our children" implies that each community member, including children and youth, would have an obligation to empower children vis-à-vis abuse of any kind—physical, sexual, or emotional. Each member would share the responsibility to pay attention to child maltreatment. The community would establish and try to carry out this policy, fully aware that it makes the boundaries of individual households much more permeable than they have been for a long time. In effect, children would become participants in constructing the conditions of their own safety, just as women would. Thus, children, like women, would become empowered to a much greater degree than at present. Today's prevailing theme is to *protect* children from violence and other negative forces. By contrast, the notion of children as social agents acting with adults to create their own safe place is only dimly perceived.

Virtually all citizens concur that the right thing to do is to free children from the threat of adults who are physically and sexually abusive. Having said that, disagreements abound regarding how to do it.[15] Many conservatives are keenly suspicious of state intervention into the nuclear family. They do not want social workers, judges, or police officers intruding into the family's privacy, thus interfering with parents' rights to discipline their own children.[16] Religious cultural conservatives are particularly anxious lest their use of corporal punishment be equated with abuse. Because they tend to believe that God wants parents to use physical force when necessary, they view state efforts to prescribe the boundaries of acceptable force with grave misgivings.[17] And in fact, many of today's political debates regarding the protection of children pivot around the issue of who gets to set those boundaries.[18]

Historian Linda Gordon reports that "child abuse was 'discovered' as a social problem in the 1870s." [19] Although adult violence toward children had clearly existed during the previous agricultural era, Gordon tells us that at that time it was frequently monitored and moderated by kin and community. A father, mother, sibling, or some other relative might slap, spank, hit, or even beat a child, but the punishment had to appear reasonable to other adults. If the hitting or violence was judged by kin and neighbors to be extreme, or beyond reasonable limits, the adult could be asked to justify it. Members of the adult's kin or community could also exert informal pressure to forestall repetition of his or her undesirable level of violence. However, by the late 1800s, the industrial-age ideal of household independence and freedom from kin control was becoming a strongly held ideal among urban families wishing to be recognized as "middle-class." [20] Among other things, household independence and privacy meant that husbands and wives sought to weave a curtain of secrecy around their own relationship and also around their relationships with their children. They wanted to shield their family from the prying eyes of kin and neighbors.

In contemporary society, domestic violence—mothers or fathers against children, men against women, siblings against each other—is viewed as "private nuclear family business." Although family members are free to strike one another, neighbors, police, and social workers hope they can keep their aggression modest and moderate. But when a child comes to school with black eyes, bruises, or welts, or goes to the hospital emergency room with broken bones, officials may be forced to react because the parents have gone too far. Nevertheless, in spite of those risks, today's parents are regarded as the ultimate arbiters of how far is "too far." If they cross that indeterminate line, officials may step in, and parents may be arrested and/or required to seek treatment from professional counselors to curb their excessive violence. Gordon notes that as professional social workers began to become involved in trying to curb domestic violence in the late 1800s, they took on the role that had historically been played by kin and community in trying to keep household aggression in check.

A Proactive Strategy

However, professionals typically become involved only after the fact—they react only after aggression has become extreme enough to command official attention. A much more proactive policy to combat domestic violence was recently proposed by the U.S. Advisory Board on Child Abuse and Neglect. Calling it a "new national strategy for the protection of children," the board in fact wants to reinvent the moderating influence of the historic First Wave community on household violence. The board's proposal is founded on the premise that physical and sexual aggression toward children should be viewed from an "environmental perspective." [21] It suggests that we discard our narrow image that child abuse is something that happens simply within household spaces. To replace that old image, we should adopt the broader view that child maltreatment is just as much a function of community spaces.

This fresh image makes child maltreatment a community issue, just as it sometimes was during the agricultural era. Whatever responsibilities are implied by speaking of "all our children," the board believes that at the very least it means that every citizen has a duty to take an active stance in keeping children in her or his neighborhood out of harm's way. The board contends that in today's society, the moderating influence of the community on household violence has greatly eroded: "Social networks have become so disrupted that, for many families, isolation is one of the realities of everyday life." [22] To overcome that isolation and thus protect children, the board asserts, "we must strengthen our neighborhoods, both physically and socially, so that people care about, watch, and support each other's families. Child protection must become a part of everyday life, a function of . . . the community." [23]

Corporal Punishment

If an NEL community would declare itself to be a violence-free zone, members could still disagree as to what precisely that means. At a very practical level, for instance, the community would have to discuss the use of corporal punishment, not only by natural parents toward their own children, but by all adults toward all community children. Gordon reports that ever since the mid-19th century, there has been a lively debate over whether or not corporal punishment is appropriate physical force. When should it be labeled violence? When, if ever, does a mild slap on the hand or a squeeze on the arm fall under the heading of aggression? What about a "gentle" spanking? Or one that's not so gentle? Some of today's most respected researchers suggest that even modest amounts of corporal punishment contribute to our national culture of violence against children.[24] Hence, they urge adults to repudiate all forms of corporal punishment and to make a deliberate commitment to the ideal of using means other than physical force to get children to cooperate.

In any event, the NEL community would have a unique opportunity to fulfill the U.S. Advisory Board's vision of the neighborhood as a proactive and moderating influence on child abuse. First of all, the community would operate as an informal but effective source of pressure on all adults to behave in a nonviolent fashion. Hence, adults retaining the right to corporal punishment would be aware that others in their neighborhood are participating with them in setting limits on any physical force toward children. An individual adult would not be the sole arbiter of when he or she has gone "too far." Trusted friends would be in place to help define those limits and to make the adult aware, either subtly or otherwise, when he or she may indeed have crossed them.

Second, others would be present not merely to advise limits but, certainly just as important, to help shoulder the frustrations that frequently trigger aggression toward children. The adult who kicks a dog after a bad day at work can just as easily lash out at a child. Or an adult's frustrations might stem from a child's seemingly obdurate and unmanageable personality. In either case, compared to "nonconnected" parents, adults in an NEL community would always have several other persons around to help them. Whether as listeners when a person needs to vent about problems at work or as active helpers when he or she needs to cope with a child's histrionics and/or unyielding behavior, trusted friends would be readily available to share frustration. Diffusing an individual's anger and frustration in this manner may in turn reduce the likelihood of his or her assaulting a child.

Bear in mind that the U.S. Advisory Board on Child Abuse and Neglect recognizes that spatial connections are just as vital as social bonds in minimizing violence toward children: "We must strengthen our neighborhoods, both physically and socially." The spatial construction of suburbia, symbolizing household independence and privacy, inadvertently advertises the ideal "inner sanctum" for force against children. But in sharp contrast, the spatial contours of NEL communities—including their common areas, where people simply "hang out"—would symbolize a commitment to the goal of minimizing aggression toward children. Their shared physical spaces would advertise parental acknowledgment that "I do not pretend to be an expert child rearer; I need and want all the help I can get for my parenting, including how to be aggression-free." In effect, their spaces would express their shared values, beliefs, and objectives regarding parenting in general and force in particular. And when the inevitable disagreements and conflicts arise between members over the use of force on children, an attempt would be made to resolve these conflicts by appealing to those shared values and objectives.

Children as Partners

Chapter 5 highlighted the notion that inventing sanctuary should not be viewed as a benefit handed *to* women. Instead, women would themselves become empowered by participating as equal partners in its ongoing construction. But what about children? Does their empowerment imply that they would be partners with adults in the creation and maintenance of the NEL neighborhood? Social scientist Elise Boulding agrees with researchers who say that we ought to cultivate a fresh image of children as social agents. Moreover, she carries the argument a significant step further by asserting that adults should view children as *partners* in the task of building the information age:

> [There needs to be a greater] emphasis on children as young citizens, capable of partnership with adults for social change. The right to play, yes; the right to one's own spaces, yes—and children often claim those rights in spaces adults never see. But the plea . . . for the recovery of childhood and innocence, while it certainly touches a deep human need for children to be children, unwittingly belittles the right of the young to draw on what they know about the societies they are growing up in, to help make them better for everyone.[25]

Despite Boulding's bold vision of the future, just how would that feature of utopian realism work? What does it mean to say that children and adults would be partners within an NEL community?

First of all, it does *not* require that children and adults be equal partners. Sociologist Bennett Berger and his colleagues spent a number of years studying communes in rural California. They have reported that the "communards" (their term for the adult members) were driven by the Western ideals of freedom and equality brought to the fore by the revolutionary spirit of the 1960s and 1970s.[26] The communards had had firsthand experience of student power, black power, women's power, gay/lesbian power, and even gray power for senior citizens. Well, then, why not children's power? "Would equality be extended to age?" asked Berger.[27] Would communards go as far in striving for age equality as they had gone in pursuing racial and gender equality? The most vital trait the communards wished to foster in their children was autonomy—a sense of being able to manage or control one's own life. Nevertheless, they found it exceedingly difficult to achieve their ideal. On the one hand, the communards staunchly defended their passionate commitment to the value of children's freedom. But on the other hand, and despite their ideals, "controversy about children was pervasive at The Ranch," the commune that Berger studied. Opinions among the Ranch's adults on how to rear children ranged "from total liberation to strict control." [28]

Berger found that children at the Ranch (like children in any commune) were never "fully autonomous persons or fully the equals of adults. They have to go to school and they have to be instructed in the skills of rural life and they have to be kept from being bored. . . . Nowhere in communal life are children as influential as adults in collective affairs." [29] Nevertheless, compared to children living in mainstream society, the children Berger observed had more independence and shared greater equality with adults. The enhanced social position of communal children was signified princi-pally by their responsibilities. They were expected to "participate in the intimacies and the mutual concern for each other's welfare that characterize the entire group." [30] Children were, in effect, expected to play a vital role in the ongoing life of the community. Children increased their stature and position in the community by proving themselves to be trustworthy par-ticipants. Unlike the nuclear families in which the communards grew up, favors did not flow along a one-way street from adults to children. Instead, children participated in a two-way flow of benefits across generations.

That sort of "limited," or "junior," partnership also seems to have characterized farm families during the agricultural era. Although children were, in a very real sense, partners with adults, they did not possess the same degree of authority, nor was their payoff the same. Nevertheless, as children (boys in particular) matured, their influence grew. And if they proved themselves to be effective farmers, their participation in family and community decision making was likely to become extensive. Eventually a father, perhaps for health reasons, might relinquish day-to-day management of the family farm to his adult son. Accordingly, the son's new authority would thus tend to indicate that, for all practical purposes, he had finally become a full partner with his father. Clearly, therefore, to say that NEL children and adults would be partners does not imply that they would be fully equal either in authority or in responsibility.

THE PRODUCTION OF CAPITAL

Nevertheless, that said, partnership does suggest that, depending on their ages, children or youths would participate actively in the life of the community. Recall that the NEL neighborhood would be a structural means for expediting gender equity, thus advancing the family revolution. Hence, it follows that if children are partners, they too would participate in the revolution. They would be contributing to, and benefiting from, the long-term objective of gender equity. And in order to do that, they would have to play a vital part in the production of what I have referred to in Chapter 5 as *social and human capital*.

Like many other social scientists, Coleman has wondered what kinds of parenting patterns might make sense for the newly emerging information age. He is not optimistic about "the mere patching up" of "old institutions," namely, the nonconnected family style. Instead, he strongly advocates the "explicit design of [new] institutions" to carry on the task of parenting.[31] He is, however, puzzled as to what those new patterns might look like: "What *does* constitute a substitute in the new social structure for the social capital that is eroding?"[32] Although unclear about their specific shapes, he is unequivocal regarding what the new patterns are supposed to do. They should generate what Coleman calls "social capital." In his view, social capital is essential for the well-being of children and society alike.

Physical Capital: Tangible Resources

Capital of any kind may be thought of as an accumulated resource, and thus has the potential to be used for certain purposes. For example, water stored in a dam is a resource that can be utilized to generate electricity on demand. Thus, water is an illustration of "physical" or tangible capital. Carpenters' tools, calculators, and computers are additional examples. Let's say a carpenter uses her tools to craft an exquisite table. She might admire and use her table or she may sell it for cash, or she may trade it for a bookcase. In any event, her tools are her physical capital—a tangible resource she uses when she wants cash or another object of some kind. Even when her tools lie on the shelf, they are nevertheless a potential resource— they are capital.

Financial Capital: Cash Resources

The most common and easily understood use of the term *capital* is that related to money. "Financial" capital consists of dollars. The cash can be used to obtain goods or services, or it can be kept in reserve (in a bank, in a shoe box) as a potential resource for future purchases—dollars are capital.

Human Capital: Internal Resources

The above-mentioned carpenter's talent for building fine furniture is an example of "human" capital.[33] Other kinds of human capital include intelligence, artistic ability (musical, painting, sculpture, literary), aptitude (math, science), and athletic prowess, as well as critical thinking skills and problem-solving capabilities. In the agricultural era, human capital included the abilities and talents necessary to being a good farmer or a good farmer's wife. In the industrial period, human capital included the aptitudes necessary for such specific occupations as bricklayer, engineer, steamfitter, auto technician, and neurosurgeon. Unlike physical and financial capital, human capital is contained *inside* the individual. But like any form of capital, these internal resources may be used whenever the person possessing them deems it necessary. When not being used, such resources are nonetheless available—as means for the person to obtain certain desired ends. Hence, these vital resources are clearly capital.

Social Capital: Shared Obligations as Resources

As Coleman describes the first three types of capital—physical, financial, and human—his readers have no trouble following him.[34] Unfortunately, his discussion of social capital has resulted in a great deal of confusion, uncertainty, and disagreement over what social capital is and how this kind of capital differs from the other three.[35] The principal reason for the confusion is that Coleman fails to define social capital in a plain and simple manner. Instead, he tells us what it is *not*. For example, social capital is *not* contained inside the individual as is human capital.[36] And even though social capital exists outside of persons, it is *not* a tangible object such as cash. Nor is social capital a physical object, such as a tool, computer, or piano. Rather than defining social capital, Coleman simply describes where it is located: "Social capital inheres in the structure of relations between persons and among persons." [37] Just as we find water in a dam, we locate social capital in the relationships between and among persons.

But not just any relationships. Many kinds of relationships, such as that between a passenger on a train and a ticket taker, involve no social capital at all. Coleman asserts that the most striking example of social capital is located in the extended family and the community in which it was embedded throughout the agricultural era. Above, I noted that children in the agricultural age contributed significantly to adults, and that adults reciprocated by contributing to children. These kinds of helping-out patterns fit Coleman's description of social capital. Social capital is found in the giving and getting of contributions, inputs, or benefits within certain kinds of situations.[38] Very often, these situations are likely to take place in what I have referred to in Chapter 4 as a primary group. Blood kin networks and fictive kin networks are both examples of primary groups.

Giving and Getting

Other researchers have described the giving and getting of benefits in a primary group as *shared obligations*.[39] The notion of shared obligations fits our definition of capital in general, namely, an accumulated resource with the potential to be used for certain purposes. Let's say, for instance, that Jill, a solo parent, belongs to an NEL neighborhood (a fictive kin network) where others are obliged to help her out with child care. Plainly, that help is a vital resource for Jill. When Jill needs child care, she can draw on the obligations of others in her group to help her out. And even when she is not drawing on them, those obligations are capital that she can use at any time—potential resources waiting to be utilized.

However, Jill does not automatically possess these resources by virtue of group membership per se. She must first earn that capital by proving herself to be trustworthy. And she does that by making inputs to her community. During the agricultural era, children were keenly aware that although they resided in particular dwellings, the full breadth of their lives encompassed several households.[40] Furthermore, they soon learned that adults and older children from those several households paid attention to them. At the same time, children observed that the adults with whom they resided (typically, but by no means always, their natural parents) paid attention to that same range of persons. And the older children became, the clearer it was that they should also pay attention to those same persons. Children were not merely expected but obliged to help out that range of persons as much as possible.

Children soon learned that trustworthiness meant being willing to receive help from, and give help to, that range of persons. They became acutely aware that a reputation for trustworthiness was among the most valuable assets one could possess. The logic that a trustworthy person must get from the group as well as give to it is compelling. A child or adult who refuses to take benefits from the group is by that action placing him- or herself outside its web of ongoing exchanges. The implication of this refusal is, "I don't need or want what you have to offer." What then is to keep the person from feeling later on that "because I take less from the group, I am thus less obliged to give"? If a number of persons were to begin thinking and behaving that way, it would not be long before the extended family's intricate web of mutual obligations would become less binding and thus ineffectual.

The Free Rider

In the agricultural age, an adult's or child's failure to discharge his or her responsibilities to the group meant that that individual faced negative sanctions. Among those, according to Coleman, was the stigma of being labeled a "free rider" or "freeloader."[41] It was not uncommon for First Wave communities to have resident examples of adult freeloaders about whom children were warned and urged not to emulate. Group members who shirked their obligations could expect censure of one sort or another, including potential exclusion from access to the group's social capital. In short, although belonging to a blood or fictive kin network is a means of obtaining social capital, access to those sorts of resources is not without cost. In order to gain social capital, one must simultaneously give it.

A recent study of a contemporary fictive kin network found that members "not fulfilling their obligations to give and receive [benefits] were placed on 'condition red' status." Because those members had allowed their reputation for trustworthiness to lapse, the remaining group members stigmatized them. Individuals who were on condition red status were fed by the group "with a long-handled spoon." They were also

> placed on probation for 3 months and forfeited the right to participate in group decision making. After that period, the group decided whether the person should be restored to the [socially constructed] family as sister or brother or be treated as "distant kin," who may expect only limited help from the family. To escape probation and/or distant kin status, a person must actively contribute to family needs. Rivers found that a distant kin who fails to participate fully in giving and receiving for an extended period is likely to be perceived as no longer belonging to the family and eventually will be "expelled," as Wilson & Pahl . . . found to be the case in their study of blood families. [42]

A "Moral" Obligation

Part of the reason free riders are dealt with in such an unflinching manner is that failure to do so threatens the life of the group. The other, and underlying, reason is that repayment itself comes to be defined as a "moral" issue.[43] Something that is "moral" is right in and of itself. A moral obligation of any kind leaves one no choice but to fulfill it. It is a duty, or responsibility, that one must not shirk. To shirk a moral obligation invariably reduces one's esteem and prestige—in one's own eyes, in the eyes of others, or both. Conversely, fulfilling moral obligations in a trustworthy manner increases one's prestige, status, esteem, and influence within the group. Accordingly, a trustworthy person is likely to maintain considerable influence in shaping group decision making. That being the case, it is in that person's own best interest to fulfill his or her obligations. As Coleman puts it, it is clearly a "rational" thing to do.

Social Capital and Group Solidarity

When one borrows financial capital from a commercial bank, one must agree in writing ahead of time what the monthly repayment (principal and interest) shall be. Once set, that figure is not the least bit squishy or vague. By contrast, the essence of social capital is squishy indeed. Its sum and substance is that fictive kin members borrow and repay "without reckoning." [44] They do not give and receive contributions on a quid pro quo, tit-for-tat, or exact equivalent basis. Because social capital is squishy, I can never feel that "I have fully discharged my obligations to my group; hence, I no longer need to contribute." Each child and adult in a fictive or blood kin network must continue making inputs or run the risk of having other members feel that she or he has started slacking off. Unlike repaying a bank loan, there is no way to gauge precisely when one has done enough to repay debts of social capital. Lacking that certainty, one tends to keep on being trustworthy. In addition, group members reciprocate by making inputs to one another, further clouding any sense that a particular member has done enough.

Self-Interest

Social capital may be squishy, but that is not to say that the social bonds it creates are flaccid in the least. To the contrary, a number of researchers believe that these are the strongest social bonds of all. [45] These bonds are particularly strong because as social capital (their fund of benefits) keeps expanding, members are likely to feel ever more strongly committed to their group. They keep inputting benefits to the group, and their inputs seem to be paying off. Group members need each other in order to keep on reaping benefits from their own past, present, and anticipated future inputs. Hence, it is in every member's own self-interest to remain with the group and to continue making inputs. On the other hand, if social capital begins to shrink because people cut back on their mutual inputs, group solidarity is likely to diminish. Accordingly, Coleman makes it abundantly clear that participants in multiperson groups are not motivated by what is usually perceived as altruism (i.e., munificently giving and expecting nothing in return).[46] Within a fictive kin network, commitment to self-interest is at least as powerful as commitment to group well-being.

In sum, within the context of a fictive kin network, or primary group, social capital is both the giving and the getting of shared obligations. It is essential that each member be trustworthy in both directions. Frequently, the obligations come to be perceived as moral—the right thing to do in and of itself. A member who fails to be trustworthy runs the risk of stigma and censure. On the other hand, a member who is trustworthy earns esteem, prestige, influence, and authority. Social capital bonds members to one another and is vital for group solidarity and stability. The extended family embedded within its community during the agricultural era is a prime example of the significance of social capital for adults and children alike. Children's participation in the production of social capital would be an essential feature of the New Everyday Life.

The Long-Term Decline of Social Capital

As the 19th- and 20th-century industrial period wore on, the typical child's family, or primary group, shrunk from a web of many persons to a very small group indeed. In comparison with the extended family, the two-parent nuclear household is a diminished structure. But it was not just size alone that distinguished the nonconnected style from its predecessor. As noted above, the new style became idealized as a cornucopia for children. It became a place where parents were obliged to supply their offspring with as many benefits as possible and where children's obligations were vague at best (e.g., children might be instructed, "Clean your room," "Rake the yard," or "Watch your sister"). In short, social capital became increasingly perceived as a one-way street. Parents were defined principally as the purveyors of benefits to children, whereas children were perceived chiefly as the beneficiaries of parental inputs.[47] To be sure, some researchers argue that today's children and youth make contributions to society through schoolwork performance as well as through part-time employment.[48] Nevertheless, the ancient notion that children should be partners with adults in a complex network whose objective is the development of their social capital (shared obligations) somehow got lost in the shuffle. Coleman believes that loss to be unfortunate, both for children and for the larger society.

Failure to offer children that unique type of partnership is negative because, first of all, the experience of creating social capital within a fictive kin setting is intrinsically rewarding in and of itself.[49] A child's own humanity is diminished if she or he lacks the day-to-day sense of being bonded with that type of we-group. Lacking the fulfillment and satisfactions that emerge from the experience of a cross-generational primary group lessens children, to say nothing of adults. As Coleman sees it, the quest for primary group experiences beyond their own households was a critical factor that drove suburban adolescents to form their own society.[50]

The second reason the fading of that unique historic experience is negative for children is that the absence of social capital might abridge children's human capital. We have learned that in the agricultural age, the contributions (social capital) of children and youth were the basis for their development of the skills and attributes (human capital) necessary for adult survival. The linkage of social and human capital is just as vital for individuals to function optimally in the information age—a point to which I return below.

Third, the fading of that unique historic experience is negative for children because it denies them the opportunity to be responsible for persons beyond their own households. The actual practice of a certain degree of duty for persons beyond one's parents and siblings is one more essential element of what it means to be fully human. Sociologist Daniel Bell calls this paying attention to the "public household." [51]

The Public Household

At the same time that inattention to the public household is negative for children, it is also contrary to the interests of the larger society. All adults, Coleman argues, "have an interest in the child becoming a moral being. The community has an interest in the child's growing up to be self-sufficient, sociable, and a contributor to the community. [Citizens] have an interest in the child's obedience to norms that lead to actions benefiting others, and thus an interest in the child's internalizing such norms." In short, parenting is not a private matter, for the obvious reason that its outcomes affect us all, both now and in the future. Every citizen has a personal stake in seeing that children are contributing members of society. Coleman adds, "The interest of the community may be seen to derive from the selfish interest of each of its members in having fellow members whose actions will benefit him when possible and will otherwise do as little harm as possible." [52] Unfortunately, owing to the structural limitations of the nonconnected style, children's contributions to society now tend to be relatively restricted. Hence, it is in the self-interest of all adults to figure out how to reinvent fictive kin networks based on shared obligations that somehow make sense for posttraditional society.

TEAMS IN THE NEL COMMUNITY

Thus far, while describing the child-adult NEL partnership, I have noted two things: First, such a partnership would not be identical to gender relations—it would not imply that children and adults are on the same footing. Second, the partnership would include the production of social and human capital. It is now time to explore how that capital might be produced within the context of NEL neighborhood "teams."

Throughout the agricultural age, children's human capital (skills necessary to survive in that type of economy) was one outgrowth of their partnership with adults in creating social capital. But in the industrial age, the nuclear family played a decreasing role in growing human capital. Children's education and job training became the chief means of generating the human capital they required to survive in that type of economy. Young people entered schools, factories, and businesses to learn the concrete skills—such as drafting, typing, welding, tool and die making—needed for particular occupations. Asking a boy, "What do you want to *be* when you grow up?" assumed that he would learn a trade or profession that would serve him (and his family) well throughout his life. In that vein of learning a valuable skill, thousands of people were, a few decades ago, trained to *be* "keypunch operators." Unfortunately for them, computer technology quickly advanced beyond the punch-card stage, and, as quickly as it had appeared, that appealing job vanished.

The New Human Capital

Currently, we are moving out of the industrial era and into the information age. It is an age in which the "powers of the mind are everywhere ascendant over the brute force of things. . . . In a Third Wave economy, the central resource . . . is knowledge . . . broadly encompassing data, information, images, symbols, culture, ideology, and values." [53]

Knowledge Workers

There seems little doubt that in today's information era, the premium once placed on learning specific skills (tool and die maker, computer operator) has dwindled virtually to zero. We are told that the key to surviving, to say nothing of thriving, in the new worldwide marketplace is to become what economist Peter F. Drucker calls a "knowledge worker." A knowledge worker is someone who possesses the "ability to acquire and to apply theoretical and analytical knowledge. . . . [He or she has] a habit of continuous [lifelong] learning." [54]

Do not misread Drucker's use of the term *knowledge.* In this sense, *knowledge* does not mean the specific content or skills requisite to do a particular job, such as computer operator or engineer. Instead, Drucker is actually describing an abstract process—a type of human capital. The human capital is the individual's capability to "think well," that is, to think in a critical and analytic fashion. Although it may be cumbersome, it would have been more exact if Drucker had stated that the information age demands "critical thinking" workers.[55] In our new age, no specific job is necessarily secure or stable. One can no longer grow up expecting to *be* a particular kind of worker throughout one's entire life. Even when a sense of security appears invulnerable—for instance, when one is a neurosurgeon—obsolescence may be just around the corner. Unless a neurosurgeon constantly absorbs the newest therapies and technologies, as well the reasoning behind them, there will be decreasing demand for her services. The upshot is that children and youth are now forced to reinvent their images of "what I want to be when I grow up": "The best way I can survive, and perhaps thrive, in the information age, is to begin now to practice a competence that I shall need to refine throughout my entire life, namely, the capability of being a knowledge, or critical thinking, worker."

Men and the New Human Capital

In comments to the national press, social scientist Theda Skocpol has described "the confusion many men presently have over what their role is supposed to be." Women's increasing independence and assertiveness have "created a confusing situation for men." [56] Indeed, confusion about and the ambiguities of male roles are common themes throughout postindustrial societies. Accordingly, in June 1993 the European Communities sponsored an international conference in Copenhagen called "Fathers in Families of Tomorrow." [57] The conference participants hoped to address the growing confusion in men's roles and to figure out how men might help shape information-age families.

One of the principal conference speakers was French sociologist François de Singly. He wondered what *unique* contribution men can bring to the lives of children and to families.[58] A religious conservative answer appeared in an essay titled "Manhood: Don't Let Your Son Leave Home Without It." [59] The essay is accompanied by an illustration of a knight in full 12th-century regalia, including lance, sword, and mailed horse. The knight's visor is lifted, and he is peering earnestly into the distance, anticipating the challenges to his male mettle. However, observes de Singly, that conventional ideal of manhood is now outmoded. Nonetheless, he concurs with Skocpol that the transition away from the " 'traditional' image of the macho father, the sort who regards the home as a sort of 'warrior's resting place,' " has been difficult indeed. The upshot has been that "in the private sphere, that traditionally female domain . . . men have lost their confidence." [60]

De Singly offers a model to restore male confidence that includes involving men in the development of children's human capital for the information age. He says that his "new model of fatherhood" stems from the marketplace qualities practiced in recent years by men in positions of responsibility. Although once found mostly among higher-status occupations, those same qualities have gradually diffused into midlevel and some lower-level occupations, including certain factory production areas. Men (and women) in those positions realize that "every day, you have to mobilize the men and women who work for the company, their intelligence, their imagination, their critical faculties, their sense of fair play, dreams, quality, their creative flair, ability to communicate, [and] observe." [61]

The Team Facilitator

Clearly, de Singly is describing the core characteristics of the knowledge worker or critical thinking worker. Another way to capture these core features is to note that this worker has a "probing inquisitiveness, a keenness of mind, a zealous dedication to reason, and a hunger or eagerness for reliable information." [62] Because the tasks they must accomplish are so complex and multifaceted, today's knowledge workers almost invariably operate in teams. One team member is designated "first as among equals"— that is, the team leader, or facilitator. Unlike the old-style industrial-age manager, foreman, or "boss," the team leader does not compel conformity on account of his or her formal authority. Instead, the leader inspires shared creativity and mutual problem solving.

According to de Singly, the concept of team leader or facilitator is the ideal model for today's "new father." One could also compare him to the coach of a sports team. Like a coach, tomorrow's new father would be " 'the team leader,' [who] must seek to harness each child's energies in such a way as to ensure that they succeed, according to their personality and their own inner resources, so that personal fulfillment goes hand in hand with . . . academic achievement." [63] Because being a team leader, or coach, is what many men have been trained to do since childhood, de Singly notes, men should be able to reproduce this role with confidence in the homeplace. For example, a certain number of men (and some women) currently serve as volunteer coaches for children's extracurricular sports teams, including baseball, softball, soccer, basketball, volleyball, and football teams. In those settings, the concept of "children's coach" is a well-known and appreciated slice of American culture.

De Singly is keenly aware that for men to cultivate this fresh identity of parent "requires both time and personal commitment. Men must make a conscious effort to develop [one-on-one] activities with their children." [64] He is also cognizant of the fact that currently in many households, both partners are employed and thus are away from home many hours a day. They are also sometimes away on weekends, for several days during the week, or for several weeks in a row. In most of these instances, it is the woman who, in addition to her occupation, is chiefly responsible for the care of the children. For example, based on in-depth observations of dual-career couples in New York City, analyst Susan Cheever has reported that the woman is virtually always the chief parent, and that her paid nanny becomes her "true significant other. It's the nanny who works with the mother to create a place where the children can thrive; the husband is at best an assistant to the team and at worst an obstacle to their aims." [65] Nevertheless, some of today's fathers are not content to be team assistants, much less obstacles. Instead, they want to share team leadership.

Although de Singly focuses on men, growing numbers of women in the marketplace are in fact currently operating as team leaders or facilitators. For example, in December 1998, General Motors appointed Cynthia Trudell to "become the first woman to head a car division [Saturn] at any domestic or foreign automaker." [66] Trudell commented, "It's near and dear to my heart that it [Saturn] values partnerships and relationships." [67] Despite the sexist nuances in de Singly's proposals, he poses a direct challenge to contemporary men. Nevertheless, he seems to overlook the reality that the nonconnected household may render his challenge meaningless. That is so even in households where men are present, to say nothing of the large numbers of households where they are not. As the industrial age winds down, critics argue that the nonconnected household is simply too small to do everything society expects it to do. Nevertheless, de Singly wants it to assume the huge responsibility of cultivating knowledge workers for the information age. Unfortunately, the isolated household does not seem to be fertile soil for cultivating the new human capital that he has in view.

The problem is that de Singly believes that fathers and mothers should be able to uproot what they do in their places of business and transplant it to their households. However, the two "soils" are very different, indeed. First of all, the marketplace team leader does not facilitate in isolation. His or her team is part of a broader network that, depending on the size of the company, includes a number of other teams. Within that broader structure, he or she works with other leaders to inspire and motivate colleagues. Second, the team members are part of a multiperson primary group bound together by its shared obligations—its social capital. No member is exempted from the moral obligation to give as well as to receive. Unfortunately, de Singly fails to address the difference in size between the homeplace and workplace teams. Nor does he question the prevailing model of the household as a repository of favors flowing toward, but not from, children. Finally, de Singly fails to consider the matter of productivity and its rewards. In the marketplace, those rewards are clear. But how would a man or woman know if he or she is being productive in generating children's social and human capital? And if he or she is productive, what rewards would follow?

Homeplace Teams

In order to address these and related issues, the NEL community would be perceived as corresponding to the man's, or woman's, marketplace team. It is *his or her homeplace team.* Hence, no household by itself would be responsible to see that its children become knowledge workers. Some neighborhoods, depending on their size, might have more than one team of children and youth. Each team would have one or more adult facilitators, or coaches, of either gender. Although every neighborhood member would have a responsibility to do so, the coach would be particularly obliged to cultivate his or her team's contributions to their community. The coach's aims would be to facilitate and monitor those contributions and to see that the children are rewarded appropriately. In effect, the coaches would be trying to produce both social and human capital. Just as they work (or worked) with a number of men and women to grow social capital and human capital in the marketplace, they would do the same thing within the neighborhood. Their long-term goal would be to cultivate children's intelligence, imagination, critical faculties, sense of fair play, creative flair, and ability to communicate.

Children's Responsibilities

But what would the NEL children actually contribute? And what would be their rewards? The coach of a child's softball team tries to inspire his or her charges to bat, pitch, field, and run well in order to win games. Each player has a fairly clear idea of what she or he is supposed to do. If a child learns to play her or his position better, that child gets the reward of positive approval from coach, teammates, and parents. And children, coach, and parents alike feel very good if and when the children win a game. And if they win, the coach gets a lot of positive feedback as well. The agricultural era's extended family was also like a team. The more proficient each child became in doing her or his tasks, the greater the child's sense of pride and the more approval she or he was likely to receive. "Winning" meant producing enough food so that the family could eat. "Winning big" meant having food left over to sell or perhaps for barter.

Jobs and People

Researchers tell us that children's inputs to present-day cohousing communities fall into two broad categories.[68] Both sets of activities rest, of course, on the children's ages, their interests and abilities, and their school responsibilities. First, some cohousing children and youth participate in activities such as gardening, landscaping, sprucing up their grounds, and routine maintenance, as well as activities in the commons such as tidying up, cleaning, and meal preparation. Second, some children pay attention to younger children playing in and around community spaces. Put another way, there are jobs that need to be done, and there are people who require attention.

Within an NEL community, children's paying attention to people would be expanded to include helping out adults of all ages who become ill or injured. It would also mean assisting adults inside their households with their children. Jobs that need to be done would be expanded to include children's helping community members with their internal household chores or running errands. Needless to say, children would not be expected to perform these jobs and people tasks by themselves. Instead, just as in the agricultural era, they would share certain neighborhood responsibilities with adults. Equally plain is the fact that, as they have been forever, fun and play would be integral to the life of every NEL child.

For the most part, paying attention to jobs and people during the industrial age has been the province of women. Hence, it is clear that children's participation in the effective performance of those tasks would be highly beneficial to women. This would be particularly so when the women who are helped are either dual-earner parents or solo parents. Accordingly, by participating actively in these tasks, children would contribute toward expediting gender equity within their community. By helping out in that manner, they would become a vital part of what has been called the NEL's "feminist vision" (see Chapter 5). They would be an integral part of the 200-year-old family revolution.

Growing Social Capital: Contributing to the Community

Nevertheless, at one time or another every child and youth will surely complain to the coach that he or she is being asked to do too much. Children will complain that they hate doing certain tasks, or that "it's not fair" that their performance is at times deemed unsatisfactory. There is no doubt that such resistance occurred during the agricultural era, and it certainly happens now on children's sports teams. Within the NEL community, the coach's response to such inevitable resistance will become the soil in which both social and human capital are cultivated. It is up to the coach, as well as to the other children on the team, to convey to the resistant child that this is a problem that must be resolved in one manner or another. Resolving it satisfactorily would likely be a way for the child to fulfill his or her obligations to contribute to their community. And by contributing, the child is participating in the group's production of social capital. On the flip side, resolving the problem also implies that the community becomes further indebted to the child. Accordingly, his or her resources, in the form of group members' obligations, are thereby increased.

Growing Human Capital: Becoming a Critical Thinker

Importantly, figuring out *how* to solve the problem contributes to the type of human capital the child needs right now. It is also the same human capital the child will require as he or she moves into the information-age marketplace. The process of resolving the conflict gives the child real-life, hands-on practice in being a knowledge or critical thinking worker, because such a process necessarily develops the child's intelligence, imagination, critical faculties, sense of fair play, creative flair, and ability to communicate. The upshot is that the child's *human capital* becomes linked with his or her community inputs, that is, his or her participation in *social capital.*

Although it is in the child's evident self-interest to cultivate her or his human capital, most children and youth also need to perceive additional, more immediate, kinds of rewards flowing from their community participation. For example, how would the child or youth draw on the resources— the social capital—that community members are obliged to give him or her? The metaphor of a sports team or a combat unit might offer some initial insights. Either setting is an example of a primary group in which members clearly belong to an entity possessing significant goals larger than themselves. Because members are a vital part of the larger whole, they have a vested interest in the group's achieving its goals and thus succeeding. They can thus identify with, and participate in, the rewards of pride, esteem, and prestige that accompany group success. Hence, the interests of the group and the members' own self-interests clearly overlap. Furthermore, during the arduous process of training to become effective participants in group success, sports team members are required to help each other out in innumerable ways. Their mutual reinforcement occurs not only while they are actually training, but off the field as well. Team members tend to become close friends in their day-to-day lives. The result is that they can count on one another for help with a whole range of personal and practical needs.

The preceding sports team scenario would apply to children and youth in the New Everyday Life. First of all, the child would identify with and share in the pride and prestige that accompanies achievement of neighborhood goals. Those goals would include the matter of increased gender equity and also some of the political issues identified in Chapter 7 (e.g., the issue of sustainability). At the same time, the child or youth would be the beneficiary of the kinds of personal and practical day-to-day help that adults and children of all ages might be able to supply to him or her. In short, the child would have friends of all ages from whom she or he could receive companionship, emotional intimacy, and practical assistance.

Besides esteem, prestige, and approval, active participation in creating social capital carries with it status and influence. This is no less true for children and youth than it is for adults. Although I said earlier that partnership does not imply children's equality, it seems clear that youth who facilitate neighborhood solidarity and goals would gain a certain degree of influence in group decision making. Thus, for youth, especially as they mature, group participation brings with it the added satisfaction of having inputs aimed at shaping the life of the group. If youth have earned their influence by being trustworthy, it would be hard to imagine denying them the right to exercise it in some meaningful fashion.

A Laboratory of Democracy

The participation of youth is particularly important if one views the NEL neighborhood as a laboratory, or workshop, of democracy. A number of thoughtful observers have bemoaned what they perceive to be the decline of the democratic process throughout contemporary American society.[69] Many suggestions have been offered to revitalize citizen participation in the hands-on dynamics of democracy. Recall from Chapter 1 that principles 3 and 4 of our proposed family policy call for increased citizen participation in the decision-making processes that affect our day-to-day lives. NEL would be a structural means of achieving those policy goals. Because peaceful democratic struggle would be central to every NEL neighborhood, it would become a means of sharpening persons' skills in achieving their goals through nonviolent means.[70] Children and youth in the NEL setting would learn firsthand that members who function as contributing citizens of their community thereby earn the right to be heard and taken seriously. Youth would also learn (perhaps painfully) that in a democracy there is no necessary correspondence between advocating an agenda and persuading others to support it.

A Workshop for Gender Equity

An indispensable feature of the NEL democracy workshop would be hands-on training in the art of gender politics. One of NEL's major benefits for girls would be its ability to provide a real-life experience in which gender equity is not merely a set of pious homilies. The NEL community's struggle to enhance the gender situation of adult women would be matched by its battle to minimize, and ideally to eliminate, differences in the ways that girls and boys participate in the giving and receiving of shared obligations.

In effect, girls and boys would grow social capital in precisely the same ways. That means that boys and girls alike would be expected to perform the same types of jobs and people tasks. And it means they would be rewarded in precisely the same ways. There are few social situations that offer girls (preteen and teen) real-life opportunities to compete with boys on a playing field that is relatively level.[71] The NEL community would be one of them.

Another, and related, feature that would motivate girls to participate actively in the NEL community has to do with the character of the new human capital. Whatever else it implies, the concept of knowledge worker is gender-free. One of the principal NEL objectives would be to encourage girls to realize that in order to be self-sufficient in the information age, they need careful training in the processes of critical thinking and problem solving. Several studies have reported that, compared with boys, today's adolescent girls tend to lack self-confidence and self-esteem.[72] Although important right now, that generalization will become even more significant in the future, because the information-age marketplace will deal more harshly than did the industrial-era marketplace with anyone lacking self-confidence and a healthy self-image.

Hence, part of the task of assisting girls to become self-sufficient knowledge workers is to target their adolescent self-image. An essential element in the process of a girl's learning to think for herself within the community context is for her to realize that "I am a capable person. In fact, I am more capable than some boys. Moreover, I can develop my talents fully enough to become a self-sufficient worker." Accordingly, an important part of the coach's task would to facilitate the self-image of each girl on his or her team. At the same time, the coach must take care not to alienate boys or to give the impression that girls are being unduly favored. The hope, after all, would be that the effects of the NEL gender equity workshop will persist once the youth become adults, whether or not they choose to reside in an NEL setting. Boys who become disaffected from the struggle are less likely to pursue it as men.

Incidentally, adolescents' participation in the NEL community would inevitably compete with the teenagers' involvement in typical peer groups. Community participation could conceivably exacerbate the unavoidable, and frequently painful, struggles between adolescents and adults. In spite of those perils, the connected neighborhood is, among other things, a conscious effort to co-opt children from *exclusive* participation in peer groups. To be sure, that objective is quite difficult to achieve. Even so, in spite of the obvious difficulties in trying to subvert negative peer group influences, parents in today's nonconnected households are being urged to do precisely that. Politicians, clergy, and the media entreat parents to "teach your children to say no to drugs, sex, alcohol, and tobacco." Adolescents and preteens, responding in a rational manner, ask, "Why? What will I gain from my restraint?" The fact is that those several pleasures are frequently the very things peers urge on one another as part of belonging to their primary group. Doing some or all of them symbolizes, and thus reinforces, the child's sense of belonging to her or his special group. And belonging means that she or he is indeed a trustworthy group member entitled to help of whatever sort and whenever needed. How can nonconnected parents hope to compete with those potent forces? Reaching beyond the boundaries of their own households to other adults at least gives them a fighting chance to compete with negative peer influences. The NEL model would be one attempt to reinvent an ancient pattern in which adults and children worked together for common ends. The neighborhood would be a real-life setting in which the child would struggle to develop social and human capital in ways that might benefit him or her and others at the same time.

Rewarding the Coach

For any number of reasons, the role of coach might be perceived as a stressful, and thus unenviable, position. An additional stressor I have not yet mentioned is how the coach might respond to the child or youth who is known to be untrustworthy for an extended period of time. What would it mean for the coach to define that person as a "free rider," and thus to place him or her on "condition red status," and perhaps to "feed him or her with a long-handled spoon"? At the very least, we could expect that the free rider might be deprived of a certain degree of community approval. Specific benefits might also be withdrawn, meaning that the child would get less of a free ride. Eventually, negative sanctions might also be applied. The emergence of the processes of stigmatization and censure would seem to be inevitable. And when they appear, they would severely test the ideal of community parenting. This would be especially so if the child's biological parent(s) come to view the censure as unfair or unwarranted.

Incidentally, there is no reason parents residing with children could not become active as coaches, or perhaps assistant coaches. Much would depend, of course, on the ages and numbers of their own children, whether or not they are lone parents, and their current employment patterns (lone parents are discussed further later in this chapter). Even parents who do not currently serve as coaches would share in the general obligation of every adult to facilitate the social and human capital of all neighborhood children. At the same time, parents residing with children might be active in making important contributions to the community other than by coaching. Moreover, if they are perceived as trustworthy, they may legitimately defer their coaching inputs to the future. The parent(s) of an infant, for instance, would not be expected to contribute very much to anything beyond their own household. In fact, they would be the recipients of a good deal of community support and inputs.

A Zone of Productivity

In any event, the role of coach within the NEL community would plainly carry a lot of stresses and strains. Why would any man or woman wish to take on that role? As I have noted in Chapter 5, the NEL community would declare itself to be a zone of productivity for social and human capital. In an effort to escape the corrosive effects of productivism, the community would aim to endow the production of both types of capital with a considerable degree of moral worth. In concert with other NEL neighborhoods, the community would need to construct the idea that it is just as vital to produce both forms of capital as it is to produce financial capital.[73] If that elusive goal can somehow be accomplished, then perhaps some men and women might be willing to take on the demanding role (and identity) of coach. An effective coach would be one whose team scores high on both social and human capital. *High* implies that the community would be able to measure or assess how much of each form of capital its teams are producing.

Because both forms of capital are essential to the life of the community, the community would respond by according an effective coach high levels of esteem, prestige, approval, influence, and authority. In order to help reinforce the shared consensus that the production of social and human capital is as worthy as the production of financial capital, the community would, among other things, gather together as a whole. Perhaps an entire federation of communities might meet together. These public meetings would be occasions to congratulate and applaud the coaches and teams that are increasing the production of both types of capital. The process of assigning moral worth to vital noneconomic productivity has long been practiced by religious groups. Members who perform highly valued and significant nonpaid service for the group are defined as doing something far more important than making lots of money. Likewise, the soldier who places his or her life in danger while trying to protect comrades is also considered to have done something far more significant than producing dollars. To demonstrate that fact, the soldier is decorated at an official public ceremony. Similarly, in the case of the NEL coach, his or her productivity would be defined as vital for children, for women, for the community, and also for the society as a whole. Because that productivity is greatly valued, it would be rewarded in significant ways at a public ceremony sponsored by the neighborhood and/or federation.

The NEL coach would, of course, enjoy the intrinsic satisfactions that any type of team leader or facilitator receives when he or she is successful in transforming both the members and the group into winners. Whether in the marketplace or on the sports field, working with and shaping one's team so as to make it more effective and thus increasingly productive supplies a great many inherent rewards. A coach's enjoyment of these sorts of benefits would be bolstered by his or her knowledge that the community as a whole recognizes and rewards his or her effectiveness within the community's zone of productivity. This individual has accepted, and is measuring up to, the awesome and vital challenge of being a coach.

Plainly, being an effective NEL community coach would demand a great deal of energy, creativity, and thought—to say nothing of time. For these reasons, I have implied in Chapter 5 that a coach would likely be someone for whom high levels of occupational achievement are, at least for the present, *not* a high priority. He or she would, nonetheless, be an economically self-sufficient person. The composition of an individual's household would not necessarily restrict her or him from serving as a coach—she or he could live alone, live with children but with no other adults, or live as part of a couple and with or without children. Moreover, there would be no particular age requirement—a coach could be a young adult, in midlife, or older.

The Caregiver

The period of infancy and the toddler stage might be called a "preteam" time for children. It would be the time before they are old enough to "feed the chickens and collect the eggs," and prior to their actual participation in the growth of social capital. Some children would, of course, be able and willing to participate sooner than others. In any case, their own parents and other community adults would presumably respond to preteam children not as coaches, but rather in the more conventional mode of caregiver. Neighborhood men and women alike would have the opportunity to serve as caregivers to preteam children. Indeed, some persons of either gender might prefer the role of caregiver to the role of coach. Given that reality, the community would first need to devise means to endow the role of caregiver with a high degree of moral worth, just as it would for the role of coach. Second, the neighborhood would also have to figure out ways to reward men and women alike who serve as effective caregivers.

A PRODUCTIVE AGING SOCIETY

As the 21st century evolves, mature citizens (midlife and older) will make up a huge pool of potential NEL community members. Not only are their numbers going to expand, they will be living longer, healthier, and more vigorous lives.[74] Accordingly, several analysts believe that it is now time for us to begin inventing a "productive aging society." [75] They assert that mature citizens have a great deal to contribute to society across a wide range of dimensions. We should, as Giddens puts it, start to regard "older people . . . as a rich resource." [76] In that vein, mature citizens—midlife and older— would in many respects be a rich resource for the New Everyday Life community. They would, for example, be likely candidates to serve either as coaches or as caregivers.

Reinventing the "Older Person"

As we enter the information age, mature citizens have a historically unique opportunity to help reinvent what it means to be an "older person." During the agricultural period, the term *older* was typically applied to persons fortunate enough to survive past their 30s or 40s. Older persons who did survive were highly respected and valued on account of their accumulated wisdom and experience. They had much to contribute to the effective functioning of their extended families and communities. But the longer the industrial era wore on, the less valuable older persons became for the well-being of their families and society alike. They became virtually obsolete. As a result, "retirement" was constructed to be a time period when persons no longer actively make contributions to the society around them. Retirement is nothing other than a social invention of the late 19th century; it simply had not existed during the agricultural period.[77]

The NEL community would offer the potential for mature citizens once again to reconstruct our notions of midlife and older life. Given the increases in their numbers, alongside their dramatic gains in health and longevity, mature citizens would be able to make a significant impact on the shape and direction of the New Everyday Life.[78] Thus far in this chapter, we have learned how vital it is to reinvent our images of children and youth. Instead of considering them as passive, dependent, and in need of protection, we must begin to view them as active social agents of their own destiny. Similarly, instead of thinking that we must do something *for* mature citizens, we must begin to ask, What can they contribute? How might they influence their own destiny? The NEL community offers a situation, or structure, within which to answer those questions.

Geographic Mobility

For example, because mature citizens are often less likely than younger persons to be geographically mobile, they may be able to assume considerable influence within the NEL community. If they move less frequently, they may turn out to be the stable nucleus of the neighborhood. A major attraction of the isolated lifestyle was its portability. Because households frequently moved from one nonconnected neighborhood to another, many persons found it difficult to form deep and lasting friendships. Hence, nuclear family members often turned inward seeking to forge long-term primary relationships with their spouses and children. Plainly, high levels of geographic mobility would work against the notion of a connected lifestyle. For one reason, the entrance of new members (as well as the loss of previous members) is a significant challenge to the development of social and human capital. Those who move out carry with them certain benefits they owed the community. Those who move in must quickly show that they are willing to begin contributing to the neighborhood, just as ongoing members must quickly show that they are willing to help them out. In short, because there is a lack of shared history of giving and receiving, a considerable amount of trust is initially required on both sides. The need for that initial mutual trust is one reason that persons must "apply" to join up. The community must assess whether or not particular persons are likely to be trustworthy in developing social and human capital. At the same time, the members of an applying household must grasp fully what they are getting themselves into, namely, the obligations as well as the benefits of the NEL style of connected living.

A core, or nucleus, of members who have lived in the community for an extended period would presumably have learned how to assess the chances of new recruits' becoming successful participants. At the same time, they would likely be inclined to invest time and energy with new members, to assist them in becoming a part of their neighborhood's patterns of giving and receiving. To the extent that midlife and older members are part of the community's stable center, they could emerge as an extraordinarily important feature of the New Everyday Life. That is not to say that NEL neighborhoods would sacrifice the diversity that accompanies having younger-aged households with children. Both lone and dual parents within the NEL might feel that their connected lifestyle is so beneficial for them and their children that they are unwilling to move, even when appealing alternatives of one sort or another present themselves. Not only would the connected lifestyle provide an incentive to stay put, it might also be an attraction for households moving into a particular locale. Having experienced that lifestyle in former locations, some households may be eager once again to live in a similar kind of neighborhood.[79] Others who have never experienced it may desire to have that lifestyle in the new location to which they are moving. Thus they might seek it out.

The cynic might remark that just as the shifting technologies of the industrial period rendered the knowledge and skills of older men and women obsolete, the same will apply many times over in the information age. However, the contributions of mature Third Wave persons to children's social and human capital would not lie in the realm of particular technologies. Indeed, even younger adults are chagrined to find themselves continually outpaced by children's grasp of the latest electronic innovations. Rather than trying hopelessly to be brokers of technology, mature adults would contribute to NEL neighborhoods in the same manner as younger adults. They would participate actively in the growth of social and human capital. The principal difference would be that, compared to younger adults with children, mature persons typically possess more time, or at least greater flexibility in arranging their time. Not having children in their own households would mean that healthy, mature persons would be able to pay considerable attention to their neighborhood's children. That being the case, we might expect that a number of them would be willing to take on the demanding role of either coach or caregiver.

A certain portion of today's retired persons live in "adults-only" housing developments (see Chapter 4). Like other varieties of the "community as commodity" phenomenon, virtually all such housing developments practice a nonconnected lifestyle. Many other mature citizens reside in urban areas and are also living a nonconnected style of life. In either setting, mature citizens risk feeling isolated and alienated from society. Relating to children in a meaningful fashion might be one way of overcoming their sense of alienation. The image of older urban citizens exchanging benefits with children other than their biological grandchildren is captured in a letter written to the editor of the *New York Times* by Vivian Fenster Ehrlich, executive director of a New York City service agency. Ehrlich censures the "adults-only" housing developments and then says that there are many older Americans who in no way resemble those who mistakenly refuse to allow children in their midst. She asserts that the "majority of elderly are starving for the company of the young. Over the past two decades our agency has experienced the greatest increase in demand for its intergenerational programs." [80] Ehrlich's central points are, first, that many of today's mature citizens need to be around children whom they can mentor and nurture, and second, that many children surely require the inputs that mature persons can make to them (as, for example, in the role of coach or caregiver).

The active participation of mature citizens in all aspects of the NEL community raises questions of injury and illness. A community member of any age may, of course, develop an illness or disability that persists indefinitely. However, older persons, even if vigorous for many years, are more prone to chronic infirmities. Hence, the issue inevitably arises as to the community's long-term obligations. Figuring out how to reward child-free adults of any age who are extensively involved as team leaders is a major challenge in and of itself. If, in addition, the community must ascertain its long-term obligations to persons who, owing to illness or disability, are no longer able to supply inputs, the challenge becomes daunting. Nevertheless, at the present time, Western societies have no clearer idea on how best to address the long-term interests of mature citizens than they do on how best to address the needs of children.[81] Although politicians and policy analysts repeatedly discuss both matters, little is actually being done of an innovative nature. The notion of an NEL neighborhood would, at the very least, stimulate a dialogue—not merely about the needs of children and mature citizens, but about their untapped potential as well.

Child-Free Adults

The situation of younger child-free persons, whether residing alone or as couples, is analogous to, yet different from, that of mature persons whose children have left home. Because of either infertility or conscious choice—based, for instance, on sustainability issues—some adults have not procreated. Nevertheless, they too might wish to participate in the unique opportunities for primary relationships and parenting options offered by the NEL neighborhood. Being child-free in no way implies that a person is antichild. It may instead signify a profound regard for parenting. Some child-free persons may have such reverence for the art of parenting that they realize they can do it better aside from a biological connection. A number of such persons might also be willing to take on the role of either coach or caregiver.

REDEFINING THE "GOOD PARENT"

A formidable obstacle to neighbors of all ages who might participate with parents in their children's lives is captured by Frederick Stoller's observation that parents "have set themselves up as expert child-rearers." [82] At this point in history, our culture expects and demands that natural parents be the principal agents of parenting, with ancillary help from teachers, clergy, kin, friends, employers, and government. Indeed, the ability to parent with minimal outside help is often considered one measure of what being a "good parent" is. Parents who look to "outsiders" for significant inputs to their children's lives risk being labeled as somehow less-than-ideal parents.

However, that ideology may simply be a vestige of the industrial age. Regardless of how adequate for children the two-parent household may or may not have been back then, we are now entering a very different age. What children seem to require today is the sort of "team" experience highlighted by de Singly. One or even two parents simply cannot generate the multiperson, primary group experience that children need to develop into effective knowledge workers. Children will increasingly require human capital in the forms of critical thinking and problem solving in order to participate optimally in the information age. The upshot is that no adult today can be an "expert child rearer" in the Second Wave sense. Hence, if every parent requires the inputs of other adults, then the conventional meanings of *good parent* lose their force. Instead, a good parent is seen as someone who works with connected adults in order to realize a single, overriding objective—the cultivation of the social and human capital of the entire neighborhood's children. A good parent is recognized as someone who nurtures children and inspires them to positive action on behalf of themselves and their team.

Lone-Parent Households

Many researchers and policy analysts have debated the adequacy of the lone-parent household compared with the dual-parent household.[83] However, the reconstruction of parenting as an obligation of the neighborhood significantly shifts the grounds of this debate. Advocates who believe that "two parents are both necessary and sufficient" for children would be required to defend their assumption. The implications of a connected lifestyle for lone parenting would be quite dramatic. Such a parent would no longer need to feel that "because I'm not married I'm an inadequate parent, and thus a second-class citizen." The issue of parenting children for the information age is far more subtle and complex than the typical image conveyed by the customary dichotomy of one versus two parents. A lone parent who chooses to live in an NEL neighborhood might be doing far more for the well-being of her or his children than she or he could do by deciding to marry or to cohabit.[84]

Needless to say, no child in the NEL community could have a parentlike, or significant other, relationship with every neighborhood adult. Certain children would connect better with some adults than with others. Implied in that statement is the reality that occasionally a child does not connect well with his or her biological parent(s). Living (or not living) in an NEL neighborhood has nothing to do with that reality. In any case, when a child and parent do not connect well, or even when there is a sound connection, a child may occasionally connect better with a community adult than with his or her own parent(s). That possibility is both threatening and comforting at the same time. It is threatening in the sense that, in terms of cultural ideals, it isn't supposed to be that way, and comforting in the sense that if it does happen, the child's needs are being met—needs that exist irrespective of the living arrangements. And that, after all, is the central issue: What is a necessary and sufficient structure for children's social and human capital in the postindustrial, information age—a time marked by increasing levels of external and manufactured risk?

Is the "necessary and sufficient" structure captured by the prevailing image of the solo- or dual-parent household struggling valiantly to do all it can, with whatever ancillary help it can muster from kin, friends, employer, or government? Or is the "necessary and sufficient" structure captured instead by the image of the household (regardless of its composition) striving to parent within a network of connected households—a network that may incorporate government participation?[85] The NEL response is that just as resolving adult gender issues requires a connected lifestyle, the same is true for many of the issues facing children and youth. Ensuring the well-being of children and youth may be yet another instance of asking the nonconnected household to do too much.

CONCLUSION

Part II of this volume is about completing the family revolution by reinventing the future. Chapter 5 focused on adult relationships within the New Everyday Life. This chapter has considered children's participation in the NEL.

During the First Wave, the agricultural era, children were expected to make significant contributions to their families (extended and nuclear) and to their communities. Their participation in the growth of social capital contributed to the development of their own human capital. Hence, their contributions benefited them both as children and later on as adults. Children's active involvement in the growth of social capital declined gradually throughout the course of the industrial period. By the post-World War II years, children's involvement had all but disappeared. Although children were viewed as the deserving recipients of parental obligations, their own responsibilities had become vague indeed. The educational system (schools, job training) was perceived to be the principal source of the kind of human capital that might enable them to survive in the marketplace. That human capital consisted largely of learning the specific skills and content required to *be* an engineer, a bricklayer, an auto technician, a teacher, a computer programmer, and so forth.

But survival in the Third Wave, postindustrial period demands a new type of human capital. Helping to develop the new capital would be a major NEL objective. The first step would be to declare that the principle of sanctuary applies to children as well as to women. After affirming that the neighborhood is a "safe place" for children, the second step would be to assert that children should be partners in the life of the community. Partnership implies participation in the growth and development of social and human capital. That means that children would participate in, among other things, the performance of the kinds of activities that have typically been the province of women. By assisting in that manner, children would enhance the long-term objective of gender equity. At the same time, by struggling to serve, they would cultivate the type of human capital that is essential for effective navigation of the information era. In effect, they would become empowered to survive, and perhaps thrive, in the new worldwide marketplace.

The new human capital is captured by such terms as *knowledge worker* and *critical thinking worker*. These labels subsume capabilities that require a lifetime to develop and are applicable to whatever specific occupational endeavor an individual might be pursuing at a particular point in her or his life. The new human capital seems to grow best within a team context in which one or more persons serve as facilitators, or coaches. Within the NEL context, certain men and women might agree to serve as coaches. The NEL objective would be to endow the production of social and human capital with a degree of social worth (esteem, prestige, respect, influence) now reserved for economic productivity. Within this zone of productivity, men and women who, for the present, do not seek to be occupational high fliers might desire a deep sense of moral worth from other than conventional sources. The projected increase in the proportion of older citizens as we enter the 21st century, alongside their expected health and longevity, indicates that older persons will have an opportunity to play a significant role in shaping the New Everyday Life. Among other things, midlife and older persons might become quite active as coaches to community teams of children or as caregivers to preteam children.

This chapter has elaborated several of the principles of family policy introduced in Chapter 1. For example, we now have a clearer picture of how the conflicting demands of independence and interdependence (self versus community) might be reconciled (principle 1). Within the NEL setting, children and adults would learn to work together for the mutual benefit (social and human capital) of both. We also now have a better idea of how women's interests might be served (principle 2). By participating in the community, children would advance the interests of adult women as well as those of girls. At the same time, children's participation would help set the stage for increased gender equity when later on they themselves become adults. In effect, NEL is not only a structural response to adult gender issues (Chapter 5), it is at the same time a situational response to the gender issues (as well as other matters) facing children and youth.

Finally, the NEL community would extend empowerment and participation in democratic dialogue to children, just as it promises to do for adults (principles 3 and 4). In effect, the community would become a laboratory of democracy, including training in some of the real-life aspects of gender politics. And because the community would declare itself to be a children's "safe place," it would squarely address the matter of violence in human affairs (principle 6). Thus far, Chapters 5 and 6 have considered all but one of the six family policy themes. Chapter 7 takes up the question of positive welfare and also discusses in greater depth the issues of empowerment and democratic participation.

7

EMPOWERING
THE COMMUNITY:
MAKING THE
PRIVATE POLITICAL

◆◆◆───────────────────────────────────

Part II of this book is about inventing the future by completing the family revolution. Chapters 5 and 6 have shown that the revolution includes empowering women, men, and children. This chapter considers how community empowerment is also very much a part of the ongoing family revolution.

At first glance, one might say that the feminists of the 1960s and 1970s succeeded in their goal of "making the private political." Formerly personal matters such as sex (heterosexual and homosexual), sexual harassment, adultery, marriage, divorce, cohabitation, children, abortion, and contraception are now on the front page of national politics.[1] Perhaps the most vivid example is the recent saga featuring President Clinton. At issue was the president's sex life and whether or not he lied about it under oath. Back in the 1960s, when the second sexual revolution was ignited, no one, even in their most outlandish psychedelic vision, could have ever imagined that the president's sex life would be forced on to the public record.[2] That was so even though certain members of the government and of the national press were fully aware of the "secret" that President Kennedy routinely slept with women other than his wife, Jackie.[3]

Nevertheless, the present state of things is *not* what feminists had in mind when they began to work to meld the private and public spheres. Their hope was that ordinary citizens—women and men alike—would participate in the sorts of political struggles that might contribute to the overriding objective of gender equity. In Chapter 3, I noted that one of the feminists' most important (and failed) agenda items was passage of the Equal Rights Amendment (ERA). Other items included passage of no-fault divorce laws and the right to choose abortion. Feminists also demanded equal opportunity for women, both in education and in the marketplace. They also sought to terminate the sexual double standard and to redefine custom and law regarding sexual harassment and rape.

THE POLITICAL VISION OF THE RELIGIOUS RIGHT

Chapter 3 noted that in reaction to these and similar objectives, a counter-revolution was mounted by cultural conservatives, especially those who are religious. The latter have come to be known as the "religious right." The religious right has grown significantly since the 1980 White House Conference on Families described in Chapter 3. They now constitute a potent force to be reckoned with in national politics.[4] Inside the Republican Party, it has become established wisdom that one must have the support of religious conservatives in order to be nominated for, and to have any hope of winning, the presidency.[5] Under the leadership of its former director, Ralph Reed, the Christian Coalition has in recent years gained what observer Katherine Seelye calls a "seat at the table of mainstream politics." [6] The Christian Coalition's 1996 budget was $200,000, and during that election year it "distributed 45 million voter guides in 125,000 churches."

A Strategy of Retreat

Several centuries ago, when conservative religious groups viewed their society as hopelessly decadent, their typical reaction was to retreat from it.[7] The most obvious examples are the Puritans who escaped England in the early 1600s. Once in the New World, their explicit aim was to create a wholly different social order from the one they had left behind. Next, in the later 1600s and the 1700s, groups such as the Quakers, the Amish, the Mennonites, the Hutterites, and the Moravians also retreated from Europe. They too sought to carve out safe havens in North America for their distinctive religious beliefs. Finally, in the mid-1800s several religious groups indigenous to the United States withdrew to remote areas in order to create their own communities with their own family values.[8] Among these were the Mormons, and one of their values, interestingly enough, was adherence to polygamy.[9]

A Strategy of Confrontation

Today's religious conservatives, however, choose not to retreat but rather to stay and fight what they view as a "corrupt" society. Part of the reason they now stay is that establishing sheltered agricultural communities is not the viable option it once was.[10] Furthermore, increasing numbers of religious conservatives agree with Ralph Reed that their legislative agenda should aim at putting an end to the alleged cultural decay that began during what they call the "abrasive" 1960s.[11] Their aim is to replace our present-day culture with "a thoroughly Judeo-Christian culture." [12] Although they are not about to flee contemporary society, they, like their forebears, feel threatened and assaulted by it. It is now as pervasive as MTV on cable television or the World Wide Web. It is everywhere present and as inescapable as the air we breathe. Indeed, the embeddedness of religious conservatives within society helps to explain their determination to confront and refashion that society in line with their own values. Currently, they continue to occupy the high moral ground on family politics that they seized at the time of the 1980 White House Conference. And to that they have now added their "seat at the table" of mainstream politics.

The political clout of the religious right is based on a model that starts at the neighborhood level and reaches upward to the highest levels of government.[13] Conservative church congregations within particular locales are aware of and often connected informally to one another, in a manner not too dissimilar from precinct linkages across urban neighborhoods in the pre-World War II era.[14] When either a perceived threat or an opportunity for action arises, the several congregations together mount a rapid response. An example of a "threat" would be a statute being considered by a city council to prohibit discrimination in jobs and housing against homosexuals solely on account of their sexual orientation. In seeking to derail such an ordinance, members of the congregations might write numerous letters to local newspapers, mount an aggressive media campaign, and send large numbers of persons to council sessions to protest the ordinance's passage.

An example of an "opportunity" occurred in the spring of 1997, when the U.S. Senate debated a bill to ban late-term abortions. As part of their strategy to pass the ban, religious conservatives called on congregations around the country to implore their own U.S. senators to support it. The first time the Senate voted, the bill fell a mere 3 votes shy of the 67 needed to override President Clinton's promised veto. However, conservatives lobbied for a second vote, and Gary Bauer, president of the Family Research Council (an umbrella political organization for the religious right), told the national press, "We're hopeful that debate will continue and that fear of unemployment will move three more votes." [15] Bauer's veiled threat was plain enough: Senators failing to support the ban the second time around may be turned out of office owing to concerted efforts organized at the local level.

The religious right's bottom-up political strategy first proved its mettle in the 1970s in the defeat of the ERA.[16] Scores of local congregations organized bus convoys from dozens of communities throughout a particular state that converged on the state capitol the very day that ratification of the amendment was up for a vote. Partisans flooded legislative halls, buttonholing their own representatives and urging them to vote against ratification. Stirring orations endorsing the ERA were being made on the steps of the capitol by celebrities such as Alan Alda at the precise moment opponents were inside, successfully pressuring their legislators to defeat it. Using local churches as their structural foundation, members of the religious right continue to fashion robust grassroots organizations with the express aim of making their vision of family policy a local, state, and national political reality.[17]

The present-day political clout of the religious right is matched by a corresponding lack of clout on the part of feminists and their allies. By and large, advocates for women's interests are now fighting a defensive action, striving simply to hold on to gains won years ago. Among other items, the religious right has been chipping away at women's abortion rights and also at their freedoms to leave a marriage (see Chapter 3). And although women's advocates do in fact have an agenda, not much is said publicly about women's interests per se (e.g., the passage of the Equal Rights Amendment). As noted in Chapter 3, the politically correct slogan is now "Kids First." One of the themes of this book, namely, that family policy should be designed to balance the competing interests of women, men, and children alike, is not widely discussed.

THE POLITICAL VISION OF THE NEW EVERYDAY LIFE

Architect Dorit Fromm reports that the European cohousing communities she studied in the 1980s were quite ambivalent about getting political. On the one side, some members argued that political action is a logical extension of their neighborhood: "When there are so many worthwhile causes, why does the community—having accomplished so much in developing itself—not organize to deal with more?" [18] But on the other side, some cohousing members argued that politics is so incredibly divisive that it could seriously threaten the success and stability of their community: "We've had sharp political discussions, and it's absolutely obvious we don't agree." [19] Hence, apart from sustainability, those members believed that it would be best for the community and its residents if they avoided such matters altogether. The upshot, says Fromm, is that most cohousing neighborhoods tend to concentrate almost totally on their prime objective, which they perceive to be difficult enough. They aim "to create a home and community that they can control, with problems they can solve, and issues on which they can reach consensus." [20]

New Social Forms

More than 30 years ago, sociologist Daniel Bell observed that "the increasing centralization of government creates a need for new social forms that will allow the citizenry greater participation in making decisions." [21] Although Bell did not have religious conservatives in mind, they have in fact created a "new social form" by which they help to shape the political outcomes of issues they care about—issues that matter a great deal to them. They have managed to combine a compelling moral vision with a pragmatic grassroots politics.

But NEL advocates believe they possess a moral vision that is much more compelling.[22] Furthermore, as Chapters 5 and 6 have clearly shown, the NEL community would constitute a new social form. Thus, it makes sense to argue that this innovative arrangement should become a vehicle for pragmatic grassroots politics. This new social form would be a means for enabling NEL advocates to take part in shaping the political status of things they care about—issues that matter a great deal to them. Hence, it follows that members of NEL communities would be interested in achieving political clout. They would hope that eventually they too might be able to achieve a "seat at the table" of mainstream politics. Analyst Ellen Willis argues that reinventing family and gaining political clout are two sides of the same coin: How can citizens, she asks, "wrest from the corporations power over economic and political decision making?" And how can "family . . . be reinvented in a world of gender equality?"[23] According to Willis, citizens must figure out how to get more control over economics and politics, *and* they must figure out how to reinvent family. Because the NEL community would aim to reinvent family by empowering adults and children, it would be in a strategic position to gain political empowerment as well. The members' objective would be to get more citizen control over a range of political and economic issues about which they care very deeply.

Sometimes ordinary citizens can and do influence government, principally by joining one or more among hundreds of special interest organizations. For example, in the mid-1940s, citizens belonging to the American Legion successfully lobbied Congress for approval of the G.I. Bill (described in Chapter 2). And today, citizens belonging to the American Association of Retired Persons lobby Congress for the protection of programs (e.g., Medicare and social security) that are beneficial to them. In 1993, the National Parenting Association was organized as a "nonprofit, non-partisan organization."[24] One of its political aims is to lobby federal and state governments on the behalf of parents. In short, it has now become obvious that citizens who do not belong to any special interest organizations run the risk of having no inputs at all into the shaping of public policy. Even citizens who do belong to such organizations may discover that they are sometimes outclassed by persons and/or associations that are able to give inordinately huge sums of money directly to elected officials.[25] Because of these and related circumstances, some political scientists have concluded that large numbers of ordinary Americans have become extraordinarily alienated from, and indifferent to, politics.[26] One indicator of political apathy in the United States is the observed long-term trend toward lower and lower voter turnouts.[27] Many citizens fail to vote because they feel politically powerless. Others vote out of a vague sense of patriotic duty, but not because they are convinced that voting will make any difference at all in the way things actually turn out.

The NEL community could offer a means for members to become actively involved in helping to decide issues that matter to them. Although community members might learn from the religious right in terms of grass-roots organization, the two sets of political visions differ drastically. Members of the religious right seek to recapture and restore features from the past. They seek to limit freedoms and to impose their view of what is right on the rest of society. Their aims involve, in Giddens's words, "tradition defended in the traditional way." Insight into the backward-looking essence of their vision can be gleaned from a 1998 pronouncement of the Southern Baptist Convention. Southern Baptists make up the largest Protestant denomination in the United States as well as one of the most influential forces within the religious right. At the 1998 convention, the Southern Baptist leadership declared that "a wife is to submit graciously to the servant leadership of her husband even as the church willingly submits to the headship of Christ." [28] At the same time, convention delegates overwhelmingly rejected an amendment that "would have had husbands and wives submit to each other." Another rejected amendment would have included "widows, widowers, and single persons as expressions of 'family.' " [29]

GRAFTING THE POLITICS OF CLASS
ONTO THE POLITICS OF GENDER

By contrast, the forward-looking NEL political vision would seek to expand both freedoms and responsibilities. Chapters 5 and 6 showed how NEL would recast the politics of gender at the community level. But what about gender politics beyond the neighborhood? And what about the politics of social class both within and beyond the community? American feminists have long sought to blunt the perennial criticism that their movement appeals mostly to women who are white and relatively privileged. Despite the movement's best efforts, working-class and lower-class women (white, black, Latina) tend to be underrepresented in its ranks. Could the NEL community somehow expand its feminist vision to take into account the interests of households that are less economically advantaged?

An Example From Cohousing

Although today's cohousing communities are not politically active and are made up largely of white, middle-class persons, there is at least one example of an innovative strategy that NEL communities might adapt and refine for their own long-range purposes. Dorit Fromm describes how one cohousing community—Santa Rosa Creek Commons, in Santa Rosa, California—actually attempted to incorporate an economically challenged household. From its inception, Santa Rosa Creek Commons was committed to the goal of diversity in terms of social class, age, household composition, and the physically challenged: "We like diversity. It makes things interesting," said one resident.[30] Nevertheless, "to appreciate diversity requires not only tolerance but a certain acceptance of conflict. . . . Perhaps the most difficult has been deciding how much the community can tolerate and how much conflict is too much." [31]

In 1982, Santa Rosa accepted a family of seven into one of the community's "low-income three-bedroom apartments." Unexpectedly, the family's five children, says Fromm, "proved to be quite overwhelming to families of only one or two children." Next, the new family ignored neighborhood norms regarding the appearance of the space surrounding their own dwelling. As one resident told Fromm, "They didn't cut the grass, they didn't weed, they hung out their wet mops and boxes of things outdoors." As a result of both types of issues, "a few members wanted to evict these tenants. A great deal of effort, and a number of years, was spent on resolving conflicts with this family." [32] Eventually, it became clear that the conflicts could not be resolved. Hence, in 1988, the "family moved into a subsidized four-bedroom house in a nearby town." Fromm reports that during their 6 years of residence in Santa Rosa, this family inflicted a great deal of damage on their dwelling unit. Some of the costs of repairing the unit were "deducted from the family's share value before it was returned to them." [33] Additional costs were covered by the community's reserve funds. Despite the community members' disappointment over the problems with this family, they were in other cases more successful in achieving their goal of diversity: "Some of the low-income members are among the most responsible contributors to the life of the community." [34]

The middle-class Santa Rosa residents were by no means wealthy. They had risked their own limited financial resources to construct and maintain the spatial features of their neighborhood. Furthermore, Fromm's statement that the five low-income children "overwhelmed" the community's middle-class children suggests an additional risk element. The middle-class parents apparently perceived that, to a certain extent, they were "risking" their children as well. Nevertheless, despite both risks, the parents were willing to continue to bring challenged households into their community. The Santa Rosa residents assumed full responsibility and risk for what they were doing. They neither asked for nor received any federal, state, or county resources.

Why Should We Care for Each Other?

Chapter 5 noted that the decline of the welfare state was one of the factors that led to the idea of constructing innovative social and spatial arrangements such as NEL communities. Chapter 3 presented discussion of the 1996 Welfare Reform Act and its potential implications for poor women and their children. The decline of government responsibility for economically disadvantaged citizens has disquieted a number of public policy analysts on both sides of the Atlantic.[35] Hugh Heclo, for instance, has remarked that many middle-class citizens are asking, "Why should we care for each other? Why should I not just live as I like?" [36] Increasingly, middle-class citizens are coming to recognize the vulnerability of their own position in the unpredictable information age. Consequently, as they and their children struggle to survive in the global marketplace, they wonder why they should worry about those who seem to be less well-off.

Today, the fragility of dyadic love relationships, the stresses of parenting, and the desire to become and remain economically autonomous per-
meate the middle, working, and lower classes alike. The sense of job stability
and security enjoyed by middle-class American men throughout the post-
World War II era now seems ephemeral, even for the better educated. And
so does the expectation of marital permanence that came with it. Because
most Americans share these and related anxieties, it is in the best interests
of all of us to figure out the most effective means to address the relentless
spread of both external and manufactured risk. Despite our common interests, is it not so that advantaged citizens want to protect what they have?
And is it not the case that disadvantaged citizens want a piece of what the
advantaged already have? The answer to both questions, obviously, is
yes.[37] But simply leaving it at that highlights the impasse in which we find
ourselves today. Programs for the disadvantaged are being downsized for
a variety of reasons. One is that middle-class citizens perceive (rightly or
wrongly) that their resources are being drained to maintain such programs.
They feel that little is being done to help those in the middle class to cope
with the anxieties, uncertainties, and insecurities of the postindustrial,
information age.

A Moral Problem

These perplexing issues have led Heclo to conclude that the "emerging
debate [over families from all social classes] is not simply about a policy
problem." It is instead "about a moral problem." [38] The ultimate puzzle is,
he says, "What is the right thing we should want to be?" The puzzle would
be solved, Heclo tells us, if we could somehow re-create, as Vannorsdall
says, "a sense . . . that we need one another . . . [to engage in] a giving and
receiving activity which is appropriate to what I am as a human being." [39]
Although these are lofty sentiments indeed, Heclo offers no clue as to how
or why middle-class and disadvantaged citizens might engage in those sorts
of giving-and-receiving patterns. Chapter 6, however, offered a clue: Mutual help patterns in the form of shared obligations called social capital
would be integral to the NEL community.

POSITIVE WELFARE

Consequently, each NEL neighborhood could, as part of its mission statement, seek to bring a limited number of less advantaged households into its orbit, including the production of social and human capital. At first, the community members would have to take this critical step on their own, as did the residents of Santa Rosa Creek Commons. Later on, however, the NEL community could aim to do this in partnership with the government. Such a joint venture, or partnership, would be an example of what Giddens calls "positive welfare" (principle 5 in Chapter 1).

A Lifestyle Alliance

Giddens explains positive welfare by asking, "Why not suppose that welfare programmes should be directed at the affluent as well as those in more deprived circumstances?" [40] Although, as noted in Chapters 2 and 3, the government has supplied certain benefits (e.g., social security, Medicare, the G.I. Bill) to advantaged persons, Giddens has something far more radical than that in mind. He advocates a new "lifestyle pact between the affluent and the poor":

> Its motivating forces would be the acceptance of *mutual* responsibility for tackling the "bads" [e.g., environmental degradation] which development has brought in its train; the desirability of lifestyle change on the part of *both* the privileged and the less privileged; and a *wide notion* of welfare, taking the concept away from economic provision for the deprived towards the fostering of the [autonomous] self.[41]

Giddens is well aware that it is quite revolutionary to ask advantaged and disadvantaged citizens to establish any sort of lifestyle alliance. To do so requires that we "reconfigure the foundations of politics and society." [42] Nevertheless, he believes that the time is ripe for public policies that encourage advantaged and disadvantaged citizens alike to take the risks of forming such an alliance, and to assume personal responsibility for doing so. The government's obligation would be to help structure the nature of those risks, and then to assist and undergird citizens as they assume them. As part of its new obligation, the government would participate in constructing ways for citizens to be rewarded for their risk taking and personal responsibility.

Giddens's ideas in no way imply that he is callous regarding the needs of the poor and the less well-off. It is obvious that citizens can never again be allowed to swing in the breeze as they were under 19th-century capitalism. Giddens leaves no doubt that there are "basic features of the welfare state [e.g., the safety net] which should be preserved against the potential ravages of cutbacks or of privatization." In the same manner, NEL advocates have never viewed their agenda as a total replacement for government responsibilities toward the disadvantaged. The NEL "approach does not eliminate basic municipal services but offers an alternative solution to the growing privatization of services and a new vision for the development of the welfare mix." [43]

The Reconstruction of Society

Giddens's conviction about the need for radical social change was expressed some years earlier by James Coleman, who said that we must engage in the "purposive reconstruction of society." [44] By that he meant, first of all, that we should aim to create multiperson arrangements that will produce social capital. To do so, they would need to operate in ways similar to those described in Chapter 6. They would require the "capacity to produce social psychological incentives . . . [such as] stigma, status, deference, and power." [45] Second, Coleman believed that these innovative social arrangements would be located midway between the macro level of government and the micro level of households. They would, in effect, be new types of neighborhoods, or communities. Third, part of their mission would be to assist persons who have needs of one kind or another: The communities would "shoulder the liabilities of dependent persons." Fourth, in order to help shoulder those liabilities, the new communities would receive financial and other kinds of "necessary resources" from government. Fifth, the new social arrangements would gain political clout: Their political "power would grow at the expense of the state, as they took over its redistributive activities." [46]

Coleman's model of the future is both similar to and different from the Santa Rosa experience. It is similar in that the members of Santa Rosa

Creek Commons tried to assist disadvantaged persons by making them part of their neighborhood production of social and human capital. Long before Giddens wrote about it, they had actually tried to establish a lifestyle alliance between mainstream and challenged citizens. Nevertheless, the Santa Rosa community neither asked for nor received any financial resources from any level of government. That was so even though it assumed some of the responsibilities generally thought to lie with government. Nor did Santa Rosa ask for or get any of the political influence that might accompany such financial resources. The community's own political power was not "growing at the expense of the state." Although Santa Rosa was forging an experimental link between everyday life and the political sphere, it was tentative, fragile, and one-sided. Santa Rosa was contributing to the interests of society and government, but in return was receiving neither resources nor political influence.

Consequently, the NEL political vision would be shaped along the lines suggested by both Giddens and Coleman. There would be a lifestyle partnership between advantaged and disadvantaged citizens, *and* there would be a partnership between government and the NEL community. As a practical matter, the politics of gender would presumably precede the politics of social class. The arrangements described in Chapters 5 and 6 would probably have to come first in time. The upshot is that social class issues would need to be grafted onto gender issues. Circumstances could change, of course, but at least in the near and intermediate future, it would seem implausible that NEL advocates could persuade government that it should participate with them in their unique approach to gender politics. If that were to be their sole agenda item, they would presumably have to pursue it apart from much if any official endorsement. The religious right would lead a vigorous charge against even the slightest hint of an official NEL-government alliance organized solely along the lines laid out in Chapters 5 and 6.

The Clanlike Federation

Currently, cohousing groups do not operate in isolation, and neither would NEL communities.[47] They would aim to construct meaningful connections across a number of NEL neighborhoods. Over time, any given geographic area might see several NEL communities become linked within some sort of loose federation. In turn, those federations might link up, and form alliances, with other NEL federations in their states and/or regions. If the NEL neighborhood by itself reinvents the enduring characteristics of an extended family, then the alliance reinvents the essential features of the clan.[48] In premodern Scotland, as well as in other places around the world, a clan consisted of a number of blood-linked extended families. Because of its size and combined wealth, the clan wields much more political (and occasionally military) muscle than any one of its extended families.[49] Hence, the image of this loose federation helps us conceive of what it might mean for NEL communities to be connected with one another.

Demonstration Programs

The immediate purpose of communities' being connected is so that they can assist one another in terms of the gender politics described in Chapters 5 and 6. Furthermore, as communities become established, they might gradually begin to experiment with programs not unlike the Santa Rosa model. Just as they would assist each other in terms of gender issues, neighborhoods would likewise help each other out with social class issues. Assuming those programs turn out to be effective, the federation would display them to the larger society as "demonstration programs." NEL advocates would make known their apparent effectiveness in addressing the interests of disadvantaged adults and children alike. A major "selling point" for these new programs is that they are not the conventional top-down dispensation of benefits.[50] They cannot be disparaged as mere "hand-outs." They are instead a grassroots effort springing from an alliance be-tween advantaged and disadvantaged citizens. They are an example of what policy analyst Paul De Sa has called the "political empowerment of the poor." [51]

Perhaps an analogy could be drawn between such efforts and the 1960s civil rights movement, which was also in large part a grassroots effort. That bottom-up movement was driven by African Americans but included the participation of many whites. Ordinary citizens (from most social classes and both races) gradually, and often painfully, moved the government toward granting the objectives of the movement in the areas of voting rights and economic opportunity. NEL communities would likewise forge alliances between middle-class citizens (white, black, Hispanic, Asian American) and less advantaged citizens. In the manner of the 1960s advocates, these new alliances would aim to influence government policies and programs. Among African Americans, NEL could, among other things, be seen as an attempt to reinvent the historic significance of fictive kin, as described in Chapter 2. In any case, as it was for the civil rights movement, the NEL agenda is empowerment, not largesse.

For example, a disadvantaged lone parent might feel that her children lack appropriate male role models and that she needs practical assistance as well as emotional support in returning to school so she can get and hold a better-paying job. The NEL community would be willing and able to make those kinds of inputs. It would be quite capable, for instance, of participating with the parent in the care of her children and in her needs for transportation regarding school and/or paid work. And it would obviously supply her and her children with first-rate housing. In return, she would be able to draw on her own unique range of capabilities, talents, and energies in order to fulfill her shared obligations to her community. As she participates in the growth of social capital, the expectation would be that her human capital would likely expand as well. Increased human capital would expedite her effective participation in education and in job situations outside the neighborhood. The ultimate outcome should be her economic self-sufficiency.

As far as this parent's children are concerned, they too would participate in the growth of social capital by becoming part of a team facilitated by a coach. Like all team members, they too would need to participate in the growth of social capital. That, in turn, should expand their own human capital, and their expanding human capital should contribute to their more effective school participation. As the children gain an ever-increasing sense of how one functions as a knowledge worker in the information era, they would become more likely later on to be capable labor force participants. It thus seems probable that they, like their mother, would be empowered to move toward economic self-sufficiency.

Bear in mind that this lone parent would be assuming a considerable degree of risk by voluntarily consenting to become part of an NEL neighborhood. The prospect of opening up the boundaries of her household in the ways described in Chapters 4, 5, and 6 would be daunting to anyone. And for challenged households, opening up their boundaries to mainstream households can be perceived as doubly threatening. Furthermore, this parent would know ahead of time that if she and her children are not eventually perceived as trustworthy members of the community, they could be asked to leave, as was the case at Santa Rosa. Policy analysts John Atlas and Peter Dreier observe that any type of collaborative neighborhood must retain this option if it is to remain viable and ongoing.[52] It must deal frankly and firmly with households perceived as "disruptive" or as free riders, that is, that fail to be responsible and trustworthy participants. Given the risks associated with such uncertainty, challenged households would need to be convinced before they join an NEL community that the incentives (gains in social and human capital resulting, hopefully, in financial capital) are indeed worthwhile.

A COMMUNITY-GOVERNMENT PARTNERSHIP

If the above-described types of demonstration programs work on a limited scale, then NEL federations might begin to advocate for community-government partnership. In the spirit of both Giddens and Coleman, NEL neighborhoods would ask the government to participate with and to support them in the refinement and expansion of those programs. NEL communities would seek government participation in the daunting task of empowering economically challenged citizens. Following both Coleman and Giddens, in exchange for the risks that mainstream households would be assuming voluntarily, the state would be asked to provide the community with incentives of some kind. Among other things, these might include guarantees of low-interest, insured loans for NEL neighborhoods, analogous to the G.I. Bill monies that fueled the expansion of post-World War II suburbia. Also included might be resources to finance the dwelling units set aside for challenged families. Those funds would be comparable to Section 8 rent supplements currently offered by the U.S. Department of Housing and Urban Development (HUD). A major difference, however, would be that the tenants would not be merely renting. Payments made on their behalf, and/or that they themselves made, would be credited toward their eventual ownership of their dwelling unit. Additional incentives might include the extension of certain tax credits to community residents and scholarships made available to community children and adults for post-secondary education—also analogous to the G.I. Bill.

Because housing is an indispensable feature of the NEL agenda, it seems likely that HUD would be the government agency with which NEL communities would have to forge their partnership, at least initially. However, for many years, HUD has been severely criticized by liberals and conservatives alike. In the wake of the 1996 Welfare Reform Act, critics have renewed their demands that HUD, too, should be reformed.[53] Upon being appointed HUD secretary in 1997, Andrew Cuomo set out to convince Congress to give HUD a "30 percent budget increase . . . to save its largest subsidized housing program for low-income people." Cuomo admitted that it would be an even harder task to change "the Department's . . . sorry image. . . . 'Known for inefficiency and ineffectiveness.' "[54] The near universal discontent with HUD adds weight to the policy objective of a fresh partnership between NEL federations and government. Any innovative program that proposes to improve significantly both the housing and the economic circumstances of disadvantaged persons would have to be viewed as more desirable than the current dismal efforts in that regard.

The Rise and Fall of HUD

Although public housing has now indeed become the "housing of last resort for the very poor—often those without jobs, skills, or hopes," it was not always so.[55] Atlas and Dreier report that in the midst of the Great Depression, public housing was simply added to an already existing jobs program. The federal government paid unemployed men to build housing just as they were building airports, roads, bridges, and beaches. Importantly, this new housing was not built for the poor. Instead, Senator Wagner, the legislation's author, declared in 1937 that it was instead for the " 'submerged middle class' . . . not the very poor with no means to pay rent. . . . There are some whom we cannot expect to serve . . . those who cannot pay the rent."[56] Nevertheless, after World War II, "recognizing the pent-up demand for housing and fearing competition from public housing . . . the real estate industry sabotaged the public housing program by pressuring Congress to limit it to the very poor."[57] In 1949, Congress succumbed entirely to this pressure, marking the "beginning of the decline of public housing." [58] A Depression-era program designed to provide temporary shelter for the "working poor and young families starting out" has now inadvertently created enclaves of "permanent housing for the very poor."

Today, those grim enclaves are inhabited largely by members of minority groups, by the destitute elderly, and by lone mothers and their children, many of whom up until recently had been receiving welfare and other government subsidies. Because they are virtually isolated from surrounding private housing, the enclaves effectively segregate their residents (many of whom are African American) from other citizens: "The look of public housing, cheap and proud of it, contributed to the isolation of its residents. . . . The program stigmatized 'government housing,' rendering it unattractive to even the lower middle class." [59] Furthermore, what makes living in these public housing projects totally undesirable to all responsible citizens, including the vast majority of their own residents, is the fact that the "projects have become the playgrounds for drug-dealing predators . . . [and] symbols of lawlessness." [60] However, Atlas and Dreier report that this was not always the case. Until the 1960s, housing developments "were places of almost excessive law and order." Project managers were "despots" who could be either benign or tyrannical. All too often they were cruel and unjust, and imposed a "vicious order" on residents, stemming from the managers' power to evict tenants without due process.[61]

But in the late 1960s, civil rights and civil liberties advocates forced HUD to change its procedures, thus ending project managers' capricious and dictatorial power over residents. Unfortunately, managerial despotism was not replaced by neighborhood democracy: "Neither were they viable, self-governing communities, nor were they any longer governed by an externally imposed set of norms." [62] The upshot was that because disruptive residents could not be disciplined, residents who could do so moved out, and "law-abiding tenants without other options became demoralized." [63]

Tenant Empowerment

In an effort to resolve that problem, in 1989 President George Bush, at the urging of his HUD secretary, Jack Kemp, made " 'tenant empowerment' the centerpiece of his agenda." [64] Empowerment had two related facets—neighborhood control and home ownership. First, the residents would govern themselves in an "effort to restore order [including the authority to evict disruptive tenants] and a sense of community." Next, opportunities would be provided for tenants to "purchase their complexes as resident-owned cooperatives." Unfortunately, Kemp's goal of empowerment met with only slight success, in part because of limited funding, but also because many local HUD officials seemed content with the status quo. Those local operatives appeared loath to give up the degree of control they retained over the lives of their residents.[65]

Atlas and Dreier are keenly aware that "resident management and ownership are not panaceas for poverty," but their argument is that if residents are able to invent their own physical spaces and household connections, then "self-reliance replaces dependency. Residents stop being victims." [66] As Atlas and Dreier see it, gaining even a small amount of spatial and social empowerment adds to residents' self-esteem, and that could result in their finding a greater degree of courage to participate more effectively in whatever job training and/or employment opportunities might be available.

To take another example, analyst Mary Davis did a study of mothers receiving AFDC (welfare benefits). She wanted to learn why, among those mothers, some were more successful than others in getting and holding jobs.[67] Davis found that mothers are hindered from participating in job training and in the labor force by the social and spatial environment of HUD projects. She also learned that two factors helped them to overcome that hindrance and to achieve job success. First, mothers who took part in a program that moved them from Chicago's black ghetto into a predominantly white neighborhood were more successful than mothers who continued to reside in the ghetto. Second, mothers who moved and then joined a support network that assisted them in job searches and in neighborhood functioning were more successful in getting and holding jobs than were comparable mothers who did not join a support group. In sum, by entering a new spatial environment, the successful mothers were, in effect, "producing space." That space also included a new social environment (their support group). By producing, or reinventing, both their spatial and their social milieu, they eventually became more effective in "producing income."

Producing Space and Income:
The Example of the G.I. Bill

Consequently, when Atlas and Dreier ask "where to break into the circle" of economic disadvantage and corrosive neighborhoods, they imply the answer to their own question.[68] Instead of trying to break in *either* at the point of producing income or at the point of producing space, why not try to do both at the same time? Why not, in the manner of the G.I. Bill, aim to empower citizens across both dimensions simultaneously? Chapter 2 showed that for millions of veterans, the capability to afford suburban lots and houses, and thus to "produce space," was a direct result of government subsidies for education and mortgages. Keep in mind that veterans were in no way perceived as the recipients of charity or "government handouts." [69] Not only was it perceived as moral to repay veterans for their inputs to society, it was also seen to be in the nation's best interest. A well-educated, and employed, populace was thus able to "produce income." That money enabled the recipients of the benefits to pay off their mortgage loans and to help grow the national economy in a number of ways.

In part, the G.I. Bill is an illustration of what Giddens seems to have in mind.[70] The federal government invented the conditions that encouraged citizens' risk taking. Hundreds of thousands of veterans were the first of their kin ever to dare take the precarious step of going to college, and/or to assume a mortgage. However, the government guaranteed neither that they would graduate from college nor that they would be able to find and hold good jobs. Nevertheless, it did bolster them while they were in school and also while they made their mortgage payments. In effect, government rewarded them for their adventuresomeness. Plainly, their spatial control could not have existed apart from their economic control. But by the same token, producing space gave meaning and impetus to producing income. Indeed, it is difficult if not impossible to separate the two symbols of empowerment. The G.I. Bill was driven by a coherent set of ideals that, among others, included the simple notion that "producing space" and "producing income" are integral to one another. It was sold to Congress and the public as a way to give substance to the American Dream by enabling veterans to gain control over the economic segment of life and control over its spatial features—both at the same time.

That identical objective would, of course, be a major selling point for an NEL community-government partnership. NEL supplies a structural setting for disadvantaged citizens to produce space *and* income at the same time. "Producing space" means that those citizens would have a financial stake in, and thus be responsible for, the physical and material features of their neighborhood.[71] They would exercise their responsibilities by participating fully in the growth of the community's social capital. In turn, their participation would contribute toward the development of their own human capital, which, in its turn, should eventually result in financial capital. In effect, they would be "producing income," leading, one would hope, toward economic self-sufficiency.

Furthermore, that manner of community participation should also contribute toward the citizens' own sense of political empowerment. *Empowerment* in this sense simply means political influence, or clout. It implies that a group is able to accomplish things that matter to the group as a whole, and thus to the individuals who make up the group. Empowerment signifies that a group and its members are not merely the objects of largesse, patronage, or handouts. Instead, they are able to negotiate with external entities (whether political, economic, or educational) for their own interests. As a result, members derive a sense of political empowerment by virtue of belonging to a group that possesses a degree of political clout.

WIDENING THE POLITICAL AGENDA

Social scientist Alan Walker has warned that the concept of the collaborative neighborhood is *not* a "panacea for all of the difficulties of the welfare state." [72] It goes without saying that in order to facilitate community interests, both in terms of gender and in terms of social class, the NEL federations must establish a set of political objectives that go beyond neighborhood boundaries. The above-described partnership with government is one such major objective. Furthermore, the well-being of girls and boys, women and men, and younger and older persons, as well as disadvantaged and advantaged citizens, requires that the federations try to bring about additional kinds of changes in the society that surrounds them.

The Public Schools

To take but one example, the wider social and political agenda of the NEL federations would necessarily target the public schools. Their long-term commitments and any political clout would lie on the side of those critics who currently argue that the public schools in the United States, along with the public colleges and universities, are not simply in need of reforms.[73] Instead, the entire educational system must be thoroughly over-hauled, reinvented, and restructured. Girls and boys from the middle, working, and lower classes alike are not adequately educated for the information age unless they become critical thinkers. Hence, the reinvented public schools would complement, and significantly extend, the efforts of the reinvented community to produce knowledge workers.

Economic Opportunities

As knowledge workers are being produced by the reinvented communities and schools, the obvious question becomes, Where would they find employment, and/or how would they become entrepreneurs? (See the discussion of the "telecottage" below.) We have learned that the postindustrial, information age is characterized by the disappearance of many kinds of jobs familiar to the industrial era. If well-educated and highly gifted persons are not exempt from the sorts of external risks imposed by these new economic realities, what about persons who are less educated and less gifted?[74] Plainly, part of the NEL federations' broader agenda would be to participate with government and the private sector in facilitating economic opportunities of all sorts. The federations, for example, might become major players in local and regional efforts to attract and hold businesses that offer a wide range of job opportunities and yet are sensitive to issues of sustainability.

Sustainability

As noted in Chapter 4, ever since the inception of cohousing, its advocates have been concerned with "green" issues. The reasoning behind the design of cohousing and NEL spatial features is not simply that greater physical proximity is likely to increase socializing, and thus enhance community bonding, as vital as that goal is. Nor are the design features meant merely to symbolize a particular vision of community, as crucial as that is. Cohousing advocates believe passionately that the overall design of cohousing communities is much more ecologically sound than the unending sprawl of today's typical suburban neighborhoods. Aside from their design, cohousing communities tend to restrict themselves to the use of "green" building materials, that is, materials that do as little damage as possible to the natural environment.[75]

Giddens believes that environmental and ecological issues are essential to his new radical center politics.[76] His rationale is that, regardless of social class standing, the best interests of children and adults of all ages demand that we pay careful attention to such matters as global warming, population control, and the quality of air, water, and soil. The well-being of people requires, moreover, that we seek to preserve irreplaceable resources such as the tropical rain forest. Fears that an "industrializing world would outgrow its resources" have been around for more than a hundred years.[77] However, the rapid spread of the global economy now makes those anxieties more salient. Latin America, Asia, and parts of Africa have now joined the West in, among other things, polluting waterways and depleting the ozone layer. A series of international conferences has been held to address possible ways to slow environmental damage, but the results have been mixed. Hence, Giddens argues that a comprehensive social policy must address the vital issue of global sustainability. Although at first glance it may seem odd to make sustainability a part of family policy, on reflection it makes perfect sense. After all, the quality of family life is significantly affected by the health of the proximate ecological environment—and increasingly, proximate means worldwide.

Consequently, the broader NEL political agenda would seek to enhance citizen participation in devising ways to sustain the natural environment on a global scale. Included in that agenda would be the related issue of revitalizing the urban areas of the United States.[78] NEL neighborhoods could be sited within densely populated cities as well as in less populous areas. But wherever they are located, NEL advocates would reach beyond their boundaries, aiming to bring about public policies and programs that would contribute to the sustainability of our local and global, natural and physical environments. Chapter 6 indicated that NEL children and youth would be a vital part of gender politics at the neighborhood level. They would, in addition, be encouraged to participate in addressing some of the wider political issues just described—issues of social class, education, employment opportunities, and the natural environment. For several decades, questions of sustainability have captured the imaginations of many children and youth. Once an NEL federation establishes a sustainability agenda, there is every reason to expect that NEL children would find it to be a particularly appealing realm in which to become politically active.

NEIGHBORHOOD PRODUCTION OF FINANCIAL CAPITAL

The Teleneighborhood

Thus far, we have assumed that "shouldering the liabilities of dependent persons" follows a prescribed logic. The reasoning has been that the ultimate NEL goal is to empower each community member to function outside the neighborhood and within the societal marketplace. A complementary logic is offered by NEL advocates Lisa Horelli and Kirsti Vespa.[79] They suggest that certain NEL communities might perhaps opt for producing financial capital internally. They point to the fact that highly sophisticated technologies (e.g., computer, modem, fax, the Internet) currently enable some people to do some or all of their economically productive work at home. Whether self-employed or employed by others, some people are now able to spend a considerable portion of their workweeks doing what writer Michael Pollan calls "living at the office." [80] Indeed, working at home has become so much a part of today's labor force that at least one large corporation has established a "telecommuting simulation lab." The lab's aim is to "teach people to work at home" in ways that allow them the "flexibility and support they are demanding, while addressing bosses' concerns about productivity, liability, and fairness." [81]

In any case, the prevailing image of the home workplace is currently limited almost exclusively to the confines of the individual's own household. Horelli and Vespa submit, however, that the image of the home workplace could be enlarged within the context of the New Everyday Life.

Some NEL neighborhoods, in cooperation with their federations, might opt to invent themselves as what Horelli and Vespa call a "telecottage" or "telecommunity." [82] Historically, most collaborative communities have engaged in joint economic activities, such as agriculture.[83] However, today's and tomorrow's technologies challenge us to stretch our creative imaginations into uncharted territory, especially when it comes to community entrepreneurship.

Let's say, for example, that a group of persons from some half dozen nonconnected households currently own and operate a small firm that assists companies in finding hardware and software solutions. At a certain point in the firm's development, the entrepreneurs realize they need to expand, including the hiring of additional employees. At the same time, they are fascinated by the idea of working where they reside, particularly if any of them have or contemplate having children and/or they resent lengthy and tedious commutes. These entrepreneurs might wish to form an NEL teleneighborhood. Consequently, their proposed alliance with government would need to comprise a range of features not found in the more typical NEL arrangement. For example, their alliance might contain the idea of identifying economically challenged persons who have the inclination and the potential to become a part of their company. Those persons would then be offered the opportunity to join the neighborhood and also the company. In order to fulfill those twin objectives, the telecommunity would require both business loans and housing/neighborhood loans. The loans might help the community build needed spaces for its economic activities, in addition to the kinds of common spaces required by every NEL neighborhood. Community members would, of course, have the option not to work for the company, and employees might choose to live off-site.

Perils and Pitfalls

One can immediately foresee all kinds of perplexing difficulties with this attempt, or indeed with any attempt, to make economic productivity a part of the New Everyday Life. What, for instance, would be the range of problems connected with living in the same closely bound neighborhood as one's coworkers? Would cleavages arise between community members who are part of the company and those who are not? Plainly, there cannot be any simple way to invent an NEL community that also includes a certain level of economic interdependence across some of its households. Nevertheless, we know far too little about the coming metamorphoses, either of technology or of the Third Wave, to predict with any degree of certainty that economic productivity could not become a viable feature of at least some connected neighborhoods.

The Not-for-Profit Partnership

The previous example of for-profit entrepreneurship is one way the NEL neighborhood might, in concert with its federation, form a partnership with government enabling some members to produce financial capital within the community's boundaries. A different option is the not-for-profit partnership with government. This kind of partnership would aim to empower citizens who have "special needs," that is, those who are challenged in ways other than economic. They might be persons with certain physical and/or developmental (mental and emotional) disabilities. Other examples might include persons with substance addiction, predelinquent youth, foster children, or women and/or children currently living in abusive situations.

Currently, national and state governments spend huge sums of money "helping" similarly challenged persons in these and other categories. However, a number of critics argue that instead of assistance or protection, the principal focus of public policy should be on the *empowerment* of challenged persons.[84] For instance, the whole thrust of the 1990 Americans with Disabilities Act (ADA) was to undermine the public perception that challenged persons are "victims" deserving of pity and requiring our help.[85] Rather than charity and largesse, most challenged persons want empowerment, and for the same reasons as those who are economically disadvantaged.

To take an example, let us say that a number of professionals are trained in the problems of persons with certain kinds of physical disabilities. They would like to form an innovative facility to empower those persons as fully as possible. The NEL neighborhood would offer them (like the entrepreneurs) the option of residing where they work. Hence, within the context of their community and its federation, the professionals would form a not-for-profit partnership with government. For its part, the government would supply a range of incentives and resources necessary to help the professionals carry out their mission. Resources might include salaries for the professionals and coverage of the costs of spaces needed for their work. As above, incentives might also include low-interest loans for constructing the more typical NEL community spaces. The long-range objective for the persons with disabilities would be the same as for persons who are economically challenged—have them (and any children they may have) participate in the production of neighborhood social and human capital so that they can move toward ultimate economic self-sufficiency.

For certain categories of challenged persons, it might be quite realistic to assume that they could eventually participate fully in the growth of social and human capital, and then later on become self-sufficient. Such persons might include adults with relatively mild disabilities, adults with substance addictions, and previously abused women. Children and youth, whether previously abused, predelinquent, or under foster jurisdiction, could participate in the growth of social and human capital, but obviously could not be expected to be self-sufficient. However, for persons with severe disabilities, it may be a long time if ever before self-sufficiency could be realized.

Consequently, a pivotal issue facing the community would be how much latitude to grant challenged members who are not able to participate as fully as others in the production of social capital. Among other things, that might require the community to think about creative ways of enlarging the implications of social capital, or the meanings of contributions to their neighborhood. For example, the simple presence of certain disabled persons clearly facilitates both the image and reality of diversity, including the inherent enrichment that accompanies it. Furthermore, the presence of disabled persons offers a unique opportunity for the neighborhood's children. It gives them the chance to make community inputs by serving persons who themselves might be able to give little in return.

Moving Toward Empowerment

As in the case of the entrepreneurship, the notion of the NEL forming a not-for-profit partnership with government in order to address persons with special needs is fraught with perils of every kind. Nevertheless, there is at present a deep discontent with most types of existing arrangements for challenged persons, whether their needs be physical or developmental. Comparable discontent abounds regarding programs for persons with substance addiction, for predelinquent youth, for foster children, and for abused women and/or children. In all of these areas, advocates now contend that public policy should move from assistance to empowerment. Accordingly, the NEL community would offer a structural context within which to try to empower varied categories of challenged persons. The foundational commitment of NEL is empowerment—of women, children, and men in general. Based on that foundation, the NEL community would propose a partnership with government in order to facilitate the empowerment, first, of economically challenged persons. In most cases, they would likely achieve financial capital outside their community. But some might possibly have the chance to do so internally. Likewise, in the case of persons with special needs, the typical goal would be for them to achieve self-sufficiency, and thus empowerment, via means outside their community. Some might not be able to do that. If so, their neighborhood might possess both the structure (social and spatial) and the resources to give them the chance to contribute whatever they can.

A DEPARTMENT OF COMMUNITY DEVELOPMENT

In the spring of 1997, President Bill Clinton, retired general Colin Powell, and numerous other dignitaries sponsored a highly publicized series of rallies in several cities urging the "rebuilding of community in America." [86] The media aside, their lofty call to rebuild community went largely unnoticed, receiving little more than a national yawn. Most citizens had no idea what they were talking about. Clinton's "call for community," though admirable, was so vague and abstract that hardly anyone got very excited about it.

Imagine that Mr. Clinton had instead made a specific recommendation to reinvent the Department of Housing and Urban Development. Assume he had proposed that we now call it the Department of *Community* Development. Suppose he had added that "societies can no longer . . . be adequately understood [merely] in terms of the individual and society." [87] He might have asserted that a middle layer of society, bridging government with its people, must somehow be constructed. Imagine that he had justified his proposals by saying that the middle layer of our globalized, posttraditional society is so vital to the well-being of our nation and its citizens that, as we move into the 21st century, we must begin to experiment with ways to reinvent it.

Mr. Clinton might have gone on to say that, currently, there are agencies at the federal and state levels representing a wide range of special interests. Those interests include, but are not limited to, real estate and other business ventures, labor, education, medicine, the military, and agriculture. But there is no national department that addresses the everyday interests of citizens within their neighborhoods.[88] Accordingly, he might have proposed that representing citizens' everyday interests would be the mission of the Department of Community Development. The new department would lead us in "reassessing the criteria that define civic interest, public responsibility, political rights, and citizenship." [89]

If Mr. Clinton had in fact made those sorts of proposals, he would surely have stirred a lot of excitement—both negative and positive. He would have also expressed yet another long-range political objective of the New Everyday Life. As NEL advocates would see it, this new department would obviously retain a number of HUD's current functions, such as the enforcement of fair housing and fair lending laws. But in addition, it would be the official agency with which communities could form partnerships for the benefit of citizens and society alike. The new department would help spell out the specific features of alliances between communities and government, and between advantaged and disadvantaged citizens. It would monitor the risks, responsibilities, resources, and rewards for all parties concerned. It would guard against the potential exploitation of all citizens participating in those communities—especially those challenged in any way, as well as children and older persons.

By no means would the new department endorse the NEL model alone. As the information age unfolds, other equally or perhaps more compelling models might evolve. The globalized, posttraditional, information era is far too much of an enigma to presume that there could be merely one strategy to empower persons, families, and communities. As NEL advocates see it, the specific model is less vital than the overall idea of creating a structural mechanism—midway between the individual and society—for the purpose of citizen empowerment. The New Everyday Life may be thought of as a stimulant for discussion and debate about ways that might somehow make the private political. Once we grant the assumption that mainstream and disadvantaged persons alike should be able to design their own families and communities, the question then becomes, How do they do it? If empowerment is the central issue, how is it accomplished?

CONCLUSION

In recent decades, members of the religious right have been able to combine their moral vision with a pragmatic grassroots politics that now influences all levels of government. NEL advocates likewise possess a compelling moral vision, and they too would seek a seat at the table of mainstream politics. They would do so by grafting the politics of social class onto the politics of gender. The magnitude of such a task has been captured by Coleman in his writing about "reconstructing" society. Giddens uses equally remarkable language when he refers to "reconfiguring the foundations of politics and society." A central tenet of his approach is a "lifestyle pact" between mainstream persons and those who are challenged in one way or another. The NEL neighborhood and its federation would supply a structural setting for that type of alliance. That alliance, furthermore, would occur within the context of a partnership between the community and government.

Prior chapters discussed five of the six principles of the "new family policy" outlined in Chapter 1. Chapter 7 blends the principle of "positive welfare" into the other five. Taken together, all six principles expedite the objective of "responsible decision making" that Giddens says must lie at the core of positive welfare. Besides enabling persons to bear the consequences of external risk, positive welfare would presumably help persons from all social classes to assume their manufactured risks in a responsible, or accountable, manner.

Alongside forging both a lifestyle alliance and its contextual partnership, the NEL would seek additional social and political objectives external to the community. Among those would be the restructuring of the public schools so that children's mastery of the skills and capabilities of critical thinking becomes their major objective, regardless of gender or social class background. Another goal would be the creation of employment opportunities for an expanding base of knowledge workers. Occasionally, it might be possible for the community to function as a teleneighborhood, thus providing on-site economic opportunities. A related possibility is for the community to form not-for-profit partnerships with government to address the interests of citizens with "special needs." Yet another vital goal of the NEL federation is the matter of ecological sustainability. Another comprehensive objective would be to help create a Department of *Community* Development to replace the current Department of Housing and Urban Development. The new department's mission would be to work on behalf of the best interests of citizens within their community contexts. It would serve as the bridge between the larger political and economic forces of society and the well-being of connected households.

8

CONCLUSION:
THE REVOLUTION
THAT NEVER ENDS

◆◆◆————————————————————————————

Despite its many virtues, the rise in the West of the individualistic, nuclear, child-oriented family which is the sole outlet of both sexual and affective bonding is thus by no means always an unmixed blessing. This [new family style] is no more permanent a phenomenon than were the economic ties of property and interest that united families in the past, even if this is the rough general direction in which Western society has been moving over the last three hundred years.[1]

Historian Lawrence Stone helps us see that the social patterns we call families never stand still. It is hard for us to imagine that what we now experience did not always exist. And it is perhaps even more difficult to picture ourselves in motion. We ourselves are now in the process of constructing families that are not mere copies of our parents'—much less our grandparents'—families. We are doing so for a variety of reasons. The fundamental one is that the nonconnected nuclear family style is not an "unmixed blessing." It has many built-in flaws, which have been the focus of this entire book. Current attempts to repair its defects are part of why Stone says that it is "no more permanent a phenomenon" than the connected family style that preceded it.

211

What is more, even if we were to manage somehow to create an innovative family style such as the New Everyday Life, that would not end the revolution once and for all (even though the title of Part II of this book implies that it might). All it would do would be to put in place a style of family that is different from the one we are now familiar with. However, that too would be a mixed blessing. It too would have its own set of flaws (some have been noted in Part II) that, invariably, people would try to fix. The new family style would thus turn out to be no more permanent than the styles that went before. In short, the family revolution never really ends. It is a work in constant progress.

And the principal reason it is ceaseless is that the revolution reflects struggle—the battle to be emancipated from the domination of others. First, it was the nuclear family (husband, wife, children) seeking freedom from the unwanted control of blood kin. In the West, at least, that is now pretty much an accomplished fact. It is analogous to the independence that the United States wrested from England in the 1780s. That was and is an unquestioned reality. But ever since that time, citizens inside the United States have been struggling for greater freedom. Those who have struggled include less-advantaged white men, women, blacks, and immigrants—first European and now Latino and Asian. Because of their past, present, and future battles to participate in the American Dream, our democracy is in continual flux, or nonviolent revolution.[2]

Similarly, although the nuclear family has been liberated from kin domination, a great deal of struggle has been occurring inside the family itself. The principal battle, of course, is between women and men. This ancient struggle predates the nuclear family's liberation and will persist no matter what styles of family the citizens of the 21st century somehow manage to devise. More recently, the issue of children's freedom has also loomed into view, and it is not at all clear how children's quest for empowerment might evolve throughout the 21st century and beyond.[3]

This book has focused principally on women's efforts to emancipate themselves from the domination of men. Their efforts began in earnest during the early 1800s. The foremost feminist goal—women's right to vote—was finally achieved in 1920 with the ratification of the 19th amendment to the U.S. Constitution. Nevertheless, at the same time, the freedom of married women to choose their own way was being severely restricted.

By the 1950s, the roles of Good Wife and Good Mother had become extremely rigid. Partly in reaction to that excessive rigidity, the feminist movement revived itself in the 1960s. Since that time, women (and their male allies) have managed to push the boundaries of gender equity in numerous and significant ways. Among other things, they have been able to involve government in the struggle, at least to a limited extent. Government, for example, is now viewed as the guarantor of women's educational and occupational opportunities, and also as the source of certain programs aimed at facilitating parenting responsibilities (e.g., child care, family leave, medical benefits). However, in the 1970s feminist efforts to get the Equal Rights Amendment ratified by two thirds of the states were stymied.[4] The source of this frustration had been foreseen a decade earlier by Margaret Mead.

Mead and other critics of the nonconnected family style of the 1950s complained that society was asking the family to do "too much." The husband-wife unit, they said, was simply too small and too deficient in resources (tangible and intangible) to do everything it was supposed to do. Furthermore, Mead warned that trying to correct these deficiencies by making the family more friendly to women could lead to irresponsible actions that might threaten the well-being of children and adults alike. If that happened, she predicted, there would be a "counterrevolution." And in the 1970s, some citizens did indeed label feminist initiatives as detrimental to children and harmful to society. The result was a movement that evolved into what is now known as the religious right. It has gradually gained a "seat at the table of mainstream politics" and, for all practical purposes, has placed the gender revolution on hold.

COHOUSING

During the 1960s and 1970s, a tiny group of people, first in Scandinavia and later in Holland and North America, conceived of "cohousing" as a way to reform the family in a responsible manner. Cohousing holds no overt feminist agenda, nor is it a political action program of any kind.[5] Participants simply wish to construct neighborhoods where persons can live in their own private households and still be connected with others, both socially and spatially. They want to give resident adults the chance to develop meaningful support networks among themselves. Adults in cohousing communities supply not only emotional help but practical assistance as well, particularly by providing a healthy and wholesome environment for their community's children. Some (but not all) cohousing neighborhoods aim to fashion themselves into "fictive kin" networks, based on a strong sense of we-ness.

Cohousing is essentially a reform movement because it seeks to cushion the shocks that adults and children feel owing to the spread of both external and manufactured risk in posttraditional society.[6] *External risk* refers to those forces over which persons have no apparent control, such as the disappearance of their jobs as a result of the increasing pace of technology. *Manufactured risk* refers to choices that persons themselves make in the pursuit of individual fulfillment. These choices could address educational or occupational matters. Frequently, such choices surround the topics considered in Chapter 3—love, sexuality, and emotional intimacy. Dyadic relationships have become infinitely more complex and thus riskier than ever before—a reality captured by the unfamiliar but pertinent label *erotic friendship*. Helping to absorb the shocks of both external and manufactured risk is something that cohousing, because of its built-in support network, can do very well.

THE NEW EVERYDAY LIFE

Like cohousing, the New Everyday Life (NEL) was born in Scandinavia.[7] Moreover, NEL advocates also share the goal of constructing neighborhoods that retain household privacy, yet offer social and spatial connectedness. Although a few cohousing communities currently exist on both sides of the Atlantic, NEL is at this point simply a proposal for *future* social policy. By calling it a "Nordic Feminist Vision," its advocates move a quantum step beyond cohousing. They view NEL as a means to bring back to life the stalled gender revolution. NEL advocates differ from most present-day feminists, who have not said a great deal about any inherent contradiction between the nonconnected family style and gender equity.[8] By contrast, advocates for the New Everyday Life do perceive an incongruity between nonconnectedness and gender equity. They argue that in addition to other resources (e.g., economic self-sufficiency based on education, occupation, and income), women must also possess the resource of residing in a neighborhood that is both socially and spatially connected.[9]

NEL promises to offer a set of structural, or situational, conditions that might empower women and thus contribute to the long-term objective of gender equity. Those same conditions offer men the option to choose a style of life other than one grounded in "productivism." Men would have an opportunity to achieve a sense of moral worth through being productive by growing children's social and human capital. Children's participation in the production of social capital (their contributions to the community) would benefit women and also the children themselves.

The first step in women's empowerment would be for the NEL neighborhood to declare itself to be a *sanctuary*—a violence-free zone. Household aggression (both physical and sexual) has been largely a private matter, and so has couple decision making in general. Accordingly, the next step in women's empowerment would be for trusted friends within the community to be allowed to participate with a couple during their negotiations and conflict resolution. Finally, because the neighborhood would mark itself as a zone of productivity (thus loosening male identity from productivism), a woman could, at any point in her life course, gain greater opportunity to participate in the labor force to the extent she desires. That same opportunity would obviously be open to men as well. The upshot is that both genders would gain considerable flexibility with regard to occupational involvement as well as participation in the lives of children.

Part of this gender flexibility would stem from the diversity of household composition within any NEL neighborhood. Although some households would contain younger, married couples with children, others might consist of couples (married or cohabiting, cross-sex or same-sex) without children. Some unmarried cohabiting couples may, of course, reside with children. Other households may consist of adults residing alone. Whether partnered or alone, adults in the community might range in age from younger to midlife to older. In any event, members of child-free households would have ample opportunity to participate in the growth of the social and human capital of the community's children. That sort of neighborhood involvement in parenting requires the opening of household boundaries in a manner similar to making the couple's own relationship more permeable. Moreover, in view of their projected increases in longevity and gains in health, midlife and older persons would constitute a potentially significant pool of NEL participants. Their involvement would signal a reinvention of what it means to "retire." For example, leaving or reducing his or her paid labor may enable a man or woman to make significant contributions to, and gain esteem, status, and influence within, the life of the NEL community.

Redefining *parent* to include a degree of adult participation in the lives of "all our neighborhood's children" carries special weight for lone parents.[10] Currently, the lone parent, like the cohabitor, is viewed as someone who ought to be en route to formal marriage. Lacking that "special" status, she or he tends to be seen as a second-class parent. However, from the NEL perspective, deciding to marry chiefly because one feels the need to share parenting is both unwise and unnecessary. To be sure, the lone parent is hard-pressed to do all that she or he needs to do, but so are dual-earner parents. Having two adults in the household is by no means a necessary and sufficient mechanism for parenting. Incidentally, parents (lone or dual) who benefit from NEL community involvement with their children would in no way be free riders. They, like everyone else, would be expected to make their appropriate contributions to community well-being.

During the several millennia of the agricultural era, children participated in the growth of the social capital (shared obligations) of their families (nuclear and extended). In turn, their participation contributed significantly to their own human capital—that is, the skills and capabilities required to function in an agrarian setting. Analogously, within NEL, children's involvement in the development of neighborhood social capital would help grow their human capital. In their case, it would be the type of human capital necessary for them to function optimally within the posttraditional, information age. As community adults ("coaches" in particular) struggle with children regarding their community inputs, the aim would be to enable each child to become a knowledge worker—that is, someone who possesses the "ability to acquire and to apply theoretical and analytical knowledge.... [He or she has] a habit of continuous [lifelong] learning." [11] Saying that the child is becoming a "critical thinker" is another label for the same thing. Analogous to the agricultural era (and quite different from the industrial period), youth empowerment in the information age stems in part from the child's contributing to something larger than him- or herself.

Furthermore, alongside being a laboratory of democracy for both adults and children, the NEL neighborhood would serve as a workshop for gender equity. In that setting, children would not merely observe adults laboring to achieve equity, they would actually participate in the struggle. For a long time, feminists have sought effective ways to cultivate in children and youth both the belief in gender equity and the actions required to bring it about. Within the context of the nonconnected family style, that ambitious goal has met with only limited success. Advocates believe that the NEL community would provide a situational means for girls and boys alike to develop hands-on experience with the complexities, frustrations, and rewards of striving for gender equity.

SIX PRINCIPLES FOR FAMILY POLICY

I have placed my approach to an NEL-based family policy within the larger context of Anthony Giddens's vision for a "reconfiguring" of society in general. I have adapted the six principles that he has proposed as the foundation for his new "radical" politics. In Giddens's sense, *radical* implies nothing more sinister than going to the root of things. The NEL community would serve as a structural context for each of his six principles. Principle 1, for instance, argues for a greater balance between group responsibility and individual autonomy. Plainly, that uneasy symmetry (asked of adults and children alike) would lie at the core of every NEL neighborhood. That said, principle 2—the continued emancipation of women—is equally salient. That goal, of course, expresses the NEL feminist vision. Principles 3 and 4 are closely allied. Being able to "make things happen" is Giddens's definition of empowerment. And by *dialogic democracy,* he means the opportunity to participate effectively in the decisions at every level of society that might affect one's daily life. Accordingly, the NEL community would facilitate personal empowerment for adults and children, and also their political empowerment, as we shall see below. It would do so in part because it would be a laboratory for democratic, or dialogic, decision making. Principle 6—the direct confrontation of violence—would also be integral to the NEL community. The community's declaring itself to be sanctuary would mean that both women and children would live in a neighborhood whose explicit aim is to construct an environment free from physical and sexual aggression.

Principle 5 emerges from the striving to empower the community (and thus its members) politically. Giddens labels this "positive welfare," and it rests on what he calls a "lifestyle pact," or an alliance between advantaged and disadvantaged citizens. Although Giddens fails to supply the details of such an alliance, the NEL federation (made up of a cluster of NEL neighborhoods) would be structurally suited to make it work. In return for doing what James Coleman calls "shouldering the liabilities of dependent persons," the NEL federation would gain from the government tangible resources and a degree of political influence. The resources would be used to increase the opportunities for disadvantaged households to participate in NEL neighborhoods. NEL communities could exert influence by trying to affect further the politics of social class as well as the politics of gender.

An additional sphere of political influence might include the restructuring of the public schools in ways that would benefit children of both genders from all social classes. This would mean, among other things, that NEL supporters would align themselves with advocates who argue that in order to fit children optimally for the information age, the public schools must make critical thinking skills their centerpiece. At the same time, Giddens places sustainability of the natural environment at the core of his vision of radical politics. Sustainability has always been a concern among cohousing advocates, and would surely endure within the NEL political agenda.

PROSPECTS FOR UTOPIAN REALISM

Even more than Europeans, notes architect Dorit Fromm, Americans fear the "greater possibility of conflict within the [cohousing] group and a loss of personal freedom." [12] In a criticism of cohousing, one U.S. citizen has captured the extraordinary allure of the intricately woven social and spatial fabric of the nonconnected lifestyle: "With all its obvious drawbacks, the single house on a suburban lot allows more control over one's territory. . . . The American Dream is not just a box on a lawn. It's a chance for a small portion of creative independence." [13] In view of such powerful ideology, what are the prospects for NEL—a version of what Giddens calls "utopian realism"?

Americans crave the privacy and the liberties afforded by the nuclear family lifestyle. Given the dilemma of balancing its freedoms with, say, the potential benefits of participation in cohousing—to say nothing of the New Everyday Life—most Americans would almost always opt for the familiar. They require the independence of the nonconnected lifestyle in much the same way they demand the autonomy afforded by the automobile. Even though many roadways in and around U.S. urban areas are all too often hopelessly choked with cars, leaving their sole occupants to vegetate idly in traffic many hours per week, most Americans fiercely resist even carpooling, to say nothing of public transportation. As long as the auto is seen as an avenue to "creative independence," it will prevail. However, should conditions in the larger society continue to change, limiting the car's potential for personal freedom much more than now, it might perhaps one day become a less attractive option.[14]

Likewise, the option of participating in the New Everyday Life might become more attractive to the extent that economic and political conditions in the posttraditional, information age make the nonconnected style increasingly less attractive. First of all, if persons perceive that more creative choices are possible within a connected lifestyle than in a nonconnected lifestyle, then the connected way of life might gain enhanced credibility. If women and men—younger, midlife, and older—begin to believe that there are greater possibilities for the development of self, children, and society within than outside of NEL, then they might start to experiment with it. A second and related factor that might stimulate NEL participation would be the continued spread of both external and manufactured risk. Although external risk implies perils over which persons have no control, manufactured risk involves hazards stemming from lifestyle liberties. The NEL community might become perceived as much more able than the nonconnected style to assist persons in managing the uncertainties intrinsic to both types of risk.

The pre-Christian Greek philosopher Plato advocated collaborative communities in his *Republic,* and they have been around in one form or other since the early days of the Roman empire. Nevertheless, such arrangements "never succeeded in catching on or in dying out." [15] They have not expired because connectedness never loses its attraction as a potential means for individuals to accomplish things together that they cannot achieve on their own. Collaborative arrangements have been called the "oldest old" and the "newest new" way of trying to make life better for people. But they do not frequently catch on because, among other things, trying to be free and connected at the same time is a herculean endeavor—a virtual contradiction in terms.

Research Questions

Determining the degree to which the present-day collaborative arrangement known as cohousing is or is not actually catching on requires considerable investigation. What are the prospects for the long-term viability of cohousing? Much needs to be discovered regarding the ways in which such communities develop and then do or do not maintain themselves. The small existing body of empirical research into cohousing must be greatly enlarged.[16] For example, what about the considerable time demands placed on cohousing participants? In one recent study, some present-day workers reported that the demands of the *nonconnected* style are so intense that they actually prefer paid work over family.[17] Given that possibility, how do cohousing members balance the time demands of their own households, their employment, *and* their community? Does having a number of people around to share the burdens of one's own household help relieve the strain, and thus reduce the intensity, of being a partner and/or parent?

And how about the consequences of households moving in and out of cohousing neighborhoods? In what ways is geographic mobility a good thing because new members bring fresh ideas? In what ways is mobility negative because it hampers the development of enduring fictive kin networks? Although mobility is a pivotal issue, it is by no means valid to argue that on account of it, living a connected lifestyle must ultimately be problematic. It may be no more problematic than living a nonconnected style, although for very different reasons. It has been noted in Chapter 6 that midlife and older persons may hold the potential for becoming the stable core of the NEL neighborhood. As posttraditional society unfolds, it may be that the benefits of living in a connected style of some kind could be compelling enough not only to attract growing numbers of persons, but also to retain them in the face of competing opportunities to move.

Participatory Action Research

Social scientist William F. Whyte and his colleagues have devised a mode of research that seems well suited to the study of cohousing and, later on, of New Everyday Life communities. They call it *participatory action research* (PAR).[18] Among other things, PAR presumes an active partnership between researchers and participants aimed at achieving the goals of both parties. Analysts Chris Argyris and Donald A. Schön use the term *action science* to describe this type of approach.[19] They believe that PAR has unique capabilities. First, it can facilitate a thorough understanding of both the people and the social situation being studied. Second, PAR enables the people themselves to figure out ways to make their own lives better. Importantly, the information garnered from the study of cohousing would in turn be the basis for subsequent research into the prospects and pitfalls of establishing NEL communities. Investigations into NEL would be based on the assumptions and strategies of participatory action research.

At the same time that research into cohousing and into NEL would be continuing, efforts to explain to citizens the usefulness of NEL-based family policy would also need to be ongoing. Currently, many would likely argue that the NEL vision is unworkable. If so, then Giddens's question looms into view: "What other possibility is there?"[20] The most visible possibilities are represented by contrasting the conservative and the liberal camps.[21] However, both perspectives have been shaped by the now rapidly fading industrial age, and each is hamstrung by drawbacks that might perhaps be more fatal than any within NEL.

Almost since the nuclear family style emerged some 200 years ago, critics have fretted over its problems and flaws. Their anxiety continues today as they worry about the ebbing of past traditions and vainly look backward for solutions. Instead, we should scan the future: "The contours of the new institutions that will emerge to take the place [of the old] are still hidden in the dawn of a new century."[22] Robert Nisbet puts it this way: "The real problem is not . . . the loss of old contexts but rather the failure of our present democratic and industrial scene to create new contexts of association and moral cohesion." [23] Stephanie Coontz notes, "We need to invent new family traditions and find ways of reviving older community ones." [24] The New Everyday Life represents an attempt to fashion innovative solutions while holding the future, not the past, in view. It is in harmony with the sentiments expressed a long time ago by the English philosopher Francis Bacon: "He that will not apply new remedies must expect new evils, for time is the greatest innovator." [25]

NOTES

◆◆◆ ───────────────────────────────────

PREFACE

1. Gregory McLauchlan, "Book Review," *Contemporary Sociology* 25 (1996): 208.

2. The reinvention of families has been going on for much longer than 200 years, of course. See Lawrence Stone, *The Family, Sex, and Marriage in England 1500-1800,* abr. ed. (New York: Harper & Row, 1979); Steven Mintz and Susan Kellogg, *Domestic Revolutions: A Social History of American Family Life* (New York: Free Press, 1988).

3. Esther Dyson, George Gilder, Jay Keyworth, and Alvin Toffler, "A Magna Carta for the Knowledge Age," *New Perspectives Quarterly* 11 (1994): 26-37.

4. Anthony Giddens, *Beyond Left and Right: The Future of Radical Politics* (Stanford, CA: Stanford University Press, 1994).

5. Boyer Commission on Educating Undergraduates in the Research University, *Reinventing Undergraduate Education: A Blueprint for America's Research Universities* (New York: Carnegie Foundation, 1998), 16.

6. Henri Lefebvre, *The Production of Space,* trans. Donald Smith-Nicholson (London: Blackwell/Oxford University Press, 1991[1974]); Lynn Stewart, "Bodies, Visions, and Spatial Politics: A Review Essay on Henri Lefebvre's *The Production of Space, Environment and Planning D: Society and Space* 13 (1995): 609-18.

CHAPTER 1

1. Gregory McLauchlan, "Book Review," *Contemporary Sociology* 25 (1996): 208.

2. See Lawrence Stone, *The Family, Sex, and Marriage in England 1500-1800,* abr. ed. (New York: Harper & Row, 1979); Steven Mintz and Susan Kellogg, *Domestic Revolutions: A Social History of American Family Life* (New York: Free Press, 1988).

3. Esther Dyson, George Gilder, Jay Keyworth, and Alvin Toffler, "A Magna Carta for the Knowledge Age," *New Perspectives Quarterly* 11 (1994): 26-37.

4. Anthony Giddens, *Beyond Left and Right: The Future of Radical Politics* (Stanford, CA: Stanford University Press, 1994), 83.

5. This process has, of course, been going on for several hundred years. According to Giddens, it has finally become fully absorbed into the fabric of everyday life.

6. Giddens, *Beyond Left and Right*; Anthony Giddens, *Affluence, Poverty, and the Idea of a Post-Scarcity Society* (Geneva: United Nations Research Institute for Social Development, 1995).

7. Mintz and Kellogg, *Domestic Revolutions*.

8. See John Scanzoni, *Sexual Bargaining: Power Politics in American Marriage*, rev. ed. (Chicago: University of Chicago Press, 1982); John Scanzoni, *Sex Roles, Lifestyles and Child-bearing* (New York: Free Press, 1975): John Scanzoni, *Shaping Tomorrow's Family: Theory and Policy for the 21st Century* (Beverly Hills, CA: Sage, 1983); John Scanzoni, "Alternative Images for Public Policy: Family Structure Versus Families Struggling," *Policy Studies Review* 8 (1989): 599-609; John Scanzoni, *Contemporary Families and Relationships: Reinventing Responsibility* (New York: McGraw-Hill, 1995); John Scanzoni and William Marsiglio, "New Action Theory and Contemporary Families," *Journal of Family Issues* 14 (1993): 105-32; John Scanzoni and Maximiliane Szinovacz, *Family Decision Making: A Developmental Sex Role Model* (Beverly Hills, CA: Sage, 1980).

9. Giddens, *Beyond Left and Right*, 1.

10. Ibid.; Giddens, *Affluence, Poverty*.

11. Giddens, *Beyond Left and Right*; Giddens, *Affluence, Poverty*. See Giddens's *Beyond Left and Right* for a discussion of the several different definitions of what it means today to be "conservative" and what it means to be "liberal."

12. On this same theme of a scarcity of new public policy ideas, see Arthur Schlesinger, Jr., "The Real Roosevelt Legacy," *Newsweek,* October 14, 1996, 43; Felix Rohatyn, "What Became of My Democrats?" *New York Times,* March 31, 1995, A15.

13. Daniel Bell, "Resolving the Contradictions of Modernity and Modernism, Part II," *Society* 27 (1990): 66-75.

14. John Naisbitt, *Megatrends* (New York: Warner, 1984).

15. Arthur B. Shostak, "Book Review," *Contemporary Sociology* 27 (1998): 388.

16. Giddens, *Beyond Left and Right*, 12.

17. Margaret Mead, "The Life Cycle and Its Variations: The Division of Roles," *Daedalus* 96 (1967): 871-75.

18. Mead previewed this possibility in her 1967 essay (ibid.).

19. Giddens, *Beyond Left and Right*, 14. Although Giddens labels his second principle "life (style) politics," I believe it is more appropriately captured by the idea of women's interests.

20. One could, of course, trace the beginnings of the "modern" struggles to the 13th-century Magna Carta.

21. Hugh Heclo, "The Social Question," in *Poverty, Inequality, and the Future of Social Policy,* ed. Katherine McFate, Roger Lawson, and William Julius Wilson (New York: Russell Sage Foundation, 1995), 665-92.

22. Ibid.

23. Giddens, *Beyond Left and Right*, 15.

24. Daniel Bell, who was among the first sociologists to talk about postindustrial society, made the same point in 1967. See Daniel Bell, "The Year 2000: The Trajectory of an Idea," *Daedalus* 96 (1967): 639-51.

25. Giddens, *Beyond Left and Right*, 16.

26. See also Scanzoni, *Shaping Tomorrow's Family*; Scanzoni and Szinovacz, *Family Decision Making*.

27. Deborah D. Godwin and John Scanzoni, "Couple Consensus During Marital Joint Decision-Making: A Context, Process, Outcome Model," *Journal of Marriage and the Family* 51 (1989): 943-56; John Scanzoni and Deborah D. Godwin, "Negotiation Effectiveness and Acceptable Outcomes," *Social Psychology Quarterly* 53 (1990): 239-51.

28. Katherine McFate, "Introduction: Western States in the New World Order," in *Poverty, Inequality, and the Future of Social Policy*, ed. Katherine McFate, Roger Lawson, and William Julius Wilson (New York: Russell Sage Foundation, 1995), 22.

29. Giddens, *Beyond Left and Right*, 18.

30. Ibid., 17.

31. Matt Richtel, "At Job Fair, American Workers Say They're Worried," *New York Times*, April 20, 1998 (on-line).

32. Harry McCracken, *PC World*, November 1995, 171.

33. Giddens, *Beyond Left and Right*, 17.

34. John Scanzoni, Karen Polonko, Jay D. Teachman, and Linda Thompson, *The Sexual Bond: Rethinking Families and Close Relationships* (Newbury Park, CA: Sage, 1989).

35. On August 29, 1998, the on-line version of the *New York Times* previewed a "soon-to-be-released Census Bureau report" that found that "for the first time, the majority of 'first births'—someone's first child—were either conceived by or born to an unmarried woman. That's up from 18 percent in the 1930s."

36. Giddens, *Affluence, Poverty*, 6.

37. Giddens, *Beyond Left and Right*, 19.

38. Ibid., 242. Giddens points out, however, that although international violence may have subsided, ethnic and intranational struggles appear to be on the rise in many parts of the world.

39. See Philip Greven, *Spare the Child: The Religious Roots of Punishment* (New York: Oxford University Press, 1991); Martha Fineman and Roxanne Mykitiuk, eds., *The Public Nature of Private Violence* (New York: Routledge, 1994).

40. Giddens, *Beyond Left and Right*, 237 ff.

41. Ibid.

CHAPTER 2

1. Jan E. Dizard and Howard Gadlin, *The Minimal Family* (Amherst: University of Massachusetts Press, 1990).

2. I prefer the term *revolution* to *evolution* because the former emphasizes human agency, or choices, as part of the explanation for the changes. See Anthony Giddens, *Beyond Left and Right: The Future of Radical Politics* (Stanford, CA: Stanford University Press, 1994). The term *evolution* tends to obscure the place of agency.

3. The chapel is located within the "Cloisters" in New York City's Palisades Park.

4. Sir Banister Fletcher, *A History of Architecture*, 19th ed., ed. John Musgrove (London: Butterworth, 1987), 186-87.

5. Lawrence Stone, *The Family, Sex, and Marriage in England 1500-1800*, abr. ed. (New York: Harper & Row, 1979).

6. David Warren Sabean, *Kinship in Neckerhausen, 1700-1870* (New York: Cambridge University Press, 1998); Stephanie Coontz, *The Social Origins of Private Life: A History of American Families, 1600-1900* (New York: Verso, 1988); John Demos, *Past, Present, and Personal: Family Life and the Life Course in American History* (New York: Oxford University

Press, 1986); Wally Seccombe, *Weathering the Storm: Working Class Families From the Industrial Revolution to the Fertility Decline* (London: Verso, 1993).

7. Edward C. Banfield, *The Moral Basis of a Backward Society* (New York: Free Press, 1958), 150.

8. Willard Waller, *The Family: A Dynamic Interpretation* (New York: Dryden, 1938), 107.

9. William J. Goode, "The Theoretical Importance of Love," *American Sociological Review* 24 (1959): 38-47; William J. Goode, *World Revolution and Family Patterns* (New York: Free Press, 1963).

10. See John Boswell, *Same-Sex Unions in Premodern Europe* (New York: Villard, 1994); John D'Emilio and Estelle B. Freedman, *Intimate Matters: A History of Sexuality in America* (New York: Harper & Row, 1988); Waller, *The Family*, 120 ff. Biblical accounts of love may be found in the stories of Jacob, Ruth, and David, and love is vividly portrayed by the poetry of the Song of Songs.

11. Stone, *The Family, Sex, and Marriage*, 414.

12. Dizard and Gadlin, *The Minimal Family*, 14.

13. Ibid., 15.

14. The Industrial Revolution took root in England in the late 18th century and spread gradually to other parts of Europe and the United States throughout the 19th century.

15. Dizard and Gadlin, *The Minimal Family*, 34-35; Coontz, *The Social Origins of Private Life*; Stephanie Coontz, *The Way We Never Were: American Families and the Nostalgia Trap* (New York: Basic Books, 1992); Seccombe, *Weathering the Storm*.

16. Sabean, *Kinship in Neckerhausen*.

17. Dizard and Gadlin, *The Minimal Family*; Eugene Litwak, "Extended Kin Relations in an Industrial Democratic Society," in *Social Structure and the Family*, ed. Ethel Shanas and Gordon F. Streib (Englewood Cliffs, NJ: Prentice Hall, 1965), 290-323; Patricia Wilson and Ray Pahl, "The Changing Sociological Construct of Family," *Sociological Review* 36 (1988): 233-72; Elizabeth Bott, *Family and Social Network: Roles, Norms, and External Relationships in Ordinary Urban Families* (London: Tavistock, 1957); Peter Willmott and Michael Young, *Family and Class in a London Suburb* (London: New English Library, 1967).

18. Robert A. Nisbet, *The Quest for Community: A Study in the Ethics of Order and Freedom* (New York: Oxford University Press, 1953), 68.

19. Dizard and Gadlin, *The Minimal Family*, 34.

20. John Scanzoni, *Contemporary Families and Relationships: Reinventing Responsibility* (New York: McGraw-Hill, 1995).

21. Dizard and Gadlin, *The Minimal Family*, 45.

22. E. Franklin Frazier, *The Negro Family in the United States*, rev. ed. (Chicago: University of Chicago Press, 1966); Andrew Billingsley, *Black Families in White America* (Englewood Cliffs, NJ: Prentice Hall, 1968); Jeanne L. Noble, "The American Negro Woman," in *The American Negro Reference Book*, ed. John P. Davis (Englewood Cliffs, NJ: Prentice Hall, 1966), 501-59.

23. Noble, "The American Negro Woman."

24. Carol Stack, *All Our Kin: Strategies for Survival in a Black Community* (New York: Harper & Row, 1974).

25. Joanne M. Martin and Elmer P. Martin, *The Helping Tradition in the Black Family and Community* (Silver Spring, MD: National Association of Social Workers, 1985); K. Sue Jewell, *Survival of the Black Family: The Institutional Impact of U.S. Social Policy* (New York: Praeger, 1988); Harold E. Cheatham and James B. Stewart, "Retrospective and Exegesis: Black Families Reconceptualized," in *Black Families: Interdisciplinary Perspectives*, ed. Harold E. Cheatham and James B. Stewart (New Brunswick, NJ: Transaction, 1990), 395-99; Bill-

ingsley, *Black Families in White America*; Joyce Aschenbrenner, *Lifelines: Black Families in Chicago* (New York: Holt, Rinehart & Winston, 1975).

26. Brenda E. Stevenson, *Life in Black and White: Family and Community in the Slave South* (New York: Oxford University Press, 1996); David Brion Davis, "White Wives and Slave Mothers," *New York Review of Books,* February 20, 1997, 35-38.

27. Rose Merry Rivers and John Scanzoni, "Social Families Among African Americans: Policy Implications for Children," in *Black Families,* 3rd ed., ed. Harriette Pipes McAdoo (Thousand Oaks, CA: Sage, 1996), 333-48.

28. Jewell, *Survival of the Black Family.*

29. Ibid.

30. Noble, "The American Negro Woman."

31. Nisbet, *The Quest for Community.*

32. Billingsley, *Black Families in White America.*

33. For an intense and penetrating first-person account of the "overcoming experience," see Henry Louis Gates, Jr., *Colored People: A Memoir* (New York: Alfred A. Knopf, 1994).

34. Frazier, *The Negro Family in the United States*; Noble, "The American Negro Woman"; John Scanzoni, *The Black Family in Modern Society: Patterns of Stability and Security,* rev. ed. (Chicago: University of Chicago Press, 1977).

35. E. Franklin Frazier, *The Negro Church in America* (New York: Schocken, 1964).

36. William O'Neill, *The Woman Movement: Feminism in the United States and England* (New York: Barnes & Noble, 1969).

37. Ibid., 22.

38. John Stuart Mill, *The Subjection of Women and Other Essays* (London: Oxford University Press, 1869).

39. Leslie Kanes Weisman, *Discrimination by Design: A Feminist Critique of the Man-Made Environment* (Urbana: University of Illinois Press, 1992), 87.

40. Ibid., 90.

41. Ibid., 87.

42. Dizard and Gadlin, *The Minimal Family,* 38.

43. Ibid.

44. Ibid.

45. Lynn Jamieson, "Theories of Family Development and the Experience of Being Brought Up," *Sociology* 21 (1987): 591-607.

46. Jessie Bernard, "The Good-Provider Role: Its Rise and Fall," *American Psychologist* 36 (1981): 1-12.

47. Yvonne Schutze, "The Good Mother: The History of the Normative Model 'Mother-Love,' " in *Sociological Studies of Child Development: A Research Annual,* vol. 2, ed. Patricia A. Adler, Peter Adler, and Nancy Mandell (Greenwich, CT: JAI, 1987), 39-78.

48. Kevin White, *The First Sexual Revolution: The Emergence of Male Heterosexuality in Modern America* (New York: New York University Press, 1993). The second sexual revolution occurred in the 1960s; see Chapter 3 of this volume.

49. D'Emilio and Freedman, *Intimate Matters.*

50. Waller, *The Family.*

51. The term *double standard* simply means that in the realm of sexuality, certain rules applied to women that did not apply to men.

52. Dizard and Gadlin, *The Minimal Family,* 30.

53. Ibid., 55.

54. Ibid.

55. Thomas L. Friedman, "The Critics Were Wrong," *New York Times,* September 25, 1996, A19.

56. Dizard and Gadlin, *The Minimal Family*.

57. David Macarov, *Social Welfare: Structure and Practice* (Thousand Oaks, CA: Sage, 1995).

58. Ibid.

59. T. H. Marshall, "Citizenship and Social Class" (Alfred Marshall Lectures given at Cambridge University, 1949), in *Class, Citizenship, and Social Development* (Garden City, NY: Doubleday, 1965); Hugh Heclo, "The Social Question," in *Poverty, Inequality, and the Future of Social Policy*, ed. Katherine McFate, Roger Lawson, and William Julius Wilson (New York: Russell Sage Foundation, 1995), 665-92.

60. Evidence for frequent occurrences of a variety of post-World War II exchanges is found in Bott, *Family and Social Network*; Litwak, "Extended Kin Relations"; Marvin B. Sussman, "Relationships of Adult Children With Their Parents in the United States," in *Social Structure and the Family*, ed. Ethel Shanas and Gordon F. Streib (Englewood Cliffs, NJ: Prentice Hall, 1965), 62-92. Johanne Boisjoly, Greg J. Duncan, and Sandra Hofferth, in "Access to Social Capital," *Journal of Family Issues* 16 (1995): 609-31, show that such exchanges continue today.

61. For a brief history of the development of suburbia since late-18th-century England, see Laura J. Miller, "Family Togetherness and the Suburban Ideal," *Sociological Forum* 10 (1995): 393-418. For a more exhaustive study, see Robert Fishman, *Bourgeois Utopias: The Rise and Fall of Suburbia* (New York: Basic Books, 1987). For a literary description of how very oppressive 1950s life could be, see Bobbie Ann Mason, "The Burden of the Feast," *New Yorker*, December 22-29, 1997, 66-73.

62. Dizard and Gadlin, *The Minimal Family*, 56. See also Kenneth Fox, *Metropolitan America: Urban Life and Urban Policy in the United States, 1940-1980* (Jackson: University of Mississippi Press, 1986).

63. Miller, "Family Togetherness."

64. Herbert J. Gans, *The Levittowners: Ways of Life and Politics in a New Suburban Community* (New York: Vintage/Random House, 1967); Herbert J. Gans, "Urbanism and Suburbanism as Ways of Life: A Reevaluation of Definitions" (1962), in *People, Plans, and Policies: Essays on Poverty, Racism, and Other National Urban Problems* (New York: Russell Sage Foundation, 1991), 51-69.

65. Dizard and Gadlin, *The Minimal Family*, 55.

66. Ibid., 56. See also Miller, "Family Togetherness," 393-94.

67. Fox, *Metropolitan America*, 61.

68. Dizard and Gadlin, *The Minimal Family*, 60.

69. Miller, "Family Togetherness."

70. Fox, *Metropolitan America*, 60-61.

CHAPTER 3

1. Mirra Komarovsky, "Cultural Contradictions and Sex Roles," *American Journal of Sociology* 52 (1946): 184-89.

2. William H. Whyte, Jr., *The Organization Man* (New York: Simon & Schuster, 1956), 392-93.

3. John R. Seeley, R. Alexander Sim, and Elizabeth W. Loosley, *Crestwood Heights* (New York: Basic Books, 1956).

4. Ibid., 181.

5. Ibid.

6. Ibid., 217-19.

7. Ibid., 218. For research revealing that working-class wives of that period, just as much as the middle-class wives discussed by Seeley et al., experienced severe constraints in and discontents with their marriages, see Lee Rainwater, R. P. Coleman, and Gerald Handel, *Workingman's Wife: Her Personality, World and Lifestyle* (New York: Oceana, 1959); Lee Rainwater and K. K. Weinstein, *And the Poor Get Children* (Chicago: Quadrangle, 1960). And working-class women also had no realistic option to divorce.

8. Seeley et al., *Crestwood Heights.*

9. Whyte, *The Organization Man*; Kenneth Fox, *Metropolitan America: Urban Life and Urban Policy in the United States, 1940-1980* (Jackson: University of Mississippi Press, 1986).

10. Fox, *Metropolitan America*, 62. Among the chief gurus of the day, according to Fox, were Benjamin Spock and Erik Erikson. The latter was heavily influenced by Freudian theories of child development.

11. Seeley et al., *Crestwood Heights*, 172.

12. Whyte, *The Organization Man.*

13. Steven Mintz and Susan Kellogg, *Domestic Revolutions: A Social History of American Family Life* (New York: Free Press, 1988); Stephanie Coontz, *The Way We Never Were: American Families and the Nostalgia Trap* (New York: Basic Books, 1992).

14. William J. Goode, *World Revolution and Family Patterns* (New York: Free Press, 1963), 380. Waller was the first to make this type of observation; see Willard Waller, *The Family: A Dynamic Interpretation* (New York: Dryden, 1938). Besides Goode, later researchers highlighting this same point include John F. Cuber and Peggy B. Harroff in *The Significant Americans: A Study of Sexual Behavior Among the Affluent* (New York: Appleton-Century-Crofts, 1964).

15. Margaret Mead, "The Life Cycle and Its Variations: The Division of Roles," *Daedalus* 96 (1967): 871.

16. Talcott Parsons, "The Kinship System of the Contemporary United States," *American Anthropologist* 55 (1943): 22-38; Talcott Parsons, "The American Family: Its Relations to Personality and to the Social Structure," in *Family, Socialization and Interaction Process*, ed. Talcott Parsons and Robert F. Bales (New York: Free Press, 1955), 3-33; Talcott Parsons, "The Normal American Family," in *Man and Civilization: The Family's Search for Survival*, ed. Seymour M. Farber, Piero Mustacchi, and Roger H. L. Wilson (New York: McGraw-Hill, 1965), 31-50.

17. Mead, "The Life Cycle and Its Variations," 872.

18. Ibid., 875.

19. Frederick H. Stoller, "The Intimate Network of Families as a New Structure," in *The Family in Search of a Future*, ed. Herbert A. Otto (New York: Appleton-Century-Crofts, 1970), 149, 148, 151.

20. Ibid., 151.

21. Ibid., 158.

22. Ibid. For an example of an innovative experiment in creating social networks apart from spatial connectedness, see Moncrief Cochran, Mary Larner, David Riley, Lars Gunnarsson, and Charles Henderson, Jr., *Extending Families: The Social Networks of Parents and Children* (New York: Cambridge University Press, 1990).

23. Stoller, "The Intimate Network of Families," 159.

24. Robert A. Nisbet, *The Quest for Community: A Study in the Ethics of Order and Freedom* (New York: Oxford University Press, 1953), 62.

25. Ibid., 70.

26. William O'Neill, *The Woman Movement: Feminism in the United States and England* (New York: Barnes & Noble, 1969). For discussion of how 19th-century feminists united around the goal of suffrage, see Chapter 2 of this book.

27. John Scanzoni, *Sexual Bargaining: Power Politics in American Marriage,* rev. ed. (Chicago: University of Chicago Press, 1982).

28. Karen R. Blaisure and Katherine R. Allen, "Feminists and the Ideology and Practice of Marital Equality," *Journal of Marriage and the Family* 57 (1995): 5-19.

29. Dorothy McBride Stetson, *Women's Rights in the USA: Policy Debates and Gender Roles* (Pacific Grove, CA: Brooks/Cole, 1991).

30. Ibid., 22.

31. Jan E. Dizard and Howard Gadlin, *The Minimal Family* (Amherst: University of Massachusetts Press, 1990).

32. John Modell, *Into One's Own: From Youth to Adulthood in the United States, 1920-1975* (Berkeley: University of California Press, 1989).

33. John D'Emilio and Estelle B. Freedman, *Intimate Matters: A History of Sexuality in America* (New York: Harper & Row, 1988).

34. Lillian B. Rubin, *Erotic Wars: What Happened to the Sexual Revolution?* (New York: HarperCollins, 1990).

35. Ibid.

36. Pepper Schwartz, *Peer Marriage: How Love Between Equals Really Works* (New York: Free Press, 1994); Marilyn Friedman, "Feminism and Modern Friendship: Dislocating the Community," in *Communitarianism and Individualism,* ed. Shlomo Avineri and Avner De-Shalit (New York: Oxford University Press, 1992), 101-19; Anthony Giddens, *The Transformation of Intimacy: Sexuality, Love and Eroticism in Modern Societies* (Oxford: Blackwell, 1992).

37. Nancy F. Cott, *The Bonds of Womanhood: "Woman's Sphere" in New England, 1780-1835* (New Haven, CT: Yale University Press, 1977).

38. Lee Rainwater, *Family Design: Marital Sexuality, Family Size and Contraception* (Chicago: Aldine, 1965), 61.

39. Charles H. Cooley, *Social Organization* (New York: Scribner, 1909).

40. Ann Swidler, "Love and Adulthood in American Culture," in *Themes of Love and Work in Adulthood,* ed. Neil J. Smelser and Erik H. Erikson (Cambridge, MA: Harvard University Press, 1980), 120-50.

41. Dizard and Gadlin, *The Minimal Family,* 56.

42. Louise DeSalvo, *Vertigo: A Memoir* (New York: Dutton Signet, 1996), quoted in *Chronicle of Higher Education,* October 18, 1996, B7.

43. Herbert A. Otto, "Introduction," in *The Family in Search of a Future,* ed. Herbert A. Otto (New York: Appleton-Century-Crofts, 1970), 1-10; Sheila Rowbotham, *The Past Is Before Us: Feminism in Action Since the 1960s* (Boston: Beacon, 1989); Marvin B. Sussman, ed., *Non-traditional Family Forms in the 1970s* (Minneapolis: National Council on Family Relations, 1972); Caroline Bird, *Born Female* (New York: David McKay, 1968); Judith B. Brown, "Female Liberation First, and Now," in *Masculine-Feminine: Readings in Sexual Mythology and the Liberation of Women,* ed. Betty Roszak and Theodore Roszak (New York: Harper & Row, 1969), 222-29; Aileen Kraditor, *Up From the Pedestal* (Chicago: Quadrangle, 1968); Roxanne Dunbar, "Female Liberation as the Basis for Social Revolution," in *Sisterhood Is Powerful,* ed. Robin Morgan (New York: Random House, 1970), 477-94.

44. Nancy E. Dowd, *In Defense of Single-Parent Families* (New York: New York University Press, 1997).

45. Don Clawson, "War on the Poor," *Contemporary Society* 26 (1997): vii.

46. Daniel Friedlander and Gary Burtless, *Five Years After: The Long-Term Effects of Welfare-to-Work Programs* (New York: Russell Sage Foundation, 1995). Visit the Web sites of the *New York Times* (http://www.nytimes.com) and the *Washington Post* (http://www.wash-

ingtonpost.com) for ongoing accounts of both the political and personal struggles that are part of these significant changes.

47. Michael T. Hannan, Nancy Brandon Tuma, and Lyle P. Groeneveld, *The Impact of Income Maintenance on the Making and Breaking of Marital Unions: Interim Report,* Research Memorandum 28 (Stanford, CA: Stanford Research Institute, June 1976); Michael T. Hannan, Nancy Brandon Tuma, and Lyle P. Groeneveld, *A Model of the Effect of Income Maintenance on Rates of Marital Dissolution: Evidence From the Seattle and Denver Income Maintenance Experiments,* Research Memorandum 44 (Stanford, CA: Stanford Research Institute, February 1977); Nancy Brandon Tuma, Michael T. Hannan, and Lyle P. Groeneveld, *Variation Over Time in the Impact of the Seattle and Denver Income Maintenance Experiments on the Making and Breaking of Marriages,* Research Memorandum 43 (Stanford, CA: Stanford Research Institute, February 1977).

48. John Scanzoni, *Opportunity and the Family* (New York: Free Press, 1970); John Scanzoni, *The Black Family in Modern Society: Patterns of Stability and Security,* rev. ed. (Chicago: University of Chicago Press, 1977); Scanzoni, *Sexual Bargaining.*

49. See Judith M. Gueron and Edward Pauly, *From Welfare to Work* (New York: Russell Sage Foundation, 1991); Janet C. Quint, Judith S. Musick, and Joyce A. Ladner, *Lives of Promise, Lives of Pain: Young Mothers After New Chance* (New York: Manpower Demonstration Research Corporation, January 1994).

50. Fox, *Metropolitan America,* 237, 238.

51. To be sure, the federal legislation failed to supply sufficient levels of backup resources, and some states are attempting to meet those needs, often with mixed enthusiasm and inadequate funding. See Robin Toner, "Senate Rejects Bid to Add Child Care to Welfare Overhaul," *New York Times,* September 12, 1995, A9.

52. For a comprehensive literature review on all of the various aspects of heterosexual cohabitation, see Marion C. Willetts, "Innovative Dyadic Relationships: A Quantitative and Qualitative Analysis" (Ph.D. diss., University of Florida, Department of Sociology, 1997). My discussion here is indebted to Willetts's work.

53. Ibid.

54. Ibid. Willetts's empirical research was based on the two waves of the National Study of Families and Households.

55. Ibid.

56. "Democratic National Committee Extends Benefits to Gay Couples," *New York Times,* May 17, 1997, 7.

57. Tim Golden, "San Francisco Near Domestic Partner Rule," *New York Times,* November 6, 1996, A9.

58. Paula L. Ettlebrick, "Since When Is Marriage a Path to Liberation?" in *Lesbian and Gay Marriage,* ed. Suzanne Sherman (Philadelphia: Temple University Press, 1992), 20-26. See also David W. Dunlap, "Some Gay Rights Advocates Question Effort to Defend Same-Sex Marriage," *New York Times,* June 7, 1996, A8.

59. Pamela Freese, "The Union of Nature and Culture: Gender Symbolism in the American Wedding Ritual," in *Transcending Boundaries: Multi-disciplinary Approaches to the Study of Gender,* ed. Pamela Freese and John M. Coggeshall (South Hadley, MA: Bergin & Garvey, 1991), 97-112; Andrew L. Roth, " 'Men Wearing Masks': Issues of Description in the Analysis of Ritual," *Sociological Theory* 13 (1995): 301-27.

60. More recent descriptions of love's flight can be found in Karen Keyser, *When Love Dies: The Process of Marital Disintegration* (New York: Guilford, 1993); and Diane Vaughan, *Uncoupling: Turning Points in Intimate Relationships* (New York: Oxford University Press, 1986).

61. Eric Schmitt, "Senators Reject Gay Marriage Bill and Job-Bias Ban," *New York Times,* September 11, 1996, A1.

62. G. Dorsey Green and Frederick W. Bozett, "Lesbian Mothers and Gay Fathers," in *Homosexuality: Research Implications for Public Policy,* ed. John C. Gonsiorek and James D. Weinrich (Newbury Park, CA: Sage, 1991), 197-214; Katherine R. Allen and David H. Demo, "The Families of Lesbians and Gay Men: A New Frontier in Family Research," *Journal of Marriage and the Family* 57 (1995): 111-27.

63. The 1997 off-Broadway play *Gross Indecency* describes Wilde's own devastating encounters with the laws of his day prohibiting sex between males.

64. Lawrence Van Gelder, "TV Comedy Makes History With First Lesbian Star," *New York Times,* May 1, 1997, A3.

65. Quoted in ibid.

66. John Boswell, *Same-Sex Unions in Premodern Europe* (New York: Villard, 1994), xxvi.

67. For numerous additional examples of public ceremonies, including lists of "ceremony officiators," see Suzanne Sherman, ed., *Lesbian and Gay Marriage* (Philadelphia: Temple University Press, 1992).

68. Walter Goodman, "Marriages That Dare Not," *New York Times,* November 7, 1996, A13. Boswell shows that throughout history, same-sex couples have typically sought marriage for precisely the same reasons (*Same-Sex Unions*). For additional contemporary examples of cross-sex unions, see Sherman, *Lesbian and Gay Marriage.*

69. "This Week in Review: Rights of Matrimony," *New York Times,* July 13, 1997; Carey Goldberg, "Judge in Hawaii Says the State Cannot Prohibit Gay Marriage," *New York Times,* December 4, 1996, A1.

70. Sam Howe Verhovek, "From Same-Sex Marriages to Gambling, Voters Speak," *New York Times,* November 5, 1998, A3.

71. Carey Goldberg, "Vermont Supreme Court Takes Up Gay Marriage," *New York Times,* November 19, 1998, A1.

72. Andrew Sullivan, *Virtually Normal: An Argument About Homosexuality* (New York: Alfred A. Knopf, 1995); Sy Adler and Johanna Brenner, "Gender and Space: Lesbians and Gay Men in the City," *International Journal of Urban and Regional Research* 16 (1992): 24-34; Kath Weston, *Families We Choose: Lesbians, Gays, Kinship* (New York: Columbia University Press, 1991); William G. Hawkeswood, *One of the Children: Gay Black Men in Harlem* (Berkeley: University of California Press, 1996).

73. Boswell, *Same-Sex Unions,* 3-4.

74. The typical kibbutz today is quite different from those of previous decades. See Chapter 4.

75. Melford E. Spiro, *Kibbutz: Venture in Utopia* (New York: Schocken, 1963), 113, 119.

76. Ibid., 119.

77. Lerke Gravenhorst, "A Feminist Look at Family Development Theory," in *Social Stress and Family Development,* ed. David Klein and Joan Aldous (New York: Guilford, 1988), 89. See also John Scanzoni and William Marsiglio, "Wider Families as Primary Relationships," *Marriage and Family Review* 17 (1991): 117-33; John Scanzoni and William Marsiglio, "New Action Theory and Contemporary Families," *Journal of Family Issues* 14 (1993): 105-32; John Scanzoni, *Contemporary Families and Relationships: Reinventing Responsibility* (New York: McGraw-Hill, 1995); John Scanzoni, Karen Polonko, Jay D. Teachman, and Linda Thompson, *The Sexual Bond: Rethinking Families and Close Relationships* (Newbury Park, CA: Sage, 1989).

78. Boswell, *Same-Sex Unions,* 4 ff.; see also Cheryl Albas, Daniel Albas, and Douglas Rennie, "Dating, Seeing and Going Out With: An Ethnography of Contemporary Courtship," *International Journal of Comparative Family and Marriage* 1 (1994): 61-81.

79. Mead, "The Life Cycle and Its Variations," 874.

80. Anthony Giddens, *Beyond Left and Right: The Future of Radical Politics* (Stanford, CA: Stanford University Press, 1994).

81. Mead, "The Life Cycle and Its Variations," 874.

82. Amitai Etzioni, *The Spirit of Community: The Reinvention of American Society* (New York: Simon & Schuster, 1993), 63. Etzioni is a leading spokesman for what is often known as *communitarianism,* a viewpoint that has numerous facets and a variety of critics. Some liberals and feminists worry that, among other things, communitarianism might tend to suppress individual liberties. That fear is surely reinforced by the implications of Etzioni's comments discussed in the above text. Nevertheless, communal values need not necessarily be conservative or repressive. Both Gutman and Friedman argue that liberals should rise to the challenge by shaping a new future through melding the best of both communal and individual values. See Amy Gutman, "Communitarian Critics of Liberalism," in *Communitarianism and Individualism,* ed. Shlomo Avineri and Avner De-Shalit (New York: Oxford University Press, 1992), 120-36; and Friedman, "Feminism and Modern Friendship." That is the position I take, as described in Part II of this book.

83. Etzioni, *The Spirit of Community,* 63.

84. Ibid. However, Popenoe *does* argue that after *each* birth, the mother should leave the labor force entirely for the infant's first 12 to 18 months. At that point, he says, she might consider part-time work for several years, or, if the husband steps in, perhaps even full-time work. David Popenoe, "Modern Marriage: Revising the Cultural Script," in *Promises to Keep: Decline and Renewal of Marriage in America,* ed. David Popenoe, Jean Bethke Elshtain, and David Blankenhorn (Lanham, MD: Rowman & Littlefield, 1996), 247-70.

85. They can have all these things, of course, with a degree of assistance from a "family-friendly" workplace and government. See National Parenting Association, *What Families Really Value: The Action Agenda of America's Parents* (New York: National Parenting Association, 1996).

86. Sara Diamond, *Roads to Dominion: Right-Wing Movements and Political Power in the United States* (New York: Guilford, 1995); William C. Martin, *With God on Our Side: The Rise of the Religious Right in America* (New York: Broadway, 1996); Judith Stacey, *In the Name of the Family: Rethinking Family Values in the Postmodern Age* (Boston: Beacon, 1996).

87. David Denby, "The Alarmist: Robert Bork," *New Yorker,* January 13, 1997, 73; see also Robert H. Bork, *Slouching Towards Gomorrah: Modern Liberalism and American Decline* (New York: Regan/HarperCollins, 1996).

88. For further discussion of Reed's and Bork's political vision, see Chapter 7.

89. Ralph Reed, "We Stand at a Crossroads," *Newsweek,* May 13, 1996, 28. Reed's forthcoming book is titled *Active Faith* (New York: Free Press).

90. Gary L. Bauer, ed., *The Family: Preserving America's Future* (Washington, DC: White House Working Group on the Family, 1986); Council on Families in America, *Marriage in America* (New York: Institute for American Values, 1995); Popenoe, "Modern Marriage." Bear in mind that not all conservatives share precisely the same sets of ideas and objectives. That obvious fact is particularly valid when one compares religious conservatives with secular conservatives.

91. Kevin Sack, "Louisiana Approves Measures to Tighten Marriage Bonds," *New York Times,* June 24, 1997, A11.

92. Ibid.

93. One big difference is that, so far at least, the binding contract is simply one option. If they wish, Louisiana citizens may choose a less binding contract.

94. Diamond, *Roads to Dominion*; Martin, *With God on Our Side.*

95. Janet K. Boles, *The Politics of the Equal Rights Amendment: Conflict and the Decision Process* (New York: Longman, 1979).

96. Sidney Blumenthal, "A Doll's House," *New Yorker,* August 30, 1996, 32.

97. Boles, *The Politics of the Equal Rights Amendment.*

98. Daniel Yankelovich, *New Rules: Searching for Self-Fulfillment in a World Turned Upside Down* (New York: Random House, 1981), 3-4.

99. White House Conference on Families, *Listening to America's Families: Action for the 80's* (Washington, DC: Government Printing Office, 1980).

100. Gilbert Y. Steiner, *The Future of Family Policy* (Washington, DC: Brookings Institution, 1981).

101. Ibid.

102. Ibid., 17.

103. Ibid., 192.

104. Popenoe, "Modern Marriage."

105. Council on Families in America, *Marriage in America.*

CHAPTER 4

1. Dorit Fromm, *Collaborative Communities: Cohousing, Central Living, and Other New Forms of Housing With Shared Facilities* (New York: Van Nostrand Reinhold, 1991); Dorit Fromm, "Collaborative Communities," *Progressive Architecture* 51 (1993): 92-97.

2. Fromm, *Collaborative Communities,* 14.

3. Ibid.

4. Ibid.

5. Mary McAleer Vizard, "Housing With a Built-In Sense of Community," *New York Times,* September 7, 1997, 29.

6. Fromm, *Collaborative Communities,* 15.

7. Ibid., 4.

8. The notion of "network participation and suicide" is an idea that Pescosolido as well as Phillips, Ruth, and MacNamara have used recently to elaborate Durkheim's original insights. See Bernice Pescosolido, "Bringing Durkheim into the 21st Century: A Network Approach to Unresolved Issues in the Sociology of Suicide," and David Phillips, Todd Ruth, and Sean MacNamara, "Missing Features in Durkheim's Theory of Suicide," both in *Emile Durkheim: Suicide—One Hundred Years Later,* ed. David Lester (Philadelphia: Charles, 1994).

9. James S. House, Deborah Umberson, and Karen R. Landis, "Social Structures and Processes of Social Support," *Annual Review of Sociology* 14 (1988): 293-318; Carol S. Aneshensel, "Social Stress: Theory and Research," *Annual Review of Sociology* 18 (1992): 15-38; Alan C. Acock and Jeanne S. Hurlbert, "Social Structural Analysis: a Structural Perspective for Family Studies," *Journal of Social and Personal Relationships* 7 (1990): 245-64; Robert M. Milardo, ed., *Families and Social Networks* (Newbury Park, CA: Sage, 1988); W. L. Parish, L. Hao, and D. P. Hogan, "Family Support Networks, Welfare, and Work Among Young Mothers," *Journal of Marriage and the Family* 53 (1991): 203-15; Duane F. Alwin, Philip E. Converse, and Steven S. Martin, "Living Arrangements and Social Integration," in *Research on the Quality of Life,* ed. Frank M. Andrews (Ann Arbor, MI: Institute for Social Research, 1984), 271-99; Lawrence A. Kurdek, "Social Support of Divorced Single Mothers and Their Children," *Journal of Divorce* 11 (1988): 167-88; R. I. M. Dunbar and M. Spoors,

"Social Networks, Support Cliques, and Kinship," *Human Nature* 6 (1995): 273-90. From another report by Cochran and his colleagues, we learn of efforts by researchers to solicit households to participate in the purposeful construction of mutual support networks within their neighborhoods. Located in a northeastern U.S. city, the neighborhoods in the study represented varying racial and social class backgrounds. Among many findings, the researchers state that households belonging to some of the constructed networks achieved a very high level of interdependence—so much so, in fact, that it would not be inaccurate to attach the label "fictive kin" to what Cochran et al. call "primary networks." Moncrief Cochran, Mary Larner, David Riley, Lars Gunnarsson, and Charles Henderson, Jr., *Extending Families: The Social Networks of Parents and Children* (New York: Cambridge University Press, 1990).

10.   Karen A. Franck and Sherry Ahrentzen, eds., *New Households, New Housing* (New York: Van Nostrand Reinhold, 1991); Caroline Andrew and Beth Moore Milroy, eds., *Life Spaces: Gender, Households, Employment* (Vancouver: University of British Columbia Press, 1988).

11.   Robert Havemann and Barbara Wolfe, *Succeeding Generations: On the Effects of Investments in Children* (New York: Russell Sage Foundation, 1994), 263.   Sara McClanahan and Gary Sandefur make the same argument in *Growing Up With a Single Parent: What Hurts, What Helps* (Cambridge, MA: Harvard University Press, 1994).

12.   Stuart C. Aitken's *Family Fantasies and Community Space* (New Brunswick, NJ: Rutgers University Press, 1998) is a welcome exception to that generalization.

13.   Milton M. Gordon, *Social Class in American Sociology* (Durham, NC: Duke University Press, 1958).

14.   Fromm, *Collaborative Communities*, 15.

15.   For a detailed discussion of the proposed cohousing, see Mary Joyce Hasell and John Scanzoni, "Cohousing in HUD Housing: Prospects and Problems," *Journal of Architectural and Planning Research* (forthcoming). For a discussion of how local HUD officials sometimes tend to stymie national policy efforts to empower poor households, see Chapter 7 of this volume.

16.   Benjamin Zablocki, *Alienation and Charisma: A Study of Contemporary American Communes* (New York: Free Press, 1980), 24 ff.

17.   Rosabeth Moss Kanter, "Commitment and Social Organization: A Study of Commitment Mechanisms in Utopian Communities," *American Sociological Review* 33 (1968): 499-517; Rosabeth Moss Kanter, *Commitment and Community: Communes and Utopias in Sociological Perspective* (Cambridge, MA: Harvard University Press, 1972); Rosabeth Moss Kanter, ed., *Communes: Creating and Managing the Collective Life* (New York: Harper & Row, 1973); Zablocki, *Alienation and Charisma.*

18.   Kanter, *Commitment and Community*, 64.

19.   Ibid., 14.

20.   Fromm, *Collaborative Communities*, 15.

21.   Mark Ontkush, *American Cohousing: The Reasons and Rationale Behind This New Form of Cooperative Living* (Washington, DC: Fannie Mae Foundation, 1997). Nevertheless, the Cantine's Island project is not necessarily representative of all U.S. cohousing. There are many significant differences among U.S. neighborhoods that use the cohousing label. Indeed, some of these neighborhoods are hardly recognizable as cohousing. See the discussion of "community as commodity" later in this chapter.

22.   Fromm, *Collaborative Communities*, 93.

23.   Ibid., 98.

24.   Ibid.

25.   Ibid., 101.

26.   Quoted in ibid.

27. Ibid., 103.

28. Ibid., 104.

29. Ibid. See also Dorit Fromm, "U.S. Cohousing: The First Five Years," *Journal of Architectural and Planning Research* (forthcoming).

30. Fromm, *Collaborative Communities*, 103.

31. Ibid., 104.

32. Ibid.

33. Quoted in ibid.

34. Billy Ray Boyd with Spring Friedlander, "Exploring the Ideology of Cohousing," *Cohousing: The Journal of the Cohousing Network* 11 (1997): 12-14.

35. Fromm, *Collaborative Communities*, 99.

36. Patricia Leigh Brown, "An Ecology-Minded Housing Complex in Cambridge, Mass.," *New York Times*, April 16, 1998 (on-line).

37. Leslie Kanes Weisman, *Discrimination by Design: A Feminist Critique of the Man-Made Environment* (Urbana: University of Illinois Press, 1992); Robert Fishman, *Bourgeois Utopias: The Rise and Fall of Suburbia* (New York: Basic Books, 1987); Graham Meltzer, "Cohousing: Verifying the Importance of Social Context in the Application of Environmentalism," *Journal of Architecture and Planning Research* (forthcoming).

38. Meltzer, "Cohousing."

39. Anthony Giddens, *Beyond Left and Right: The Future of Radical Politics* (Stanford, CA: Stanford University Press, 1994). See also Chapter 1 of this volume.

40. Quoted in Fromm, *Collaborative Communities*, 89.

41. Charles H. Cooley, *Social Organization* (New York: Scribner, 1909); Kanter, *Commitment and Community*, 93; Ellsworth Faris, "The Primary Group: Essence and Accident" (1937), in *Sociological Theory*, ed. L. A. Coser and B. Rosenberg (New York: Macmillan, 1957), 298-303; John Scanzoni, *Contemporary Families and Relationships: Reinventing Responsibility* (New York: McGraw-Hill, 1995), 23 ff.

42. Elizabeth Bott, *Family and Social Network: Roles, Norms, and External Relationships in Ordinary Urban Families* (London: Tavistock, 1957), 217.

43. Lee Rainwater, *Family Design: Marital Sexuality, Family Size and Contraception* (Chicago: Aldine, 1965).

44. Robert Wuthnow, *Sharing the Journey: Support Groups and America's New Quest for Community* (New York: Free Press, 1994); Robert Wuthnow, ed., *"I Came Away Stronger": How Small Groups Are Shaping American Religion* (Grand Rapids, MI: W. B. Eerdman, 1994). Kanter reports in *Commitment and Community* that small support groups were an attractive feature among many of the mid-19th-century communities she studied.

45. Michael Gordon, *The American Family: Past, Present, and Future* (New York: Random House, 1978), 265.

46. Kanter, *Commitment and Community*, 86.

47. Gordon, *The American Family*, 267.

48. Kanter, *Commitment and Community*, 87. The 19th-century Mormons practiced polygamy, and although the practice is now officially banned in the state of Utah, according to Altman, some persons in the rural areas still practice it. Irwin Altman, "Challenges and Opportunities of a Transactional World View: Case Study of Contemporary Mormon Polygynous Families," *American Journal of Community Psychology* (forthcoming)

49. Gordon, *The American Family*, 262.

50. Kanter, *Commitment and Community*, 88.

51. Ibid., 90.

52. Kanter, *Communes*, 353.

53. Ibid. Noyes's essay was based on materials he first copyrighted in 1937.

54. Melford E. Spiro, *Kibbutz: Venture in Utopia* (New York: Schocken, 1963), 110 ff. Much has changed in many kibbutzim since the 1950s. See, for example, Aryei Fishman, *Judaism and Modernization on the Religious Kibbutz* (New York: Cambridge University Press, 1992); Menachem Rosner, Itzhak Ben David, Alexander Avnat, Neni Cohen, and Uri Leviatan, *The Second Generation: Continuity and Change in the Kibbutz* (Westport, CT: Greenwood, 1990).

55. Spiro, *Kibbutz,* 123.

56. Ibid., 135.

57. Ibid., 11.

58. Ibid., 29.

59. Melford E. Spiro, *Children of the Kibbutz* (New York: Schocken, 1965), 20.

60. Bennett M. Berger, *The Survival of a Counterculture: Ideological Work and Everyday Life Among Rural Communards* (Berkeley: University of California Press, 1981); Kanter, *Commitment and Community*; Kanter, *Communes*; Zablocki, *Alienation and Charisma*.

61. Todd Gitlin, *The Sixties: Years of Hope, Days of Rage* (New York: Bantam, 1987).

62. Quoted in Zablocki, *Alienation and Charisma,* 346.

63. See Chapter 3 for a discussion of John R. Seeley, R. Alexander Sim, and Elizabeth W. Loosley, *Crestwood Heights* (New York: Basic Books, 1956); and William H. Whyte, Jr., *The Organization Man* (New York: Simon & Schuster, 1956).

64. Berger, *The Survival of a Counterculture,* 59 ff.; Kanter, "Commitment and Social Organization"; Kanter, *Commitment and Community*; Kanter, *Communes*; Gilbert Zicklin, *Countercultural Communes: A Sociological Perspective* (Westport, CT: Greenwood, 1983); Gitlin, *The Sixties*; Lillian B. Rubin, *Erotic Wars: What Happened to the Sexual Revolution?* (New York: HarperCollins, 1990); Yaacov Oved, *Two Hundred Years of American Communes* (New Brunswick, NJ: Transaction, 1988); John Case and Rosemary C. R. Taylor, eds., *Experiments in Social Change in the 1960s and 1970s* (New York: Pantheon, 1979).

65. Gitlin, *The Sixties.*

66. Rubin, *Erotic Wars.*

67. Zablocki, *Alienation and Charisma,* 7.

68. Philip Selznick, *The Moral Commonwealth: Social Theory and the Promise of Community* (Berkeley: University of California Press, 1992), 367.

69. Dennis R. Judd, "The Rise of the New Walled Cities," in *Spatial Practices: Critical Explorations in Social/Spatial Theory,* ed. Helen Liggett and David C. Perry (Thousand Oaks, CA: Sage, 1995), 159.

70. Ontkush, *American Cohousing.*

71. Judd, "The Rise of the New Walled Cities," 156.

72. Ibid.

73. Ibid., 159.

74. Advertisement for Las Campanas Santa Fe, *New Yorker,* August 26-September 1, 1997, 137.

75. Judd, "The Rise of the New Walled Cities," 155.

76. Ibid., 159.

77. Quoted in Fromm, *Collaborative Communities,* 93.

78. Judd, "The Rise of the New Walled Cities," 160.

79. Ibid.

80. Ibid., 161, 162.

81. Ibid., 162.

82. Thomas L. Friedman, "Tinted Windows," *New York Times,* June 23, 1997, A19.

83. "Adult Community Told to Let Teen-Ager Stay," *New York Times*, February 23, 1997, 19Y.

84. James Brooke, "Young Unwelcome in Retirees' Haven," *New York Times*, February 16, 1997, 10Y.

CHAPTER 5

1. Joan Alway, "The Trouble With Gender: Tales of the Still-Missing Feminist Revolution in Sociological Theory," *Sociological Theory* 13 (1995): 209-28; Karen R. Blaisure and Katherine R. Allen, "Feminists and the Ideology and Practice of Marital Equality," *Journal of Marriage and the Family* 57 (1995): 5-19; David Bradley, "Perspectives on Sexual Equality in Sweden," *Modern Law Review* 53 (1990): 283-302.

2. Katherine McFate, "Introduction: Western States in the New World Order," in *Poverty, Inequality, and the Future of Social Policy*, ed. Katherine McFate, Roger Lawson, and William Julius Wilson (New York: Russell Sage Foundation, 1995), 1-28.

3. Hugh Heclo, "The Social Question," in *Poverty, Inequality, and the Future of Social Policy*, ed. Katherine McFate, Roger Lawson, and William Julius Wilson (New York: Russell Sage Foundation, 1995), 669; Jessie Bernard, "The Good-Provider Role: Its Rise and Fall," *American Psychologist* 36 (1981): 1-12.

4. Heclo, "The Social Question," 669.

5. Marlis Buchmann, *The Script of Life in Modern Society: Entry Into Adulthood in a Changing World* (Chicago: University of Chicago Press, 1989).

6. Heclo, "The Social Question," 668.

7. Ellen Willis, "Down With Compassion," *New Yorker*, September 30, 1996, 4, 5.

8. Ibid., 5.

9. Gregory McLauchlan, "Book Review," *Contemporary Sociology* 25 (1996): 208.

10. John Naisbitt, *Megatrends* (New York: Warner, 1984).

11. Anthony Giddens, *Beyond Left and Right: The Future of Radical Politics* (Stanford, CA: Stanford University Press, 1994), 250.

12. Wendell Bell, *Foundations of Futures Studies*, vol. 1, *History, Purposes, and Knowledge* (New Brunswick, NJ: Transaction, 1997); Wendell Bell, *Foundations of Futures Studies*, vol. 2, *Values, Objectivity, and the Good Society* (New Brunswick, NJ: Transaction, 1997).

13. Arthur B. Shostak, "Book Review," *Contemporary Sociology* 27 (1998): 388.

14. Giddens, *Beyond Left and Right*, 197.

15. Gilbert Y. Steiner, *The Future of Family Policy* (Washington, DC: Brookings Institution, 1981), 179.

16. Ibid., 192.

17. For a discussion of the same goal in a North American context, see John Scanzoni, *Shaping Tomorrow's Family: Theory and Policy for the 21st Century* (Beverly Hills, CA: Sage, 1983).

18. Phyllis Moen, *Working Parents: Transformations in Gender Roles and Public Policies in Sweden* (Madison: University of Wisconsin Press, 1989); Linda Haas, *Equal Parenthood and Social Policy: A Study of Parental Leave in Sweden* (Albany: State University of New York Press, 1992).

19. Harriet Holter, *Sex Roles and Social Structure* (Oslo, Norway: Universitet-Forlaget, 1970). For a review of this literature, see John Scanzoni, *Sexual Bargaining: Power Politics in American Marriage*, rev. ed. (Chicago: University of Chicago Press, 1982).

20. Lisa Horelli and Kirsti Vespa, "In Search of Supportive Structures for Everyday Life," in *Women and the Environment,* ed. Irwin Altman and Arza Churchman (New York: Plenum, 1994), 202.

21. Ibid.

22. Ibid.

23. Ibid.; see also Barbara J. Risman and Danette Johnson-Sumerford, "Doing It Fairly: A Study of Post-Gender Marriages," *Journal of Marriage and the Family* 60 (1998): 23-40.

24. McFate, "Introduction," 22.

25. Nordic Council Research Group, *The New Everyday Life: Ways and Means* (Stockholm: Nordic Council, 1991), 9.

26. Horelli and Vespa, "In Search of Supportive Structures," 204.

27. Ibid., 215.

28. Dolores Hayden, *The Grand Domestic Revolution: A History of Feminist Designs for American Homes, Neighborhoods, and Cities* (Cambridge: MIT Press, 1981); Leslie Kanes Weisman, *Discrimination by Design: A Feminist Critique of the Man-Made Environment* (Urbana: University of Illinois Press, 1992); Daphne Spain, *Gendered Spaces* (Chapel Hill: University of North Carolina Press, 1992); Daphne Spain, "Gendered Spaces and Women's Status," *Sociological Theory* 11 (1993): 137-51; Elizabeth Wilson, *The Sphinx in the City: Urban Life, the Control of Disorder, and Women* (Berkeley: University of California Press, 1992); AnnMarie Adams, *Architecture in the Family Way: Doctors, Houses, and Women, 1870-1900* (Montreal: McGill-Queen's University Press, 1996); Irwin Altman and Arza Churchman, eds., *Women and the Environment* (New York: Plenum, 1994); Joan Forester Sprague, "More Than Housing: Life Boats for Women," *Inland Architect* 10 (1991): 56-61; Karen A. Franck and Sherry Ahrentzen, eds., *New Households, New Housing* (New York: Van Nostrand Reinhold, 1991); J. Cecora, ed., *Changing Values and Attitudes in Family Households With Rural Peer Groups, Social Networks, and Action Spaces: Implications of Institutional Transition in East and West for Value Formation and Transmission* (Bonn: Society for Agricultural Policy Research and Rural Sociology, 1994).

29. Amy S. Wharton, "Review of Andrew & Milroy," *Contemporary Sociology* 22 (1993): 172, emphasis added. Miller is one recent example of a sociologist who seeks to analyze linkages between social features and the physical spaces of suburbia. See Laura J. Miller, "Family Togetherness and the Suburban Ideal," *Sociological Forum* 10 (1995): 393-418.

30. In an essay on the portrayal of gender relations in the media, including serious writing and serious filmmaking, Kuczynski concludes that "between the sexes, it's World War III out there." Alex Kuczynski, "Between the Sexes, It's World War III Out There," *New York Times,* July 19, 1998.

31. Giddens, *Beyond Left and Right,* 190.

32. Horelli and Vespa, "In Search of Supportive Structures," 203.

33. Ibid., 210.

34. Marilyn Friedman, "Feminism and Modern Friendship: Dislocating the Community," in *Communitarianism and Individualism,* ed. Shlomo Avineri and Avner De-Shalit (New York: Oxford University Press, 1992), 101-19; Amy Gutman, "Communitarian Critics of Liberalism," in *Communitarianism and Individualism,* ed. Shlomo Avineri and Avner De-Shalit (New York: Oxford University Press, 1992), 120-36. Giddens also expresses misgivings about "communitarian" approaches toward reinventing society (*Beyond Left and Right,* 124 ff.). However, NEL proposals tend to be more radical and future oriented than those typically found under the present-day communitarian umbrella. (I use *radical* here as defined in Chapter 1—in the sense of "going to the root of things.")

35. Recall the discussion of the "Kids First" slogan in Chapter 3 and its connection with Etzioni's evaluation of mothers' employment trends. See Amitai Etzioni, *The Spirit of Community: The Reinvention of American Society* (New York: Simon & Schuster, 1993).

36. Friedman, "Feminism and Modern Friendship," 112 ff. For a brief description of how some women in the past have sought to forge communities of choice, see Sheila Rowbotham, *The Past Is Before Us: Feminism in Action Since the 1960s* (Boston: Beacon, 1989), 266-93.

37. Gutman, "Communitarian Critics of Liberalism," 134. Stephanie Coontz, in *The Way We Never Were: American Families and the Nostalgia Trap* (New York: Basic Books, 1992), 277-78, makes the same argument.

38. David Island and Patrick Letellier, *Men Who Beat the Men Who Love Them: Battered Gay Men and Domestic Violence* (New York: Haworth, 1991); Claire M. Renzetti, *Violent Betrayal: Partner Abuse in Lesbian Relationships* (Newbury Park, CA: Sage, 1992); Janis Weber, "Lesbian Dyads as Families" (Ph.D. diss., University of Florida, Gainesville, 1998).

39. For a discussion of how existing spatial features shield domestic aggression, see Weisman, *Discrimination by Design*. For general discussions of privacy and violence, see Martha Fineman and Roxanne Mykitiuk, eds., *The Public Nature of Private Violence* (New York: Routledge, 1994); Sara Ruddick, "Injustice in Families: Assault and Domination," in *In the Company of Others: Perspectives on Community, Family, and Culture,* ed. Nancy E. Snow (Lanham, MD: Rowman & Littlefield, 1996), 65-90.

40. Robert A. Nisbet, *The Quest for Community: A Study in the Ethics of Order and Freedom* (New York: Oxford University Press, 1953).

41. Nancy F. Cott, "Eighteenth-Century Family Life as Revealed in Massachusetts Divorce Records," in *A Heritage of Her Own: Toward a New Social History of American Women,* ed. Nancy F. Cott and Elizabeth H. Pleck (New York: Simon & Schuster, 1979), 107-35.

42. Wally Seccombe, *Weathering the Storm: Working Class Families From the Industrial Revolution to the Fertility Decline* (London: Verso, 1993); Stephanie Coontz, *The Social Origins of Private Life: A History of American Families, 1600-1900* (New York: Verso, 1988); Coontz, *The Way We Never Were.*

43. Linda Gordon, "Family Violence, Feminism, and Social Control," in *Women, the State, and Welfare,* ed. Linda Gordon (Madison: University of Wisconsin Press, 1990), 190.

44. Barbara B. Smuts, "Commentary: Apes of Wrath," *Discover Magazine,* April 1995, 37.

45. Ibid.

46. Barbara B. Smuts, *Sex and Friendship in Baboons* (New York: Aldine, 1985).

47. Smuts, "Commentary," 37.

48. Murray A. Straus with Denise A. Donnelly, *Beating the Devil Out of Them: Corporal Punishment in American Families* (Lexington, MA: Lexington, 1994).

49. Ellen Goodman, "Out From Under the Rule of Thumb," *Washington Post,* September 30, 1980 (on-line). See also Scanzoni, *Shaping Tomorrow's Family,* 104-5.

50. Waller was the first social scientist to analyze it in a systematic manner; see Willard Waller, *The Family: A Dynamic Interpretation* (New York: Dryden, 1938). However, the work of Blood and Wolfe was a major influence on subsequent research; see Robert O. Blood and Donald M. Wolfe, *Husbands and Wives* (New York: Free Press, 1960).

51. For literature reviews, see John Scanzoni and Maximiliane Szinovacz, *Family Decision Making: A Developmental Sex Role Model* (Beverly Hills, CA: Sage, 1980); Deborah D. Godwin and John Scanzoni, "Couple Consensus During Marital Joint Decision-Making: A Context, Process, Outcome Model," *Journal of Marriage and the Family* 51 (1989): 943-56; John Scanzoni and Deborah D. Godwin, "Negotiation Effectiveness and Acceptable Out-

comes," *Social Psychology Quarterly* 53 (1990): 239-51; John Scanzoni, *Contemporary Families and Relationships: Reinventing Responsibility* (New York: McGraw-Hill, 1995).

52. Rosabeth Moss Kanter, *Commitment and Community: Communes and Utopias in Sociological Perspective* (Cambridge, MA: Harvard University Press, 1972), 64.

53. Lawrence Stone, *The Family, Sex, and Marriage in England 1500-1800,* abr. ed. (New York: Harper & Row, 1979), 426.

54. Blood and Wolfe, *Husbands and Wives*; Maximiliane Szinovacz, "Family Power," in *Handbook of Marriage and Family,* ed. Marvin B. Sussman and Suzanne K. Steinmetz (New York: Plenum, 1987), 651-94.

55. Godwin and Scanzoni, "Couple Consensus"; Scanzoni and Godwin, "Negotiation Effectiveness."

56. John R. Seeley, R. Alexander Sim, and Elizabeth W. Loosley, *Crestwood Heights* (New York: Basic Books, 1956). (See the discussion in Chapter 3 of this volume.) See also Lee Rainwater, R. P. Coleman, and Gerald Handel, *Workingman's Wife: Her Personality, World and Lifestyle* (New York: Oceana, 1959); Lee Rainwater and K. K. Weinstein, *And the Poor Get Children* (Chicago: Quadrangle, 1960).

57. Needless to say, some erotic friendships (marriages, cohabitations) continue to be characterized in that manner.

58. Scanzoni and Szinovacz, *Family Decision Making*; Scanzoni, *Contemporary Families and Relationships.*

59. Blaisure and Allen, "Feminists and the Ideology"; Alway, "The Trouble With Gender."

60. Jonathan G. Shailor, *Empowerment in Dispute Mediation: A Critical Analysis of Communication* (Westport, CT: Praeger, 1994); Kenneth Kressel, Dean G. Pruitt, and Associates, *Mediation Research: The Process and Effectiveness of Third Party Intervention* (San Francisco: Jossey-Bass, 1989).

61. Horelli and Vespa, "In Search of Supportive Structures." Such arrangements, however, do not give the couple a "free ride." See Chapter 6 for a discussion of the production of social capital.

62. Use of this term started with Blood and Wolfe, *Husbands and Wives.*

63. Although my discussion of couple decision making is limited largely to cross-sex couples, the principle of neighborhood participation applies just as firmly to the decision making of same-sex couples. See Peter J. Carter, "An Exploratory Study of Decision-Making Among Three Non-traditional Sets of Couples: Gay, Lesbian, and Heterosexual Cohabitors" (M.A. thesis, Department of Sociology, University of Florida, Gainesville, 1992).

64. See note 31 and the connected text, above.

65. Scanzoni, *Contemporary Families and Relationships.*

66. Anthony Giddens, *The Transformation of Intimacy: Sexuality, Love and Eroticism in Modern Societies* (Oxford: Blackwell, 1992); Kenneth Clatterbaugh, *Promise-Keepers: An Evangelical Christian Men's Movement* (Boulder, CO: Westview, 1997).

67. Giddens, *Beyond Left and Right,* 175. Giddens acknowledges, of course, that his ideas are drawn from the early-20th-century pioneer sociologist Max Weber.

68. Ibid.

69. I have defined self-sufficiency above as the person's own capability—actual and/or potential—to care for the economic needs of him- or herself and any children for which he or she is responsible.

70. Giddens, *Beyond Left and Right,* 177.

71. Joyce Purnick, commencement address, Barnard College, reprinted in *Chronicle of Higher Education,* June 12, 1998, B9.

72. Ibid. Purnick's observations are strongly supported by existing social science data. See Alway, "The Trouble With Gender"; Blaisure and Allen, "Feminists and the Ideology."

73. David Macarov, *Social Welfare: Structure and Practice* (Thousand Oaks, CA: Sage, 1995), 239 ff.; Jerry Watts, "The End of Work and the End of Welfare," *Contemporary Sociology* 26 (1997): 409-12; Jeremy Rifkin, *The End of Work: The Decline of the Global Labor Force and the Dawn of the Post-market Era* (New York: Putnam, 1995).

74. Giddens, *Beyond Left and Right*, 178.

75. Ibid., 180.

76. See, for example, the magazine *Focus on the Family*, which is published by James Dobson, a leading national spokesman for religious cultural conservatives.

77. James S. Coleman discusses monetary rewards for parenting in "The Rational Reconstruction of Society," *American Sociological Review* 58 (1993): 1-15.

78. Clifford Adelman, *Women at ThirtySomething: Paradoxes of Attainment* (Washington, DC: U.S. Department of Education, Office of Research, 1991), 21.

79. Giddens, *Beyond Left and Right*, 180.

80. In Chapter 7, I address another significant dimension of productivity, namely, political empowerment of the community.

81. I am obviously indebted to the work of James Coleman, who identifies the differences between these two labels as well as their significance for children. See James S. Coleman, "Social Capital in the Creation of Human Capital," *American Journal of Sociology* 94 (1988): S95-120; James S. Coleman, *Foundations of Social Theory* (Cambridge, MA: Harvard University Press, 1990).

82. In *Foundations of Social Theory*, published in 1990, Coleman argued that adults producing children's capital should be rewarded in nonmonetary terms. However, by 1993 he was discussing options for monetary compensation as well ("The Rational Reconstruction of Society").

83. I develop these ideas (based on Coleman's work) further in Chapter 6.

84. "Providing" is, of course, open to a wide range of interpretations. Increasingly, middle-class Americans are coming to include such elements as retirement planning in their concepts of providing for oneself. Additional matters might be included as well.

85. Risman and Johnson-Sumerford, "Doing It Fairly."

86. Giddens, *Beyond Left and Right*, 197.

CHAPTER 6

1. Lisa Horelli and Kirsti Vespa, "In Search of Supportive Structures for Everyday Life," in *Women and the Environment*, ed. Irwin Altman and Arza Churchman (New York: Plenum, 1994), 201-26.

2. William A. Corsaro, *The Sociology of Childhood* (Thousand Oaks, CA: Pine Forge, 1997), 58. Corsaro's sources are Lester Alston, "Children as Chattel," in *Small Worlds: Children and Adolescents in America, 1850-1950*, ed. Elliott West and Paula Petrik (Lawrence: University of Kansas Press, 1992), 208-31; David Wiggins, "The Play of Slave Children in the Plantation Communities of the Old South, 1820-60," in *Growing Up in America: Children in Historical Perspective*, ed. N. Hiner and J. Hawes (Urbana: University of Illinois Press, 1985), 173-92.

3. Corsaro, *The Sociology of Childhood*, 58.

4. Elliott West, "Children on the Plains Frontier," in *Small Worlds: Children and Adolescents in America, 1850-1950*, ed. Elliott West and Paula Petrik (Lawrence: University of Kansas Press, 1992), 26-41, as cited in Corsaro, *The Sociology of Childhood*, 60-61.

5. West, "Children on the Plains Frontier," as cited in Corsaro, *The Sociology of Childhood*.

6. Corsaro, *The Sociology of Childhood,* 61.

7. For a review of this literature, see ibid., 61 ff.

8. Ibid., 8-47.

9. Sylvia Blitzer, " 'They Are Only Children, What Do They Know?' A Look at Current Ideologies of Childhood," in *Sociological Studies of Child Development: A Research Annual,* vol. 4, *Perspectives on and of Children,* ed. Patricia A. Adler and Peter Adler (Greenwich, CT: JAI, 1991), 11-28. In the 1970s, the children's rights movement theme was represented by the contributors to two edited volumes: Beatrice Gross and Ronald Gross, eds., *The Children's Rights Movement* (Garden City, NY: Anchor, 1977); Albert Wilkerson, ed., *The Rights of Children* (Philadelphia: Temple University Press, 1973). The children's liberation theme was expressed by the essays in David Gottlieb, ed., *Children's Liberation* (Englewood Cliffs, NJ: Prentice Hall, 1973).

10. James S. Coleman, *The Adolescent Society: The Social Life of the Teenager and Its Impact on Education* (New York: Free Press, 1961); John R. Seeley, R. Alexander Sim, and Elizabeth W. Loosley, *Crestwood Heights* (New York: Basic Books, 1956). Earlier research into adolescent peer groups appeared in the Middletown studies: Robert S. Lynd and Helen Merrell Lynd, *Middletown: A Study in American Culture* (New York: Harcourt, Brace, 1929); Robert S. Lynd and Helen Merrell Lynd, *Middletown in Transition* (New York: Harcourt, Brace, 1937).

11. Kenneth Fox, *Metropolitan America: Urban Life and Urban Policy in the United States, 1940-1980* (Jackson: University of Mississippi Press, 1986).

12. Coleman, *The Adolescent Society,* 4.

13. Ibid.

14. Gaines argues that by the late 1980s, many suburban adolescent peer groups had wandered into what she calls a "teenage wasteland." Donna Gaines, *Teenage Wasteland: Suburbia's Deadend Kids* (New York: Pantheon, 1991).

15. Penelope K. Trickett and Cynthia J. Schellenbach, eds., *Violence Against Children in the Family and the Community* (Washington, DC: American Psychological Association, 1998); Richard J. Gelles, *The Book of David: How Preserving Families Can Cost Children's Lives* (New York: Basic Books, 1996).

16. James P. Lucier, "Unconventional Rights: Children and the United Nations," *Family Policy* 5 (1992): 1-16.

17. Philip Greven, *Spare the Child: The Religious Roots of Punishment* (New York: Oxford University Press, 1991); Murray A. Straus with Denise A. Donnelly, *Beating the Devil Out of Them: Corporal Punishment in American Families* (Lexington, MA: Lexington, 1994).

18. Lucier, "Unconventional Rights"; Barbara Vobejda, "House Approves Bill to Speed Adoption of Abused Children," *Washington Post,* May 1, 1997, A1. The United States is one of only three countries in the world that has not ratified the United Nations 1989 Convention on the Rights of the Child. Paul Lewis, "A Re-engineered Unicef Wins Rights for Children," *New York Times,* April 27, 1997, A9.

19. Linda Gordon, "Family Violence, Feminism, and Social Control," in *Women, the State, and Welfare,* ed. Linda Gordon (Madison: University of Wisconsin Press, 1990), 184.

20. Wally Seccombe, *Weathering the Storm: Working Class Families From the Industrial Revolution to the Fertility Decline* (London: Verso, 1993).

21. U.S. Advisory Board on Child Abuse and Neglect (Deanne Tilton Durfee, chair), *Neighbors Helping Neighbors: A New National Strategy for the Protection of Children* (Washington, DC: U.S. Department of Health and Human Services, Administration for Children and Families, 1993), 18.

22. Ibid., 6.

23. Ibid., 3.

24. Straus, *Beating the Devil Out of Them*; Rebecca R. S. Socolar, Desmond K. Runyon, and Lisa Amaya-Jackson, "Methodological and Ethical Issues Related to Studying Child Maltreatment," *Journal of Family Issues* 16 (1995): 565-86.

25. Elise Boulding, "Book Review," *Contemporary Sociology* 25 (1996): 590.

26. Bennett M. Berger, *The Survival of a Counterculture: Ideological Work and Everyday Life Among Rural Communards* (Berkeley: University of California Press, 1981); Bennett M. Berger, Bruce M. Hackett, and Mervyn Millar, "Child-Rearing Practices of the Communal Family," in *Communes: Creating and Managing the Collective Life*, ed. Rosabeth Moss Kanter (New York: Harper & Row, 1973), 356-64. See Chapter 4 of this volume for a brief overview of the communes of the 1960s and 1970s.

27. Berger, *The Survival of a Counterculture*, 53.

28. Ibid., 63.

29. Ibid., 63, 72.

30. Ibid., 63.

31. James S. Coleman, "The Rational Reconstruction of Society," *American Sociological Review* 58 (1993): 10.

32. James S. Coleman, *Foundations of Social Theory* (Cambridge, MA: Harvard University Press, 1990), 653.

33. Ibid.

34. Ibid., 300 ff.

35. How to define *social capital* is currently the subject of much debate among scholars from a variety of disciplines. For a review and summary of that debate, see Michael W. Foley and Bob Edwards, eds., "Escape From Politics? Social Theory and the Social Capital Debate" (special issue), *American Behavioral Scientist* 40, no. 5 (1997). To try to clarify the essence of social capital, political scientist Robert Putnam has borrowed the term *favor bank* from Tom Wolfe's 1987 novel *The Bonfire of the Vanities*. Wolfe uses the term in describing the social support networks formed by young businesspersons struggling to make it in the corporate world. Each network consists of a dozen or so participants who engage in an ongoing series of mutual favors, favors they need granted to help them do their jobs more effectively. Putnam observes that each network's guiding principle is "I'll do this for you now, in the expectation that down the road you *or someone else* [in your group] will return the favor." See Robert D. Putnam, *Making Democracy Work: Civic Traditions in Modern Italy* (Princeton, NJ: Princeton University Press, 1993); Robert D. Putnam, "The Prosperous Community: Social Capital and Public Life," *American Prospect* 13 (1993): 35-42.

36. Coleman, *Foundations of Social Theory*, 302.

37. Ibid.

38. For a full range of approaches toward trying to define this construct, see Foley and Edwards, "Escape From Politics?"

39. Desmond P. Ellis, "The Hobbesian Problem of Order: A Critical Appraisal of the Normative Solution," *American Sociological Review* 36 (1971): 692-703; Peter Ekeh, *Social Exchange Theory* (Cambridge, MA: Harvard University Press, 1974); Claude Lévi-Strauss, "The Principle of Reciprocity," in *Sociological Theory*, ed. Lewis A. Coser and Bernard Rosenberg (New York: Macmillan, 1957), 84-94; Janet Finch, *Family Obligations and Social Change* (Cambridge, MA: Blackwell, 1989).

40. Coleman, *Foundations of Social Theory*.

41. In his writings, Coleman assigns considerable significance to stigma and censure as a means to ensure ongoing member contributions and thus continued group solidarity. See especially ibid. and James S. Coleman, "Social Capital in the Creation of Human Capital," *American Journal of Sociology* 94 (1988): S95-120.

42. Rose Merry Rivers and John Scanzoni, "Social Families Among African Americans: Policy Implications for Children," in *Black Families,* 3rd ed., ed. Harriette Pipes McAdoo (Thousand Oaks, CA: Sage, 1996), 342. For a striking example of stigma and censure among contemporary blood kin, see Patricia Wilson and Ray Pahl, "The Changing Sociological Construct of Family," *Sociological Review* 36 (1988): 233-72.

43. Ellis, "The Hobbesian Problem"; Coleman, "Social Capital."

44. Coleman, "Social Capital"; Ekeh, *Social Exchange Theory*; Lévi-Strauss, "The Principle of Reciprocity"; Finch, *Family Obligations.*

45. Putnam, *Making Democracy Work*; Coleman, *Foundations of Social Theory*; Robert A. Nisbet, *The Quest for Community: A Study in the Ethics of Order and Freedom* (New York: Oxford University Press, 1953).

46. Coleman, *Foundations of Social Theory*; Ellis, "The Hobbesian Problem." For a discussion of economist Gary Becker's views on altruism among households, see H. Elizabeth Peters, "An Economic Approach to the Study of Child Well-Being: Gary Becker on Altruism and Household Production," *Journal of Family Issues* 16 (1995): 587-608.

47. In recent years, a number of researchers have utilized Coleman's notion of social capital to describe parental inputs to children. But as far as I can tell, little if any attention has yet been paid to the issue of children's contributions to their natural parent(s), much less to adults outside their households. See Cornelia Butler Flora and Jan L. Flora, "Entrepreneurial Social Infrastructure: A Necessary Ingredient," *Annals of the American Academy of Political and Social Science* 529 (1993): 48-58; Frank F. Furstenberg, Jr., "How Families Manage Risk and Opportunity in Dangerous Neighborhoods," in *Sociology and the Public Agenda,* ed. William Julius Wilson (Newbury Park, CA: Sage, 1993), 231-58; Frank F. Furstenberg, Jr., and Mary Elizabeth Hughes, "Social Capital and Successful Development Among At-Risk Youth," *Journal of Marriage and the Family* 57 (1995): 580-92; Lionel J. Beaulieu and David Mulkey, "Human Capital in Rural America: A Review of Theoretical Perspectives," in *Investing in People: The Human Capital Needs of Rural America,* ed. Lionel J. Beaulieu and David Mulkey (Boulder, CO: Westview, 1995), 3-21; Johanne Boisjoly, Greg J. Duncan, and Sandra Hofferth, "Access to Social Capital," *Journal of Family Issues* 16 (1995): 609-31; Toby L. Parcel and Elizabeth G. Menaghan, "Family Social Capital and Children's Behavior Problems," *Social Psychology Quarterly* 56 (1993): 120-35; Toby L. Parcel and Elizabeth G. Menaghan, *Parents' Jobs and Children's Lives* (Hawthorne, NY: Aldine de Gruyter, 1994); Mark H. Smith, Lionel J. Beaulieu, and G. Israel, "Effects of Human Capital and Social Capital on Dropping Out of High School in the South," *Journal of Research in Rural Education* 8 (1992): 75-87; Mark H. Smith, Lionel J. Beaulieu, and Ann Seraphine, "Social Capital, Place of Residence, and College Attendance," *Rural Sociology* 60 (1995): 363-80; John Hagan, Ross MacMillan, and Blair Wheaton, "New Kid in Town: Social Capital and the Life Course Effects of Family Migration on Children," *American Sociological Review* 61 (1996): 368-85; Jay D. Teachman, Kathleen Paasch, and Karen Carver, "Social Capital and Dropping Out of School Early," *Journal of Marriage and the Family* 58 (1996): 773-83; Suzanne M. Bianchi and John Robinson, "What Did You Do Today? Children's Use of Time, Family Composition, and the Acquisition of Social Capital," *Journal of Marriage and the Family* 59 (1997): 332-44.

48. Jens Qvortrup, Marjatta Bardy, Giovanni Sgritta, and Helmut Wintersberger, eds., *Childhood Matters: Social Theory, Practice and Politics* (Avebury, VT: Aldershot, 1994); Corsaro, *The Sociology of Childhood*; Jeylan T. Mortimer and Michael D. Finch, eds., *Adolescents, Work, and Family: An Intergenerational Developmental Analysis* (Thousand Oaks, CA: Sage, 1996). Researchers adopting this point of view are very much a part of the "empowerment" perspective on children discussed above. For a range of studies describing various facets of the empowerment perspective, see James E. Cote and Anton L. Allahar, *Generation on Hold: Coming of Age in the Late Twentieth Century* (New York: New York

University Press, 1995); Allison James and Alan Prout, "Re-Presenting Childhood: Time and Transition in the Study of Childhood," in *Constructing and Reconstructing Childhood: Contemporary Issues in the Sociological Study of Childhood,* ed. Allison James and Alan Prout (New York: Falmer, 1990), 216-38; Viktor Gecas, "The Social Psychology of Self-Efficacy," *Annual Review of Sociology* 15 (1989): 291-316; Jenny Kitzinger, "Who Are You Kidding? Children, Power, and the Struggle Against Sexual Abuse," in *Constructing and Reconstructing Childhood: Contemporary Issues in the Sociological Study of Childhood,* ed. Allison James and Alan Prout (New York: Falmer, 1990), 157-83; Bonnie E. Robo, "Children of Divorce: Some Do Cope," in *Why Some Children Succeed Despite the Odds,* ed. Warren A. Brown and Waln K. Brown (New York: Praeger, 1991), 7-22; Leena Alanen, "Rethinking Socialization, the Family and Childhood," in *Sociological Studies of Child Development: A Research Annual,* vol. 3, ed. Nancy Mandell (Greenwich, CT: JAI, 1990), 13-28; Warren A. Brown and Waln K. Brown, eds., *Why Some Children Succeed Despite the Odds* (New York: Praeger, 1991); Harry Hendrick, "Constructions and Reconstructions of British Childhood: An Interpretive Survey, 1800 to the Present," in *Constructing and Reconstructing Childhood: Contemporary Issues in the Sociological Study of Childhood,* ed. Allison James and Alan Prout (New York: Falmer, 1990), 35-59; Myles I. Friedman and George H. Lackey, Jr., *The Psychology of Human Control: A General Theory of Purposeful Behavior* (New York: Praeger, 1991); Robin Lynn Leavitt, "Power and Resistance in Infant-Toddler Day Care Centers," in *Sociological Studies of Child Development: A Research Annual,* vol. 4, *Perspectives on and of Children,* ed. Patricia A. Adler and Peter Adler (Greenwich, CT: JAI, 1991), 91-112; John Scanzoni, *Contemporary Families and Relationships: Reinventing Responsibility* (New York: McGraw-Hill, 1995), 383 ff.

49. Coleman, *Foundations of Social Theory.*

50. Coleman, *The Adolescent Society.*

51. Daniel Bell, "Resolving the Contradictions of Modernity and Modernism, Part II," *Society* 27 (1990): 66-75.

52. Coleman, *Foundations of Social Theory,* 599.

53. Esther Dyson, George Gilder, Jay Keyworth, and Alvin Toffler, "A Magna Carta for the Knowledge Age," *New Perspectives Quarterly* 11 (1994): 26.

54. Peter F. Drucker, "The Age of Social Transformation," *Atlantic Monthly,* November 1994, 62.

55. Peter A. Facione, *Critical Thinking: What It Is and Why It Counts* (Millbrae: California Academic Press, 1996); Gerald Nosich, "Educational Virtue: Becoming a Critical Thinker," in *Critical Thinking: How to Prepare Students for a Rapidly Changing World,* ed. Jane Willsen and A. J. A. Binker (Santa Rosa, CA: Foundation for Critical Thinking, 1995), v-x. Some educators and critics argue that the public schools should shift their emphasis from content-based learning to a focus on critical thinking. See, for example, Theodore R. Sizer, *Horace's School: Redesigning the American High School* (New York: Houghton Mifflin, 1992); Theodore R. Sizer, *Horace's Hope: What Works for the American High School* (New York: Houghton Mifflin, 1996). A recent critique of research universities makes the same point for them; see Boyer Commission on Educating Undergraduates in the Research University, *Reinventing Undergraduate Education: A Blueprint for America's Research Universities* (New York: Carnegie Foundation, 1998).

56. Theda Skocpol, cited by E. J. Dionne, Jr., "A Good Word for Promise Keepers," *Washington Post,* October 3, 1997, A19. Skocpol's comments were part of an assessment of the Promise Keepers. See Kenneth Clatterbaugh, *Promise-Keepers: An Evangelical Christian Men's Movement* (Boulder, CO: Westview, 1997).

57. Danish Ministry of Social Affairs, ed., *Fathers in Families of Tomorrow* (Cophenhagen: Danish Ministry of Social Affairs, 1993).

58. François de Singly, "The Social Construction of a New Paternal Identity," in *Fathers in Families of Tomorrow*, ed. Danish Ministry of Social Affairs (Copenhagen: Danish Ministry of Social Affairs, 1993), 42-75.

59. Robert Lewis, "Manhood: Don't Let Your Son Leave Home Without It," *Focus on the Family*, June 1997, 6-7.

60. De Singly, "The Social Construction," 42.

61. Ibid., 53.

62. Facione, *Critical Thinking*, 5.

63. De Singly, "The Social Construction," 53.

64. Ibid., 60.

65. Susan Cheever, "The Nanny Track," *New Yorker*, March 6, 1995, 94.

66. Keith Bradsher, "Woman Chosen to Head G.M.'s Saturn Division," *New York Times*, December 15, 1998, B1.

67. Quoted in ibid.

68. Dorit Fromm, *Collaborative Communities: Cohousing, Central Living, and Other New Forms of Housing With Shared Facilities* (New York: Van Nostrand Reinhold, 1991); Horelli and Vespa, "In Search of Supportive Structures."

69. Putnam, "The Prosperous Community"; Robert D. Putnam, "Bowling Alone: America's Declining Social Capital," *Journal of Democracy* 6 (1995): 65-78.

70. I pursue the issue of the community in politics in Chapter 7.

71. The military is one setting that strives to create a level playing field for young women.

72. Myra Sadker and David Sadker, *Failing at Fairness: How America's Schools Cheat Girls* (New York: Scribner, 1994).

73. For further discussion of NEL federations, see Chapter 7.

74. Fred C. Pampel, *Aging, Social Inequality, and Public Policy* (Thousand Oaks, CA: Pine Forge, 1998).

75. Scott A. Bass, Francis G. Caro, and Yung-Ping Chen, eds., *Achieving a Productive Aging Society* (Westport, CT: Auburn House, 1993); Matilda White Riley, "On the Significance of Age in Sociology," in *Social Structures and Human Lives*, ed. Matilda W. Riley, Bettina J. Huber, and Beth B. Hess (Newbury Park, CA: Sage, 1988), 24-45; Nancy Dailey, *When Baby Boom Women Retire* (Westport, CT: Praeger, 1998).

76. Anthony Giddens, *Beyond Left and Right: The Future of Radical Politics* (Stanford, CA: Stanford University Press, 1994), 170.

77. Riley, "On the Significance of Age"; David Macarov, *Social Welfare: Structure and Practice* (Thousand Oaks, CA: Sage, 1995).

78. Horelli and Vespa, "In Search of Supportive Structures."

79. Among other things, the currently existing national organization of cohousing communities assists households in determining whether or not a particular locale contains that kind of neighborhood. (See www.cohousing.com)

80. Vivian Fenster Ehrlich, letter to the editor, *New York Times*, February 23, 1997, 12E. See also Dorothy Noyes's "My Turn" essay, "Senior-Teener, a New Hybrid: The Elderly Have a Lot in Common With Teenagers," *Newsweek*, September 5, 1994, 15.

81. Riley, "On the Significance of Age"; Pampel, *Aging, Social Inequality*.

82. Frederick H. Stoller, "The Intimate Network of Families as a New Structure," in *The Family in Search of a Future*, ed. Herbert A. Otto (New York: Appleton-Century-Crofts, 1970), 148. See Chapter 3 in this book.

83. See, for example, Sara McClanahan and Gary Sandefur, *Growing Up With a Single Parent: What Hurts, What Helps* (Cambridge, MA: Harvard University Press, 1994); Nancy E. Dowd, *In Defense of Single-Parent Families* (New York: New York University Press, 1997); Council on Families in America, *Marriage in America* (New York: Institute for American Values,

1995). As mentioned previously, on August 29, 1998, the on-line version of the *New York Times* previewed a "soon-to-be-released Census Bureau report" that found that "for the first time, the majority of 'first births'—someone's first child—were either conceived by or born to an unmarried woman. That's up from 18 percent in the 1930s."

84. This is especially true when a woman marries principally because she believes that either her son or her daughter requires a man around the house for material and/or emotional reasons.

85. For a discussion of government participation, see Chapter 7.

CHAPTER 7

1. For evidence of that assessment, one need only consult the Web sites of the *New York Times* (http://www.nytimes.com) and the *Washington Post* (http://www. washingtonpost.com) on a regular basis.

2. For a discussion of the 1960s sexual revolution, see Chapter 3.

3. See Gayle Worland, "Scandals Throughout Presidential History," *Washington Post,* February 11, 1998 (on-line).

4. Sara Diamond, *Roads to Dominion: Right-Wing Movements and Political Power in the United States* (New York: Guilford, 1995); William C. Martin, *With God on Our Side: The Rise of the Religious Right in America* (New York: Broadway, 1996).

5. Guy Gugliotta, "GOP Moves to Bolster Ties to Evangelicals," *Washington Post,* May 9, 1998, A6.

6. Katherine Q. Seelye, "Christian Coalition's Reed Quits for New Political Role," *New York Times,* April 24, 1997, A7.

7. Rosabeth Moss Kanter, "Commitment and Social Organization: A Study of Commitment Mechanisms in Utopian Communities," *American Sociological Review* 33 (1968): 499-517; Rosabeth Moss Kanter, *Commitment and Community: Communes and Utopias in Sociological Perspective* (Cambridge, MA: Harvard University Press, 1972).

8. Kanter, *Commitment and Community.*

9. Stuart A. Queen, Robert W. Habenstein, and Jill Sobel Quadagno, *The Family in Various Cultures,* 5th ed. (New York: Harper & Row, 1985), 241-42. Altman notes that although polygamy is now officially banned in Utah, some persons in the state's rural areas still practice it. Irwin Altman, "Challenges and Opportunities of a Transactional World View: Case Study of Contemporary Mormon Polygynous Families," *American Journal of Community Psychology* (forthcoming). Altman's findings seem to be verified by a recent report in the national press: "In this conservative state [Utah], 'don't ask, don't tell' means that sheriffs and judges turn a blind eye to polygamy, a felony that has not been prosecuted here in almost half a century." James Brooke, "Utah Struggles With a Revival of Polygamy," *New York Times,* August 23, 1998 (on-line).

10. Recent studies have found that even the Amish and (other) Mennonite communities are forsaking agriculture for more lucrative endeavors as nonfarm entrepreneurs. See Donald B. Kraybill and Steven M. Nolt, *Amish Enterprise: From Plows to Profits* (Baltimore: Johns Hopkins University Press, 1995); Calvin Redekop, Stephen C. Ainlay, and Robert Siemens, *Mennonite Entrepreneurs* (Baltimore: Johns Hopkins University Press, 1995).

11. Gary L. Bauer, ed., *The Family: Preserving America's Future* (Washington, DC: White House Working Group on the Family, 1986).

12. Ralph Reed, "We Stand at a Crossroads," *Newsweek,* May 13, 1996, 28. Reed's forthcoming book is titled *Active Faith* (New York: Free Press). I have described one example of what Reed has in mind in Chapter 3, namely, the 1997 Louisiana legislation severely restricting the freedom to terminate marriages.

13. Diamond, *Roads to Dominion*; Martin, *With God on Our Side*; Louis A. Zurcher, Jr., and R. George Kirkpatrick, *Citizens for Decency: Antipornography Crusades as Status Defense* (Austin: University of Texas Press, 1976); Janet K. Boles, *The Politics of the Equal Rights Amendment: Conflict and the Decision Process* (New York: Longman, 1979).

14. Herbert J. Gans, "Urbanism and Suburbanism as Ways of Life: A Reevaluation of Definitions" (1962), in *People, Plans, and Policies: Essays on Poverty, Racism, and Other National Urban Problems* (New York: Russell Sage Foundation, 1991), 68.

15. Quoted in Katherine Q. Seelye, "Abortion Opponents Hunt for 3 More Votes in Senate," *New York Times*, May 22, 1997, A10.

16. See Chapter 3 of this volume as well as Boles, *The Politics of the Equal Rights Amendment*; Pamela Johnston Conover and Virginia Gray, *Feminism and the New Right: Conflict Over the American Family* (New York: Praeger, 1983).

17. In November 1997, the antichoice forces in Congress were able to prevent allocation of the funds needed for the U.S. contributions to the United Nations and the International Monetary Fund. Jerry Gray, "Congress Deprives Clinton of Money for U.N. and I.M.F.," *New York Times*, November 14, 1997, A3.

18. Dorit Fromm, *Collaborative Communities: Cohousing, Central Living, and Other New Forms of Housing With Shared Facilities* (New York: Van Nostrand Reinhold, 1991), 15.

19. Quoted in ibid.

20. Ibid. Strange as it now seems, that same type of reasoning once permeated religiously conservative churches. One has only to study the sermons of Billy Graham (an internationally known evangelist from the 1950s to the early 1980s) to see that during that time most religious conservatives diligently avoided taking concerted political action. Church members might become politically involved as individuals, but conservative congregations, denominations, and groups of churches did not express political views, lobby public officials, or endorse the election of particular candidates. They certainly did not perceive themselves as either wanting or needing a "seat at the table" of mainstream politics. In Chapter 3, I discussed how conservative Christians' political reluctance was overcome in the 1970s by the threats to their way of life that they saw coming from the women's movement. They now believe it is necessary to be politically active in order to reinforce their values and beliefs. They are convinced that putting their ideals into practice would make life better both for individuals and for the larger society. For an example of how this reasoning is presented to laypersons, see Tom Minnery, "The Relationship Between Church, Family and Government," *Focus on the Family*, July 1998, 10-11.

21. Daniel Bell, "The Year 2000: The Trajectory of an Idea," *Daedalus* 96 (1967): 645.

22. Chip Berlet, ed., *Eyes Right! Challenging the Right-Wing Backlash* (Boston: South End, 1995).

23. Ellen Willis, "Down With Compassion," *New Yorker*, September 30, 1996, 5.

24. National Parenting Association, *What Families Really Value: The Action Agenda of America's Parents* (New York: National Parenting Association, 1996). The NPA calls itself "a nonprofit, non-partisan organization . . . founded . . . [in 1993] by Sylvia Ann Hewlett." See Sylvia Ann Hewlett, *When the Bough Breaks: The Costs of Neglecting Our Children* (New York: Basic Books, 1991).

25. The cost of the 1996 national elections has been reported to be a record-setting $2.2 billion. Jill Abramson, "Costs of '96 Campaigns Sets Record at $2.2 Billion," *New York Times*, November 25, 1997, A3. For detailed reports on how the 1996 national elections were financed, and the implications thereof, see Dan Froomkin, "Campaign Finance," part 1 of 6, "Big Money: The Cost of Winning," *Washington Post*, September 15, 1997, A7.

26. Robert D. Putnam, *Making Democracy Work: Civic Traditions in Modern Italy* (Princeton, NJ: Princeton University Press, 1993); Robert D. Putnam, "The Prosperous Community:

Social Capital and Public Life," *American Prospect* 13 (1993): 35-42; Robert D. Putnam, "Bowling Alone: America's Declining Social Capital," *Journal of Democracy* 6 (1995): 65-78.

27. Harold W. Stanley and Richard G. Niemi, *Vital Statistics on American Politics*, 4th ed. (Washington, DC: Congressional Quarterly Press, 1994).

28. Quoted in Gustav Niebuhr, "Married Couples Should Be Led by Husband, Say Southern Baptists," *New York Times*, June 10, 1998 (on-line).

29. Kristen Moulton, "Southern Baptists Urge Wives to 'Submit,' " *Washington Post*, June 10, 1998.

30. Quoted in Fromm, *Collaborative Communities*, 104. See also David B. Wong, "Community, Diversity, and Confucianism," in *In the Company of Others: Perspectives on Community, Family, and Culture*, ed. Nancy E. Snow (Lanham, MD: Rowman & Littlefield, 1996), 17-37.

31. Fromm, *Collaborative Communities*, 104.

32. Ibid.

33. Ibid., 107.

34. Ibid., 105.

35. Katherine McFate, "Introduction: Western States in the New World Order," in *Poverty, Inequality, and the Future of Social Policy*, ed. Katherine McFate, Roger Lawson, and William Julius Wilson (New York: Russell Sage Foundation, 1995), 1-28.

36. Hugh Heclo, "The Social Question," in *Poverty, Inequality, and the Future of Social Policy*, ed. Katherine McFate, Roger Lawson, and William Julius Wilson (New York: Russell Sage Foundation, 1995), 686.

37. Wong, "Community, Diversity, and Confucianism."

38. Heclo, "The Social Question," 687.

39. Ibid., 686. Heclo quotes from John Vannorsdall, *The Best of John Vannorsdall* (Chicago: Evangelical Lutheran Church, Office of the Bishop, 1991).

40. Anthony Giddens, *Beyond Left and Right: The Future of Radical Politics* (Stanford, CA: Stanford University Press, 1994), 193.

41. Ibid., 194.

42. Giddens as cited in Robert S. Boynton, "The Two Tonys: Why Is the Prime Minister So Interested in What Anthony Giddens Thinks?" *New Yorker*, October 6, 1997, 67.

43. Lisa Horelli and Kirsti Vespa, "In Search of Supportive Structures for Everyday Life," in *Women and the Environment*, ed. Irwin Altman and Arza Churchman (New York: Plenum, 1994), 222.

44. James S. Coleman, *Foundations of Social Theory* (Cambridge, MA: Harvard University Press, 1990), 652.

45. Ibid., 657-58.

46. Ibid., 658.

47. Nordic Council Research Group, *The New Everyday Life: Ways and Means* (Stockholm: Nordic Council, 1991); Horelli and Vespa, "In Search of Supportive Structures." Currently, there is in North America an organization of persons interested in cohousing, the Cohousing Network (P.O. Box 2584, Berkeley, CA 94702), that holds a yearly international conference and also publishes quarterly the *Cohousing Journal*. (See www.cohousing.com)

48. A brief description of the significance of the clan is found in Kingsley Davis's classic work *Human Society* (New York: Macmillan, 1955), 407-9.

49. A recent example of clan military power can be seen in a territory of Somalia where, after many years of anarchy and bloodshed, "the local military and political leaders have established a regional government controlled by clan elders." James C. McKinley, Jr., "In One Small Somali Town, Clan Rule Has Brought Peace," *New York Times*, June 22, 1997, A13.

50. Giddens, *Beyond Left and Right*, 18.

51. Paul De Sa, "The Politics of Poverty" (letter to the editor), *New York Times*, August 5, 1998. De Sa is a Harvard research fellow, and his letter was written in response to an essay by Nadine Gordimer, the goodwill ambassador for the U.N. Development Program's "Decade for the Eradication of Poverty." Nadine Gordimer, "Dare to Dream of Eradicating Poverty," *New York Times*, August 1, 1998 (on-line).

52. John Atlas and Peter Dreier, "From 'Projects' to Communities: Redeeming Public Housing," *Journal of Housing* 50 (1993): 21-36. See the discussion below in the context of Jack Kemp's "tenant empowerment" proposals.

53. Jason Turner, "Public Housing Needs Reform Too," *New York Times*, April 8, 1997, A17; Lizette Alvarez, "House Passes Bill to Change Public Housing," *New York Times*, May 15, 1997, A3.

54. Michael Janofsky, "HUD and Its New Chief Face His High Ambitions," *New York Times*, April 13, 1997, A8.

55. Atlas and Dreier, "From 'Projects' to Communities," 21. See also Gail Radford, *Modern Housing for America: Policy Struggles in the New Deal Era* (Chicago: University of Chicago Press, 1996). In August 1998, Secretary Cuomo and congressional leaders were reportedly near agreement on legislation to allow more working-class families once again to live in public housing. James Dao, "U.S. Plan Would Shift More Working Families Into Public Housing," *New York Times*, August 19, 1998 (on-line).

56. Atlas and Dreier, "From 'Projects' to Communities," 25-26.

57. Ibid., 26.

58. Ibid.

59. Ibid.

60. Ibid., 22, 28.

61. Ibid., 28, 29.

62. Ibid., 27.

63. Ibid.

64. Ibid., 33.

65. Ibid. See Chapter 4 of this volume, especially Exhibit 4.1 and surrounding text. For an actual case study of how efforts to use cohousing as a means to empower a group of disadvantaged lone mothers living in a HUD project were stymied by its local officials, see Mary Joyce Hasell and John Scanzoni, "Cohousing in HUD Housing: Prospects and Problems," *Journal of Architectural and Planning Research* (forthcoming). For a discussion of how current HUD regulations are a striking example of imposing impossible burdens on residents and Section 8 persons seeking financial independence, see Paul H. Messenger, "Public-Housing Perversity: A View From the Trenches," *Public Interest* 12 (1992): 132-43. For a discussion of community empowerment in a Scottish context, see Alan Barr, "Empowering Communities: Beyond Fashionable Rhetoric? Some Reflections on Scottish Experience," *Community Development Journal* 30 (1995): 121-32.

66. Atlas and Dreier, "From 'Projects' to Communities," 35.

67. Mary Davis, "The Gautreaux Assisted Housing Program," in *Housing Markets and Residential Mobility*, ed. G. Thomas Kingsley and Margery Austin Turner (Washington, DC: Urban Institute Press, 1993).

68. Atlas and Dreier, "From 'Projects' to Communities," 22.

69. Theda Skocpol, "Targeting Within Universalism: Politically Viable Policies to Combat Poverty in the United States," in *The Urban Underclass*, ed. Christopher Jencks and Paul E. Peterson (Washington, DC: Brookings Institution, 1991), 411-35.

70. There was, of course, no lifestyle alliance between advantaged and disadvantaged persons.

71. Lynn Stewart, "Bodies, Visions, and Spatial Politics: A Review Essay on Henri Lefebvre's *The Production of Space," Environment and Planning D: Society and Space* 13 (1995): 609-18; Henri Lefebvre, *The Production of Space,* trans. Donald Smith-Nicholson (London: Blackwell/Oxford University Press, 1991[1974]).

72. Alan Walker, "From Welfare State to Caring Society? The Promise of Informal Support Networks," in *Support Networks in a Caring Community,* ed. J. A. Yoder (Dordrecht, Netherlands: Martinus Nijhof, 1985), 42.

73. Peter A. Facione, *Critical Thinking: What It Is and Why It Counts* (Millbrae: California Academic Press, 1996); Theodore R. Sizer, *Horace's School: Redesigning the American High School* (New York: Houghton Mifflin, 1992); Theodore R. Sizer, *Horace's Hope: What Works for the American High School* (New York: Houghton Mifflin, 1996). See also Chapter 6 of this volume. For discussion of the reinvention of research universities, see Boyer Commission on Educating Undergraduates in the Research University, *Reinventing Undergraduate Education: A Blueprint for America's Research Universities* (New York: Carnegie Foundation, 1998).

74. Kathryn Marie Dudley, *The End of the Line: Lost Jobs, New Lives in Postindustrial America* (Chicago: University of Chicago Press, 1994); Jerry Watts, "The End of Work and the End of Welfare," *Contemporary Sociology* 26 (1997): 409-12; Jeremy Rifkin, *The End of Work: The Decline of the Global Labor Force and the Dawn of the Post-market Era* (New York: Putnam, 1995).

75. Fromm, *Collaborative Communities;* Dorit Fromm, "Collaborative Communities," *Progressive Architecture* 51 (1993): 92-97; Richard L. Crowther, *Ecologic Architecture* (Boston: Butterworth Architecture/Heinemann, 1992), 4; Leslie Kanes Weisman, *Discrimination by Design: A Feminist Critique of the Man-Made Environment* (Urbana: University of Illinois Press, 1992); Robert Fishman, *Bourgeois Utopias: The Rise and Fall of Suburbia* (New York: Basic Books, 1987); Graham Meltzer, "Cohousing: Verifying the Importance of Social Context in the Application of Environmentalism," *Journal of Architecture and Planning Research* (forthcoming); Patricia Leigh Brown, "An Ecology-Minded Housing Complex in Cambridge, Mass," *New York Times,* April 16, 1998 (on-line).

76. Giddens, *Beyond Left and Right;* Anthony Giddens, *Affluence, Poverty, and the Idea of a Post-Scarcity Society* (Geneva: United Nations Research Institute for Social Development, 1995).

77. Giddens, *Beyond Left and Right,* 202.

78. Dolores Hayden, *The Grand Domestic Revolution: A History of Feminist Designs for American Homes, Neighborhoods, and Cities* (Cambridge: MIT Press, 1981); Crowther, *Ecologic Architecture,* 4.

79. Horelli and Vespa, "In Search of Supportive Structures."

80. Michael Pollan, "Living at the Office," *New York Times,* March 14, 1997, A17.

81. Kirk Johnson, "Offices Placing Limits on the 'Work at Home' Life," *New York Times,* December 17, 1997, B3.

82. Horelli and Vespa, "In Search of Supportive Structures," 213-14.

83. The Oneida community was one exception, having engaged in a variety of business activities over the years, including trap manufacturing, bag making, fruit preserving, a silk works, and a foundry. Constance Noyes-Robertson, *Oneida Community: An Autobiography, 1851-1876* (Syracuse, NY: Syracuse University Press, 1970).

84. V. J. Bradley, J. W. Ashbaugh, and B. C. Blaney, eds., *Creating Individual Supports for People with Developmental Disabilities: A Mandate for Change at Many Levels* (Baltimore: Paul H. Brookes, 1994). See the *Newsweek* "My Turn" essay in which Lee makes his case for the benefits to society of empowering physically challenged persons such as himself. Jerome Lee, "A Good Investment," *Newsweek,* June 21, 1997, 21.

85. Robert R. Grist, Mary Joyce Hasell, Rocke Hill, James L. West, Tony R. White, and Sara Katherine Williams, *An ADAAG Guide for Designing and Specifying Spaces, Buildings, and Sites* (New York: McGraw-Hill, 1996).

86. Blaine Harden, "Summit on Volunteerism Ends With Calls to Keep the Promise to Help Children," *Washington Post,* April 30, 1997, A7.

87. Bob Edwards and Michael W. Foley, "Social Capital and the Political Economy of Our Discontent," *American Behavioral Scientist* 40 (1997): 677.

88. For examples of a few scattered federal initiatives aimed at communities, see Robin Kimbrough, "Strengthening Communities Through Federal Policy," *Family Futures* 1 (1997): 25-27.

89. Anne B. Shlay, "Housing in the Broader Context in the United States," *Housing Policy Debate* 6 (1995): 713.

CHAPTER 8

1. Lawrence Stone, *The Family, Sex, and Marriage in England 1500-1800,* abr. ed. (New York: Harper & Row, 1979), 427.

2. Because they are struggles for freedom, I prefer the label *revolution* to *evolution* because the latter seems to place less emphasis on human agency as an element in bringing about important social and cultural changes, including those in families.

3. Anthony Giddens, *Beyond Left and Right: The Future of Radical Politics* (Stanford, CA: Stanford University Press, 1994), 188-89; Bennett M. Berger, *The Survival of a Counterculture: Ideological Work and Everyday Life Among Rural Communards* (Berkeley: University of California Press, 1981), 56 n.

4. See Chapter 3 for the full text of the Equal Rights Amendment.

5. The closest thing to a political agenda among cohousing advocates is their concern for ecological sustainability. See Graham Meltzer, "Cohousing: Verifying the Importance of Social Context in the Application of Environmentalism," *Journal of Architecture and Planning Research* (forthcoming).

6. Giddens discusses the two types of risk at length. See Giddens, *Beyond Left and Right*; Anthony Giddens, *Affluence, Poverty, and the Idea of a Post-Scarcity Society* (Geneva: United Nations Research Institute for Social Development, 1995).

7. Currently there are only two publications available in English that describe NEL: Nordic Council Research Group, *The New Everyday Life: Ways and Means* (Stockholm: Nordic Council, 1991); and Lisa Horelli and Kirsti Vespa, "In Search of Supportive Structures for Everyday Life," in *Women and the Environment,* ed. Irwin Altman and Arza Churchman (New York: Plenum, 1994), 201-26. In Chapters 5, 6, and 7 of this book I have built on their foundation and expanded their vision considerably.

8. There are exceptions, of course. Among others, these include Leslie Kanes Weisman, *Discrimination by Design: A Feminist Critique of the Man-Made Environment* (Urbana: University of Illinois Press, 1992); Caroline Andrew and Beth Moore Milroy, eds., *Life Spaces: Gender, Households, Employment* (Vancouver: University of British Columbia Press, 1988); Amy S. Wharton, "Review of Andrew & Milroy," *Contemporary Sociology* 22 (1993): 172-73; Karen A. Franck and Sherry Ahrentzen, eds., *New Households, New Housing* (New York: Van Nostrand Reinhold, 1991); Daphne Spain, *Gendered Spaces* (Chapel Hill: University of North Carolina Press, 1992); Daphne Spain, "Gendered Spaces and Women's Status," *Sociological Theory* 11 (1993): 137-51.

9. NEL is foreign to any and all versions of "communitarianism" that fail to expedite women's historic struggles for gender equity. See Marilyn Friedman, "Feminism and Modern Friendship: Dislocating the Community," and Amy Gutman, "Communitarian Critics of Liberalism," both in *Communitarianism and Individualism,* ed. Shlomo Avineri and Avner De-Shalit (New York: Oxford University Press, 1992).

10. As I have noted previously, on August 29, 1998, the on-line version of the *New York Times* previewed a "soon-to-be-released Census Bureau report" that noted that "for the first time, the majority of 'first births'—someone's first child—were either conceived by or born to an unmarried woman. That's up from 18 percent in the 1930s."

11. Peter F. Drucker, "The Age of Social Transformation," *Atlantic Monthly,* November 1994, 62. *Coach* refers to a person who facilitates a team of community children (see Chapter 6).

12. Dorit Fromm, *Collaborative Communities: Cohousing, Central Living, and Other New Forms of Housing With Shared Facilities* (New York: Van Nostrand Reinhold, 1991), 91.

13. N. I. Hilliard (of Berkeley, California), letter to the editor, *San Francisco Examiner,* August 23, 1987, as quoted in ibid., 91-92.

14. Those conditions might, for instance, include excessive congestion, declines in the supply of fossil fuels and thus higher monetary costs, and increasingly hazardous pollution (e.g., threats to the ozone layer) caused by the use of fossil fuels (including electric cars). Accordingly, it would be advisable for us to begin planning now for transportation realities that could be a half century or more away.

15. Benjamin Zablocki, *Alienation and Charisma: A Study of Contemporary American Communes* (New York: Free Press, 1980), 24. For a discussion of Plato's views on the matter, see Rosabeth Moss Kanter, "Introduction," in *Communes: Creating and Managing the Collective Life,* ed. Rosabeth Moss Kanter (New York: Harper & Row, 1973), 1 ff.

16. One example of the kind of cross-disciplinary work that is needed is found in Dorit Fromm and John Scanzoni, eds., "Interdisciplinary Perspectives on Cohousing" (special issue), *Journal of Architectural and Planning Research* (forthcoming). This journal issue, coedited by an architect and a sociologist, includes contributions by scholars from several fields.

17. Arlie Russell Hochschild, *The Time Bind: When Work Becomes Home and Home Becomes Work* (New York: Metropolitan, 1997). However, a contrasting viewpoint appears in John P. Robinson and Geoffrey Godbey, *Time for Life: The Surprising Way Americans Use Their Time* (University Park: Pennsylvania State University Press, 1997).

18. William Foote Whyte, Davydd J. Greenwood, and Peter Lazes, "Participatory Action Research: Through Practice to Science in Social Research," in *Participatory Action Research,* ed. William Foote Whyte (Newbury Park, CA: Sage, 1991), 19-55. For a recent example of PAR with regard to a proposed cohousing arrangement, see Mary Joyce Hasell and John Scanzoni, "Cohousing in HUD Housing: Prospects and Problems," *Journal of Architectural and Planning Research* (forthcoming).

19. Chris Argyris and Donald A. Schön, *Theory in Practice* (San Francisco: Jossey-Bass, 1974); Chris Argyris and Donald A. Schön, "Participatory Action Research and Action Science Compared: A Commentary," in *Participatory Action Research,* ed. William Foote Whyte (Newbury Park, CA: Sage, 1991), 85-96.

20. Giddens, *Beyond Left and Right,* 197.

21. In the conservative camp I include those forms of communitarianism that look chiefly to the past rather than the future. See Gutman, "Communitarian Critics of Liberalism."

22. Katherine McFate, "Introduction: Western States in the New World Order," in *Poverty, Inequality, and the Future of Social Policy,* ed. Katherine McFate, Roger Lawson, and William Julius Wilson (New York: Russell Sage Foundation, 1995), 22.

23. Robert A. Nisbet, *The Quest for Community: A Study in the Ethics of Order and Freedom* (New York: Oxford University Press, 1953), 73.

24. Stephanie Coontz, *The Way We Never Were: American Families and the Nostalgia Trap* (New York: Basic Books, 1992), 278.

25. Francis Bacon as quoted in Arthur Schlesinger, Jr., "The Real Roosevelt Legacy," *Newsweek,* October 14, 1996, 43. Bacon lived in the late 16th and early 17th centuries.

INDEX